# TOLLERTON
# AN AIRFIELD
# FOR NOTTINGHAM
# 1929 - 2007

Howard Fisher

Bob Hammond

Nigel Morley

KEYWORTH AND DISTRICT LOCAL HISTORY SOCIETY

First published in 2008 by Keyworth & District Local History Society
c/o Keyworth Library, Church Drive, Keyworth, Nottingham, NG12 5FF.

Made and printed in Great Britain by
Adlard Print & Reprographics Limited,
Telephone (0115) 921 4863.

ISBN 0-9524602-3-8.

British Library Cataloguing in Publication Data available.

# Contents

## Part III: Post-War - 1945 to 2007 - by Bob Hammond

# Foreword

Since October 1980, when my brother and I purchased Truman Aviation Ltd of Tollerton from Derek Truman, I have been the Managing Director of the company. I have therefore been invited to write this brief foreword.

After the airfield was derequisitioned by the Air Ministry during the 1950s we were fortunate enough to become involved with the resumption of flying at Tollerton when my brother Raymond became a member of the Sherwood Flying Club to commence flying training under the supervision of the then Chief Flying Instructor Paul Cash, one of the founders of the Club in 1956. Raymond's first flight was on 1 July 1956 in a Tiger Moth G-AOFO, the first aircraft the Club purchased. Since then our connection with Tollerton Airfield has been maintained continuously. My own first instructional flight at Tollerton was on 30 July 1961 in Auster G-AJRN and this eventually resulted in the issue of a Private Pilot Licence. Over the years further flying experience was logged which resulted in my gaining an Instructor Rating on 3 January 1975. This was to prove useful later in 1980 after the acquisition of Truman Aviation, which came with two new aircraft, a Piper Aztec Twin Seater and Piper Tomahawk Trainer. The Aztec was sold and a new flying training establishment was created in 1981, employing the Tomahawk as the first of a Company fleet, which now numbers ten aircraft.

Following on from this the Company has flourished with the development of aviation services including professional aircraft maintenance and helicopter operations right up to 19 December 2006 when the purchase of the freehold of the airfield was achieved by the formation of a new company, Nottingham City Airport plc. The new owner is dedicated to the development of future flying activity as well as to addressing the potential of replacing many of the old buildings with newly purpose-built units in a landscaped and secure environment which will be a credit to Nottingham and the local community.

The history of the airfield has been carefully researched and recorded by the authors of this book and provides a most interesting and authentic account of flying activities and achievements, so forming a remarkable archive of the past, from when it all began in 1929 right up to the present.

Derek Leatherland
Truman Aviation Ltd
September 2007.

# Acknowledgements

This book would not have been possible without the generous help and support of a large number of people and organisations. The writers may be at the top of the triangle but there are a great many people whose input has been essential to the project and who have worked equally hard to bring it to a successful fruition.

Members of Keyworth and District Local History Society have given great background support but some have had a greater input than others and need to be specifically mentioned. Jeanne Stevens had the original idea for the project and made some initial contacts for information; Jeanne's enthusiasm has been of great benefit to the group and her questions helped to focus minds on more than one occasion. Alan Atkinson has been a stalwart researcher, wading through the Nottingham newspaper files held at the Local Studies Department of the Nottingham Central Library, month after month. Working alongside Alan was John Atkins: together they have unearthed much fascinating information. Other members of the team behind the book whose input has been invaluable are: Jill Chapman, Joan Speed and Margaret Wright who conducted interviews, Jean Batte who transcribed interview tapes, Derrick Hattersley who regularly searched current issues of the Nottingham Evening Post and Sue Manley who kept our accounts.

Alan Spooner has been essential to the project as Editor, bringing together the work of the three writers and ensuring that our natural wish to include as much as possible has been brought to a semblance of cohesion whilst allowing for individual idiosyncrasies.

One person deserves particular and special mention. A most enthusiastic member of the team from the outset has been Rod Gill. Rod has organised the contacts made from various sources; carried out interviews having mastered our recording equipment; driven many miles up and down the M1 for research work at The National Archives, Colindale Newspaper Archive, Newark Air Museum, Duxford and Old Warden. He has been an absolute stalwart and essential member of the team. Rod's input has been essential to the success of the work.

We are also grateful to Margaret Lawson of the Ruddington Local History Society who gave us initial guidance in getting the project started.

Dr. Anne Tarver has patiently coped with our requirements and amendments in producing the maps and diagrams.

We have received tremendous help and co-operation from many other people, all of whom are listed below in alphabetical order and who have always been most encouraging and supportive of the project. We are very grateful to them all for their memories, the loan and donation of photographs, scrapbooks, minute book, newsletters and other memorabilia:

George Alford, Denise Amos, Fred Beresford, David Birch, Ron Blake, Roy Bonser, Ron Bramley, Derrick Brookes, Douglas Burton, Peter Clark, Arthur Clay,

Don Coaster, Eric Cox, Graham Crisp, Arthur Cronk, Wilf Dale, John Davis, Jim Davies, Kerry Donlan, Alf Evans, Arthur Faulks, Gordon Ferriman, Derek Foot, Jim Flint, Zane Gani, George Gardiner, Albert Gunn, Harold Hall, Brian Hancock, Bunney Hayes, Keith Hayward, Len Henson, Stan Hibbert, Daisy Hills, Keith Hodges, Keith Hodgett, Harry Holmes, Herbert Houldsworth, David Horsman, Harry James, Guy Jefferson, Bill Joynes, Diana Kidger, David Kidger, Cyril King, Fred Kitchen, Michael Knight, Jan Krupa, Derek Leatherland, Charles Loakes, Terence Lucas, Edith M Lyons, John McCallum, Vera McLean, Dennis Marshall, Ned Marshall, Peter Marwood, Moshahid Miah, Mrs J Morfen, Rex Morris, Michael Moss, Peter Mounser, Tom Myall, Larry Parker, Jim Patrick, Barbara Pearson, Melvis Phenix, Peter Phenix, Jenny Phimister, Alan Purdy, Richard Randall, Jeff Redshaw, J. E. Rigden, Brian Scott, Betty Shelton, Ken Shipside, Caroline Smith, Ken Smith, Phil Speachley, Bearnice Squires, Len Stapleton, June Stevens, Anne Sweet, Raymond Towler, Valerie Truman, Mary-Rose Vandervord, Brian Wells, Jack White, Graham Whitehead, Gordon Williams, S Woodroffe, Mrs P Wright, Norma Yates.

Various organisations have been of tremendous help and we are grateful to the staffs of the BAA Museum, British Library Newspaper Section at Colindale, Central Helicopters, Cobham plc, Hunting plc, National Archives at Kew, Newark Air Museum, Nottinghamshire Archives Office, Nottingham Local Studies Library, Nottingham Evening Post, RAF Hendon, and The University of Nottingham Department of Manuscripts and Special Collections.

If anyone has been inadvertently omitted from this list we are truly sorry and ask for forgiveness.

Credit for the photographs has been given where known and every effort has been made to contact copyright holders for permission to reproduce images.

Whilst every care has been taken to check and validate the information contained in the book, the authors accept final responsibility for any errors which may have escaped the rigorous editing process.

This book is only a part of the project: in addition there are exhibitions and talks to interested parties.

None of this would have taken place without the support of The National Lottery through the Heritage Lottery Fund and the help of their staff when we were putting together our funding application. The grant which we received enabled us to carry out research on a broad basis and, most importantly, to keep the price of this book at a low amount.

# Introduction

There are two Tollertons with airfields in England, one in North Yorkshire and the other in Nottinghamshire. This book is about the Nottinghamshire Tollerton.

The Nottinghamshire Tollerton is a village to the south-east of Nottingham, just beyond the ring road (A52) which here marks the boundary between the built-up area of the city's suburb of West Bridgford and its Green Belt. The airfield lies wholly within Tollerton parish, north of the village, and wholly within Nottingham's Green Belt (Figure 1). It is less than four miles from Nottingham – ten minutes by car from the city centre on a good day. It is accessed by a country lane, but except during special events like air pageants, it has never generated enough traffic to cause congestion problems. A catchment population (people for whom it is the nearest civilian airport) of about a million has kept it in business for nearly eighty years, though mostly through private and club flying rather than larger scale commercial flying. It got off to an early start, being one of the first licensed commercial airports in the country.

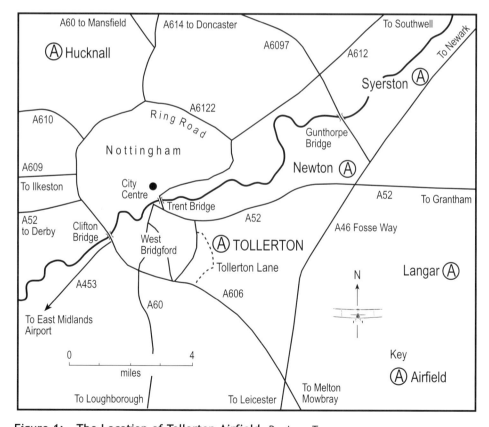

**Figure 1: The Location of Tollerton Airfield** *Dr. Anne Tarver*

On the other hand, it is small – early aircraft required only short take-off and landing distances - and can only be used by light, propeller-driven aircraft. Positioned between a canal and stream to the north and east, and by a village and housing to the south and west, the possibility of physical expansion is limited. This has constrained commercial development, which in turn has led the airfield operators, particularly since World War II, to look for additional sources of revenue, some unrelated to aviation. Tollerton is more than an airport where aircraft take off and land and are parked and serviced in hangars; it also encompasses what amounts to a small trading estate. While the airport occupies most of the airfield's space, the trading estate area has usually employed many more people – during the war and for most of the following twelve years, several hundreds more.

This book attempts to deal with all aspects of the airfield's history from its inception to the present, including activities unrelated to aviation. It is divided into three sections covering periods of very unequal length: pre-war, wartime and post-war; ten, six and 62 years respectively. They are all dependent on a combination of documentary and oral sources, but in different proportions. The pre-war period has proved the richest in documentary material - official reports, articles in aviation journals and newspapers. Flight was still in its formative phase, and Tollerton was then, in relative terms, more important than it became during and after the war – aviation in general advanced and expanded rapidly while Tollerton did not. Personal reminiscences for this period are few however: most who were then involved at Tollerton are no longer alive.

With regard to wartime, when Tollerton, along with other airfields, was requisitioned and became RAF Tollerton, documentary sources have proved surprisingly and disappointingly elusive, perhaps because of official secrecy or because of the airfield's unglamorous role in pilot training and aircraft repair. It is also over sixty years since the war ended so that those with relevant memories are again not numerous. On the other hand the circumstances of war and the role played by Tollerton in it were so different from those of the pre- and post-war periods that more space is given to describing these in general terms – for instance, the strengths and weaknesses of some of the military aircraft that used the airfield.

The more recent post-war and contemporary period has relied heavily on people's memories, the more so because documentary sources to which we have had access, while not sparse, are uneven in their cover.

## Before Tollerton

Nottingham Airport, as the airfield was then known, was opened in 1929, when commercial flying was in its infancy, and powered flight was less than thirty years old. Before launching into Section I of the book on pre-World War II Tollerton, let us look briefly at the thirty pioneer years of aviation that preceded it.

There were many attempts at heavier-than-air flight before the first successful flight by Orville and Wilbur Wright in the USA on 17 December 1903. Following their success others developed aeroplanes and the first officially recognised flight in the UK was on 16 October 1908 by Colonel Samuel F. Cody. The first British subject to fly an all-British machine was Alliott Verdon Roe who flew his Roe Triplane at Lea Marshes, Essex on 13 July 1909, just two weeks before Louis Bleriot flew across the Channel. Flying meetings were held at Doncaster on 15-25 October 1909 and at Blackpool on 18-29 October 1909. It is said that over 50,000 people attended both events. The first recorded landing of an aeroplane at Nottingham occurred on 30 September 1910 when Paul de Lesseps landed his Bleriot monoplane at Colwick Park, having lost his way when flying from Burton-on-Trent. It was such a curiosity that when it flew over Notts County football ground while a match with Bristol City was in progress, players and spectators alike were so astounded by the apparition that the referee stopped play until it had passed.

However, it was the Great War which was the catalyst for the rapid development of aircraft design for military purposes and for subsequent attempts to raise awareness of the benefits of civil flying. Military actions often drive technological advances and the First World War was no exception, especially in terms of aviation. At the outbreak of war in 1914 Britain possessed few aircraft. France and Germany had many more, with the former having over 200 aircraft and the latter 30 airships. Britain had no formal military air service until the formation in 1911 of the Air Battalion of the Royal Engineers. In May 1912 this battalion became the Royal Flying Corps (RFC). In parallel the Admiralty formed the Royal Naval Air Service (RNAS) in June 1914 and both merged into the Royal Air Force in 1918.

When the RFC went to France in support of the Army Expeditionary Force in August 1914 it possessed 63 aeroplanes, none of which carried a gun or had bomb-carrying capabilities. The function of the RFC was perceived to be that of a reconnaissance unit in support of the army, using a mixture of BE2, BE8, Avro and Henry Farman bi-planes and Bleriot monoplanes. The function of the RNAS was seen to be the defence of Great Britain although some of its aircraft were stationed on the Continent and its Sopwith Tabloid biplanes carried out the first British bombing raid on airship sheds at Düsseldorf in October 1914.

The needs of aerial warfare saw the development of aircraft for specific purposes such as fighters, bombers and reconnaissance aircraft. The ability to mount guns and bombs quickly developed on both sides of the conflict with first one side and then the other gaining technical superiority. Bomb loads increased and the ability of fighters to have guns which synchronised with the propeller was a major advance. Engine power and general manoeuvrability of the aeroplanes developed through the war years.

By the end of the war the RAF had become the largest air force in the world comprising 290,000 personnel, 180 operational squadrons and 3,300 aeroplanes.

Its aircraft were technically superior in every way to those with which the RFC and RNAS had started the war: more powerful engines, greater range and separated into specific fighter and bomber functions. The needs of warfare had driven forward changes and developments during the four years which perhaps would not have happened for very many more years had war not broken out.

Civil flying was allowed to resume on 1 May 1919 and it is estimated that out of about 22,000 trained RAF pilots demobilised in that year, only one per thousand could find work in civil aviation. About 50 ex-service pilots tried to earn a living by giving flights to the public at one guinea (105p) a time but this was well out of the reach of most people and so the enterprises failed. One enterprise which did survive was that of Alan Cobham who, with others, founded the Berkshire Aviation Company. Cobham was to become famous for his daring and pioneering long distance flights for which he was later knighted.

Sir Alan Cobham decided he ought to try and make the UK population more 'air-minded' and in 1926 he wrote to all the major municipalities in the country suggesting a network of municipal aerodromes. There was little civil airline flying at the time, although there were already private flying clubs in existence. Little came of this but some municipalities began turning their minds towards aviation and how it could benefit their areas. Nottingham had a private airfield at Hucknall which was used by the Nottingham Aero Club after its formation in 1926, but it was taken over by the RAF as a military airfield on 26 March 1928. Shortly after that, in 1929, Nottingham Corporation bought land at Tollerton for a civil aerodrome. It is here that the story of Tollerton airfield begins.

# PART I: PRE-WAR 1929 to 1939

## Chapter 1

# A Municipal Aerodrome for Nottingham

In the late 1920s the Air Ministry circulated town and city authorities in the United Kingdom urging them to consider developing municipal airfields to support an anticipated expansion of civil aviation. It was anticipated that every major city and town in the country would need an airfield to support a network of internal airline operations. As a result Nottingham City Council formed a sub-committee in 1928 to examine the possibilities of an airfield to serve the City. Sites at Bestwood, Clifton Pastures and Tollerton were soon identified as potentially suitable places and were put forward for an inspection by the Air Ministry. Sir Sefton Brancker, the Head of Civil Aviation, made an unofficial visit to the Tollerton site in October 1928 at the invitation of Sir Albert Ball, a member of the sub-committee, and subsequently wrote to Sir Albert:

> I consider the site you showed me to be eminently suitable for the purpose [of an airfield], and I feel that Nottingham will be missing a great opportunity of providing a really fine air port at a most convenient distance from the city if it does not take advantage of the possibility of taking up this site.

Sir Sefton's opinion of Tollerton was confirmed on 25 January 1929 when Major Mealing, the Air Ministry's Inspector, reported his findings to the Council's sub-committee following his inspection of the three places. He recommended the site at Tollerton as the most suitable for an aerodrome.

In January 1929 the *Nottingham Guardian's* Annual Trade Review carried an interview with the Lord Mayor of Nottingham, Alderman Atkey, in which he discussed the merits of a municipal aerodrome for the City. His view was that an aerodrome was likely to prove as important to the development of Nottingham, and particularly its businesses, as a recently completed project to provide new wharfage facilities on the River Trent which had been funded by the Corporation. He did, however, suggest that the Corporation should not spend any more on an aerodrome than it had on the river development, and that, apart from providing the basic aerodrome landing ground, further development was more properly a matter for private initiative than a public responsibility. He summarised his view:

> For many years Nottingham has enjoyed an enviable position as a centre with convenient access by railways. To this is already added waterways, and when it has placed facilities at the disposal of the users of airways then surely it will hold pride of place in the Midlands as a centre of progressive effort.

There was, of course, an element of civic pride involved in the decision to develop an aerodrome for Nottingham and this was to become a rather contentious issue when neighbouring authorities started to develop their aerodromes. Nottingham businesses were strong advocates for an airfield and, particularly, The Nottingham Junior Chamber of Commerce publicly said that the City could only benefit from an early decision to develop the Tollerton site for this purpose.

Counter arguments were expressed in the *Nottingham Guardian* of 27 February 1929, a week before the City Council was due to consider the matter, when it said that the development of municipal aerodromes in Britain was not as important as on the Continent and in the USA because distances here were not as great and that rail travel was quicker than flying. Railway stations were sited within town and city boundaries and airfields, of necessity, were a distance away and required extra travelling time to reach them. With some prescience the article said 'this part of the problem [the siting of airfields] may, of course, be solved some day by the discovery of a method by which aeroplanes can safely rise from and descend to the centre of a city'.

On Monday 4 March 1929 the General Purposes Committee presented its report to the Nottingham City Council in which it recommended the development of an aerodrome at Tollerton, stating that it was essential for Nottingham to have such a facility if the City was to maintain a position of prominence in the country. The Town Clerk had made enquiries about the land at Tollerton which could be bought from the owner, Albert Ball (Nottingham) Ltd, at a figure of £34 per acre. The Corporation was empowered to buy this land and borrow the cost under the terms of the Air Navigation Act, 1920.

The Deputy Lord Mayor, Alderman E. Huntsman, opposed the proposal on the grounds that he thought the Air Ministry was trying to get local authorities to fund aerodromes because the Government was not prepared to invest in the RAF. He felt the motive was for the expansion of military rather than civil aviation. W. Crane said that his Labour Party had not approved such schemes either nationally or locally and, backed by R. Bury, he proposed a deferral for twelve months. Despite this opposition the Council's decision was to proceed with an aerodrome at Tollerton and authorised the borrowing of £4,806 to facilitate it.

## From Farmland to Aerodrome

The files of the Town Clerk held at the Nottinghamshire Archive Office hold full details of the negotiations between the Council and Albert Ball (Nottingham) Ltd for the purchase of the land. The first approach to the Company was on 19 January 1929 and two days later a price of £36 per acre was quoted. The Company said this was the value of the land as agricultural rather than development land. Vacant possession was offered for 8 April because the long-term tenant had given notice to quit his tenancy on that date. Negotiations over the price continued until 12 February when Sir Albert Ball said that £34 per acre would be accepted although he considered this price 'to be very bad'. Sir Albert was a member of the City Council at the time which, perhaps, is why he sold at a price below what he thought reasonable. The land had been owned by Albert Ball (Nottingham) Ltd for less than a year, having been bought as part of a larger parcel from the Trustees of the Tollerton Estate. The Estate provided the Rector of Tollerton with an annual fee of £300 and the Corporation had to agree to contribute a proportionate annual amount of £35.7s.0d to the Rector.

The Ministry of Health was responsible for local authority affairs at that time and on 11 March 1929 the City Council consequently requested permission from the Ministry to borrow the money for the land purchase. The Air Council had given its prior consent under Section 8 of the Air Navigation Act, 1920 and the District Valuer had provided a report regarding the land. The latter described the land as covering 141.359 acres in a block extending from the eastern side of the Nottingham to Tollerton road, as far as the Polser (or Poulter) Brook and

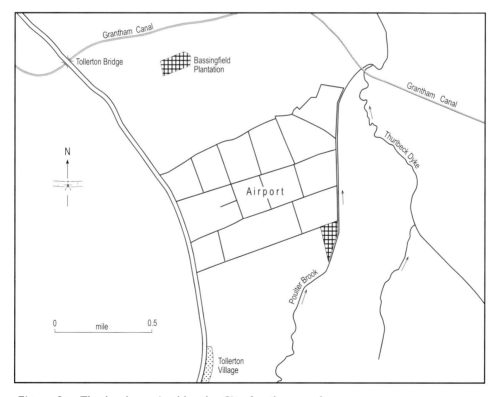

**Figure 2:   The land acquired by the City for the aerodrome.**
*Dr. Anne Tarver; Nottinghamshire County Archive Service*

the Tollerton and Holme Pierrepont parish boundaries. Of the total acreage 30.632 acres were used as pasture and the remainder arable land; the proposed purchase price was said to be fair and reasonable.

The Ministry of Health needed confirmation that the proposals were generally known in the locality and the Town Clerk gave assurances that there had been extensive coverage in the Nottingham newspapers and that the general public appeared to welcome the aerodrome. Official sanction to proceed was given on 9 April 1929 and the land purchase completed on 24 April 1929.

An Air Ministry pamphlet of June 1929 entitled *How To Establish An Aerodrome* set out the expected requirements. Tollerton eventually complied with most of these which included the need for aerodromes to be as close to town centres as possible and to be on the side of a town where the prevailing wind would blow smoke and dust away from the airfield. It was recommended that the site should not be close to a river for fear of frequent fogs and a situation on a plateau, providing it was not too high, was to be preferred. There should be no high obstacles such as chimneys or church spires close by, nor should it be at the foot of or near to a hill. A telephone at the site was essential as was water and light.

In these days of advanced technology it is amusing to read of the recommended way of assessing the surface for smoothness and its suitability to handle the weight of an aircraft. In the former case it was said that a car had to be capable of being driven across the ground at 20 mph without inconveniencing its passengers. For the test of weight-bearing capabilities if a fully laden 3 ton lorry could be driven across the land without its wheels sinking, the weight of an aircraft's wheels and tail skid could be sustained.

The initial work to prepare Tollerton for use by aircraft involved the removal of some trees and hedges from the site as well as to mole-drain about two thirds of it. Two surface drains totalling 1,500 yards were piped and filled in. The land was then ploughed, rolled and seeded to produce a flying area, called the flying-ground, of about 99 acres. This work cost £3,150.

The Air Ministry published a booklet called the *Air Pilot* which gave details of all operating aerodromes to assist pilots in using them. On 29 August 1929 the Nottingham Town Clerk provided the information that Tollerton had a grass surface, was well drained with a slight slope to the east. Its boundaries were formed of hedges up to ten feet high with some trees extending to 15 feet. There was a plantation of trees in the south-eastern corner of 30 feet in height and, additionally, there were telegraph wires on the west side at 20 feet. The aerodrome was not equipped with radio communications and flying was only done between sunrise and sunset. No landing fees had been set at that time.

It had been hoped that the aerodrome could be ready for the Lord Mayor, Alderman A. R. Atkey, to use when he had to go to the annual meeting of the British Waterworks Association at Plymouth in early July 1929. Unfortunately Tollerton was not ready and so he was flown from 'the landing ground by the side of the Trent at Lady Bay'. This quotation suggests that there was regular flying from Lady Bay, although no further proof of this has been found. Alderman Atkey was flown to Plymouth by E.D. Winn using the Nottingham Aero Club's Moth aeroplane which was then based at Hucknall airfield.

The opening date for Tollerton was set for Saturday 27 July 1929 and it had been arranged that the famous aviator, Sir Alan Cobham, would land his DH Grand Moth aircraft, named 'Youth of Britain', at Tollerton in which he would then fly the Lord Mayor to London where he would be presented with the Air Ministry's licence for Tollerton to be used for aviation. The plan was that the Lord Mayor would return to Tollerton to officially open the aerodrome. There would then be a civic reception and later in the afternoon Cobham would give some of the dignitaries a flight and then a flight for some school children selected by the City's Director of Education. The cost of the children's flights was said to have been covered by an anonymous donor who was, in fact, Lord Wakefield who was a strong supporter of aviation. After the children's flights, Cobham was to give pleasure-flights to the general public.

In the event, Cobham was unable to fulfil the first part of these arrangements due to his aeroplane having been damaged at Doncaster on the day before the official opening. Parts were urgently flown from Stag Lane, London, but the repairs were not completed in time. Alderman Atkey, wearing his ceremonial robes as Lord Mayor, was therefore flown to London by Flight Lieutenant R. Lee Bateman, the Flying Instructor of the Nottingham Aero Club, in the Club's DH 60 Moth, G-EBQW. This was an open-cockpit aircraft and therefore much less comfortable than Cobham's Grand Moth cabin aeroplane would have been.

Leaving Hucknall aerodrome at 8 a.m. on 27 July the aircraft reached Stag Lane aerodrome at Edgware, London, thirty-five minutes before the scheduled time of 10 a.m. In order to kill time Flight Lieutenant Bateman flew over London, returning to Stag Lane for 10 a.m. where Air Vice-Marshall Sir Sefton Brancker and the Under-Secretary of State for Air, F. Montague MP, were waiting to present Tollerton's licence to Alderman Atkey. This ceremony concluded at 10.15 a.m. and to avoid reaching Tollerton before the official opening time of 12.30 p.m., the Lord Mayor was given a tour of the de Havilland factory. The aircraft still arrived back in Nottingham early and had to fly over the City for a short while before landing at Tollerton at the appointed time.

The aerodrome was declared officially open, the licence handed to the Town Clerk for safe keeping and the party of dignitaries given an official luncheon at Tollerton Hall which had recently opened as a Country Club. Sir Alan Cobham flew from Doncaster in a Moth to attend the luncheon and then immediately returned to Doncaster to collect the by then repaired 'Youth of Britain' so that he could, at least, fulfil that part of the original arrangements to provide flights for the school children and public. Whilst awaiting the arrival of Cobham, free flights were provided in the two Moths owned by Nottingham Flying Club and Flight Lieutenant Bateman provided a display of stunt flying.

Cobham arrived at 5 p.m., the dignitaries were flown over the City, the children given their flights and the public then bought flights until it was almost dark. The following day flights were available from 11 a.m. lasting until dusk despite some inclement weather. A reporter from the *Nottingham Journal* took a flight and reported:

> The trip was a glorious adventure which should certainly be experienced by everyone. Not only was the flight extremely exhilarating, but it afforded one an unusual, though very excellent view of Nottingham and its surroundings, a view which could not possibly be obtained in any other way and indeed would not have been dreamed of a few years ago. Practically everyone seemed surprised when they stepped into a large, roomy cabin to be seated in a luxurious armchair. The comfort of the giant machine was most impressive.

The school children given the free flights were selected by drawing lots; only 132 of the 700 who applied could receive a flight. 40 teachers applied but only 12 received flights. The lucky children were from Ilkeston Road Girls, St. Marks Senior, Trent Bridge Girls, People's College, Bosworth Road Boys, Sneinton Boulevard Boys, St. Matthias Senior, Berridge Road Girls, St. Anne's Senior and All Saints Senior schools. They gathered at the Education Offices on South Parade, Nottingham and were taken to Tollerton in motor buses.

In 2006 Daisy Hills of Nottingham recalled the excitement of a flight with Cobham on this occasion:

**Plate 1:     The Lord Mayor's arrival at Tollerton with the Air Ministry licence to operate the aerodrome.** He is showing the licence to the Sheriff, William Green and Alderman Albert Ball. *Roy Bonser collection*

In 1929, when I was 10 years old we had a competition [at school]. We had to write an essay about the Empire. I liked writing essays and I won first prize. The prize was a trip in an aeroplane and the pilot was to be Sir Alan Cobham. I was so excited about going in an aeroplane. My mother arranged for my niece to have a ride with me. She was only five years old but she wanted to come, so my Mum paid five shillings for her to come with me.

My sister took us to Tollerton to meet Sir Alan Cobham. He was very handsome and he said he had never had such young passengers before. Tollerton airfield was just an empty field. I can't remember any buildings or runways. Our plane was a biplane with three cockpits. We were lifted over the side into our seats. I sat in the middle seat and my niece sat at the back. Sir Alan was in front. We were not strapped in and we didn't have a helmet or any special clothes. There was no cover over the cockpit so it was windy, blowing in our faces. We were too small to see out over the sides, but there was a hole in the floor so I looked out of that. When we were in the air I could see the river and fields. We went over the countryside not over Nottingham. It was a really great experience and I shall never forget it.

Tollerton was the second municipal aerodrome in the UK to receive an operating licence and the first with a permanent site. The first licence was issued to Manchester in April 1929 but the site there was a temporary one; its permanent site came a little later.

## National Flying Services Ltd

After the aerodrome was opened decisions still had to be made by the City Council regarding the infrastructure. They had an aerodrome without buildings; in effect only a more-or-less level grass field which was capable of being used by aeroplanes. A far cry from the completed facilities available when East Midlands Airport opened many years later. Not only had decisions to be made about the type of buildings required but how they were to be funded had to be decided. During the land acquisition period various Council members had expressed the opinion that it was not necessarily the responsibility of the Council to fund buildings; private enterprise should play a part with the Council's duty ending with the provision of the basic airfield. Other views were that the Council should retain full control and provide all the required facilities. In hindsight it is unfortunate that the latter opinion did not prevail. The eventual decision led to subsequent disputes and dissatisfaction on the part of the Council's staff and elected members over how the aerodrome was being developed and used. The vision of men such as Sir Albert Ball and Alderman Atkey, who had driven the Council towards the development of an aerodrome, was for a busy commercial airport which would enhance the status of Nottingham and aid its businesses. This vision was never fulfilled and Tollerton's commercial importance was eclipsed by neighbouring aerodromes which were developed later and where the relevant Corporations retained full control.

Important to the story of Tollerton airport was the formation of National Flying Services Ltd (NFS) which was announced in *Flight* magazine of 10 January 1929, with further details given in the issue of 7 February 1929. There were people influential in aviation circles involved with the company from the outset. The unpaid chairman was Captain the Honourable F. R. Guest, who had been Air Minister in 1921-2. The Managing Director was Lieutenant Colonel A. A. E. Edwards who had been Chief Technical Advisor to the Director of Civil Aviation. The Board of Directors included Colonel the Master of Sempill and Sir Alan Cobham. The title 'Master' was traditionally given to Scottish heirs apparent or heirs presumptive, and the Colonel eventually became the 19th Lord Sempill upon the death of his father in 1934. Before he inherited the title he was universally known as 'The Master of Sempill'.

The NFS headquarters were located at Hanworth aerodrome and the Company's intention was to train pilots and develop civil aviation through a network of 22 aerodromes at the larger provincial centres. In addition they planned to have 100 smaller aerodromes which would be regarded as intermediate landing-grounds where only petrol, oil supplies and a telephone would be available. The 22 main places would have a clubhouse serving meals and where dances and other social events would be arranged for club members. Each of these sites would have four aeroplanes, two pilot instructors, two ground engineers, two assistants and clubhouse staff. This rather grandiose launch aim was to prove far too ambitious; the reality was to be much different.

The Company succeeded in obtaining an Air Ministry subsidy of £10 per pilot trained during the first three years and £5 per pilot for the succeeding five years. This was subject to a maximum sum of £15,000 per annum for the first three years and £7,500 for five years thereafter.

Nottingham Corporation saw NFS as a means of gaining infrastructure at Tollerton without the need for public expenditure. Negotiations were started which led to NFS occupying the aerodrome at the end of September 1929 although the lease was not finally signed until 2 January 1930. The lease term was for 21 years from September 1929 with an option for a seven year extension. NFS were to erect hangars, build a clubhouse and provide fuel and servicing facilities. They could only use the land as an aerodrome and the hangars were to be completed by 25 March 1930. The Corporation's duties were to level and fence the landing-ground, to limit the height of any buildings on adjacent land and to construct a white circle at the centre of the landing-ground in accordance with Air Ministry requirements. It is clear from the Corporation's records that it fully expected NFS to encourage commercial flying at Tollerton as well as private club flying.

Because Nottingham was such an early developer of a municipal aerodrome, many local authorities who were considering an airfield in the early and mid

1930s contacted the Town Clerk for information about how it had been achieved and was being operated. On 20 February 1930 the Town Clerk answered such an enquiry from Cheltenham Council which provides an overview of the airfield at that time. By then NFS had completed a hangar and the clubhouse and had sunk a well for water supplies; cables from the Derbyshire and Nottinghamshire Power Company's mains about half a mile away had been run to the aerodrome for the electricity supply.

The Nottingham papers strongly supported the developments happening at Tollerton. The *Nottingham Guardian* Trade Review of 1 January 1930 said that NFS would be running air-taxis from the airfield at 1s.6d a mile for two passengers in addition to the club operation. The *Nottingham Evening Post* said on 18 January 1930 that it would be possible for a businessman to have breakfast in Nottingham, lunch in Paris and do business there in the afternoon before flying back to Nottingham for dinner the same evening. This paper reported the formal inauguration of the NFS air-taxi service on Friday 14 February at the London Air-Park, where twenty aircraft were based with others at Hull, Leeds, Reading and, soon, at Tollerton. The charges had been fixed at 1s.0d a mile for single passenger aeroplanes such as the Moth or Bluebird and 9d a mile per person for larger passenger machines such as the Desoutter. Destinations could be to any of 90 UK aerodromes.

Details of the aerodrome were given to the Air Ministry in August 1930 for inclusion in an updated *Air Pilot*. The hangar, which is still in use at the airfield, was built of corrugated iron and measured 90 feet in breadth and 60 feet in depth. The door was 15 feet high and 40 feet wide. It was completed early in April 1930 and would house eight aircraft or 16 of the folding wing type. The

**Plate 2: The clubhouse and hangar in 1930.** The Moth Major has been superimposed and bears a spurious registration mark. *Roy Bonser collection*

clubhouse was completed shortly after the hangar. Meteorological reports for Tollerton were obtainable from Cranwell aerodrome. Landing fees were 2s.6d upwards depending on the size of the aeroplane concerned.

## The Official NFS Opening

NFS celebrated their occupation of Tollerton aerodrome with a ceremony on Thursday 19 June 1930, when the airfield was officially opened by Sir Sefton Brancker, the Director of Civil Aviation, followed by an Air Pageant. Sir Sefton flew to Tollerton from Hanworth in a Desoutter air-taxi, arriving at 1 p.m. He was greeted by a group of civic dignitaries from Nottingham led by the Lord Mayor (Councillor W. Wesson). Also in the party were the Sheriff of Nottingham (Councillor W. Hooley), the Town Clerk (W. J. Broad), Alderman Sir Albert Ball and Alderman Sir Bernard Wright, several wives and other guests. Representing NFS were the Chairman, Lieutenant Colonel Edwards, and the Deputy Managing Director, Captain G. E. G. Boyes.

The opening ceremony was conducted at 2 p.m. with speeches by Sir Sefton and the Lord Mayor followed by a varied programme of events to entertain the

**Plate 3:**    **Sir Sefton Brancker fires a Very pistol to officially open the aerodrome.**
*Guardian Journal, 20 June 1930*

large crowd of onlookers. A competition for the first private aircraft to arrive after 12 noon was won by S. B. Cliff from the Hampshire Aero Club who landed his Cirrus-Moth only five seconds after noon. The afternoon's handicap race held over a 30 mile circuit had only three starters due to poor weather on the previous day preventing several entrants from reaching Tollerton. The three who competed were Flying Officer A. G. Store in a Breda monoplane, Flying Officer W. A. Andrews in a Spartan and Flight Lieutenant S. David flying a de Havilland Puss Moth owned by W. L. Everard, the MP for Melton Mowbray and President of the Leicestershire Aeronautical Club. Andrews completed the course first in 19 minutes 30 seconds, with David second and Store third, two and 15 seconds behind respectively. However, Andrews and Store were disqualified for flying too low and so the winner was David.

The crowd were thrilled by a demonstration of the Autogiro, a precursor of the helicopter, given by Flying Officer Egglesfield. Flight Lieutenant Schofield gave an aeronautical display in a Cirrus-Moth which included 'a wonderful inverted falling-leaf' movement. Members of the Nottingham Gliding Club amused the crowd by demonstrating short glides with an 'avion sans moteur' as *Flight* put it.

'Crazy' flying and 'how not to fly' demonstrations were performed by Flight Lieutenant Styran and Schofield performed aerobatics again, but this time in a Hermes-Desoutter which drew comment because it was a 'business-like cabin machine' which 'looked strange performing all manner of contortions'. An aerobatic competition for private owners was won by Mr Wynn of the Leicestershire Aeronautical Club. Mr Winn of the Nottingham Aero Club was second and S. B. Cliff of Hampshire third, all three flying Moths.

A feature of this event, and a standard feature of most NFS organised pageants, was a staged raid on a railway level crossing which was bombed from

Plate 4: Advert for the opening air pageant of 19 June 1930.

*Roy Bonser collection*

the air and 'exploded in a spectacular fashion'. An item which was novel to the crowd was a parachute descent by John Tranum using a Russell Lobe parachute. This was his first descent from a Desoutter and he consequently misjudged his range, landing outside the aerodrome but still in full view of the spectators.

After the prizes were presented by the Lady Mayoress the public were able to purchase pleasure-rides during the rest of the evening.

## The Demise of NFS

NFS never reached its very optimistic original target for the number of aerodromes under its control. Almost from the start there were financial difficulties. Letters dated April and May 1930 in the Air Ministry files at The National Archives indicate some of the problems. On 11 March 1930 Colonel Edwards of NFS visited the Air Ministry to explain the Company's financial state and to ask for an advance of £15,000 against future subsidy payments. Internal Air Ministry reports suggest that at least part of the problem was that NFS had not raised enough money from the issues of debentures and shares to fulfil their programme. They had hoped for £300,000 but had a shortfall of £15,000. Building work at Hanworth, Hull, Reading, Stoke-on-Trent and Tollerton was £30,000 over estimate and the trading account showed a loss of £30,000. The Air Ministry estimated that the likely figure the Company would require was between £5,000 and £15,000 higher than Edwards was requesting. The Ministry's conclusion was that, although it was in no-one's interests to see NFS fail, the required funds should come from its own resources, perhaps a bank overdraft or from supporters. The Ministry could not advance any more than £2,500.

The figures given for Tollerton in the NFS document showed that capital expenditure to date was £3,100. £4,000 was owed to E. D. Winn & Co Ltd with a further £350 required to furnish the clubhouse.

Despite this worrying financial situation NFS had aerodromes operating at Hull, Sherburn-in-Elmet, Blackpool, Reading and Nottingham by 1931. The clubs associated with these places had flourishing memberships of between 70 and 200 who seemed to be well served by NFS staff. Harold Penrose, the well known aviation writer, quotes F. D. Bradbrooke as saying that after a tour of the NFS stations, 'the staffs are genial, competent and keen and fault will not be at their door if the new NFS does not cope with ... a bad beginning ... the fundamental idea of a really national flying service, given a chance, will show its worth with such excellent material and personnel at hand.'

In an attempt to bolster the Company's prospects the Board was reconstituted with The Master of Sempill and Sir Alan Cobham becoming more involved in the management. *Flight* of 10 April 1931 suggested the Company was emerging from its difficulties. This article also gave a very favourable review of the Flying Club at Tollerton and its facilities.

However, in Nottingham there was some disquiet about how NFS was using the aerodrome. The Air Correspondent of the *Nottingham Journal* questioned on 23 May 1931 how useful the aerodrome was to the City. He said that the sporting side was being developed but the commercial aspects were largely ignored. He argued that it was the commercial element which was of much greater importance to Nottingham City than private flying and that, by ignoring the commercial aspects, 'one of the most important industrial centres in the world was in danger of being antiquated'. His criticisms were not solely directed at NFS; the Corporation came in for its share. He thought the Corporation, together with NFS, did not show interest in the commercial development of aviation at Tollerton and advocated that an Aviation Committee utilising political and business men with aviation knowledge should be formed as had, apparently, happened with success at Bristol. This committee would dedicate itself to ensuring that Tollerton was properly developed for commercial aviation. The other Nottingham papers were equally critical, the *Nottingham Guardian* saying on 1 January 1931 that the Corporation had not been prepared to find money to develop the airfield but had 'turned their aerodrome over to National Flying Service with a pious blessing for their success in converting it into a paying proposition'.

On 26 March 1932 Captain Shepherd, the Chief Instructor of the Nottingham Flying Club, was forced to answer criticisms of the state of the airfield which related to half of it being unsafe for landing. He said this was untrue because he experienced no difficulties using the airfield in either the Club's aircraft or the Hawker Horsley and Fairey 111F day-bombers which he was flying at Tollerton for Rolls-Royce Ltd. However, in the same year, a report by Sir Albert Ball, then Chairman of the Council's Aerodrome sub-committee, said that he and the City Engineer had visited the airfield and work was required to improve it. The City Engineer was then authorised to have the airfield levelled which suggests an element of spin on the part of Captain Shepherd.

Meanwhile, NFS's financial problems were far from over. At the AGM held on 16 March 1932 the chairman stated that there was an operating loss for the financial year of £68,000. He blamed this on abnormal weather and the national industrial depression saying, 'I can assure shareholders that if their interests were scourged with whips in 1930 they have been chastised with scorpions in 1931.' Comments which, whilst truthful, were hardly likely to give confidence to shareholders or the Air Ministry. The subsidy agreement with the Air Ministry expired on 31 July 1932 and files at The National Archives show that the Company was seeking support from the Government by a loan and annual subsidy of £16,000. At this time NFS was operating seven air parks. It employed 12 'B' licensed commercial pilots, 22 certified engineers and 139 non-technical staff. In August of that year The Master of Sempill told the Air Ministry that staff had been ruthlessly cut: even the Company Secretary, Noel Smith, had gone. The Air Ministry was unmoved and a memo of December 1932 suggested that

NFS was nearly bankrupt and no additional payments should be made unless a full reconstruction of the Company could be effected.

Earlier, in March 1932 Noel Smith of NFS had met the Nottingham Town Clerk and Captain Shepherd of the Nottingham Flying Club. His purpose was to refer to the loss reported at the NFS's AGM and to say that it was not possible for the company to continue under its then operating conditions. NFS were seeking the co-operation of municipalities in assisting its recovery. Although Tollerton was one of the better sites showing a very slight financial loss of only £68.8s.5d, he asked for a reduction in the annual rent. The City Treasurer advised the Town Clerk that a reduction would, in effect, be a contribution by the citizens of Nottingham towards the Company's losses at other aerodromes and should be refused.

NFS struggled on into the next year. On 22 February 1933 The Master of Sempill told the *Nottingham Guardian* that the Company had been reorganised and that important negotiations would soon reach a satisfactory conclusion with NFS being on a much firmer footing for the future. The newspaper accepted this statement and assured its readers that NFS would continue at Tollerton.

However, things did not work out as The Master had predicted and the appointment of a Receiver for NFS was announced in *The Times* of 21 June 1933. This did not immediately end the Company's relationship with Tollerton and on 6 September the Town Clerk invited The Master of Sempill to attend a sub-committee meeting to discuss the future commercial use of the aerodrome. The Master accepted the invitation but was prevented from attending after being involved in a serious road traffic accident in the USA. Before the accident he had told the *Nottingham Journal* that he felt the Corporation should take a greater interest in developing Tollerton. He predicted that if it did not then the new aerodrome at Braunstone which was being built and funded by Leicester Corporation would eclipse Tollerton.

Events were to prove these remarks correct but they were made only shortly before the NFS Receiver was seeking offers for the NFS assets at Tollerton and the Corporation was receiving enquiries from individuals about the transfer of the lease.

\*

Both NFS and Nottingham Corporation were pioneers in the development of municipal aerodromes in Great Britain. Neither was successful in achieving the aims of those men who started the development of the organisations. NFS was not successful in raising the capital it required even to fully operate those few aerodromes where it forged partnerships with the municipal owners. Shortly after it started in business there was an industrial depression in the country but, even without that downturn, it is unlikely that it would have achieved its original objects. Nottingham Corporation failed to achieve its commercial aims for the aerodrome in its early phase because it was not prepared to invest in the infrastructure and passed on that responsibility to a third party in NFS.

Being at the forefront of the development of municipal aerodromes was not necessarily the business advantage originally anticipated. Later municipalities obviously learned from the Nottingham experience and retained control of their airfields. As a consequence they were more successful but, even so, this was only in the short term. The real reasons why internal commercial flying in Great Britain was not a lasting success were simply that there was no real need for it and the swift advancement of aircraft performance in the 1930s meant that the vision of a municipal airfield at every major town and city, based on the performance of the aircraft of the 1920s, was never going to be required.

# Chapter 2

# Successes and Failures

The Official Receiver began to seek offers for the assets of NFS. In connection with those at Tollerton the first person to contact the Town Clerk about the possibility of taking over the lease and purchasing the NFS equipment was H. J. Ashworth of The Nook, Lowdham, who met the Town Clerk to discuss the matter on 23 October 1933 when he said his intention was to develop Tollerton for both private and commercial flying and to retain the services of the present pilot instructor and engineers.

The Town Clerk stated the attitude of the Corporation to the sale and lease transfer in his reply of 31 October 1933 in which he emphasised the importance of the commercial development of the aerodrome:

> There is no objection to the lease being assigned from NFS to a responsible individual or Company on the distinct understanding that active steps are taken to popularise the Aerodrome and to provide an efficient and regular service for commercial and other purposes.
>
> The intention of the Corporation when it purchased land for, and established, the aerodrome was that it should be an active centre of Aviation and that Air services should be such as to make Nottingham the most important centre of Flying in the East Midlands.
>
> The following is an extract from a letter which I received recently from a Nottingham gentleman interested in the question who has had considerable experience of the Flying Services both on the Continent of Europe and America:-
>
> Nottingham would be an ideal centre. I strongly urge that whoever is in charge should work to the end of getting the Air Port for Great Britain established within a very short distance of the centre of Nottingham.
>
> Geographically Nottingham is central: Commercially it is not yet, but it should be. If we could get the Customs Authorities to have their Headquarters in Nottingham, it would greatly help the scheme.
>
> All large planes would leave Nottingham for France, Belgium, Holland, Germany. It is my belief that in future, night flying will be as common as day flying, also that air-craft will not be allowed to fly over large Cities when landing or taking off. Therefore, places like Croydon will be useless.
>
> An Air Port in Nottingham would introduce new ideas both for business and pleasure. There would have to be a first class hotel for the Air Port which would act as a Clearing House for human beings, and there would be a large Warehouse which would be a Clearing House for Goods, Mail etc.
>
> An Air Port in Nottingham would bring all Foreigners first to Nottingham and then re-distribute them by smaller craft to their places of destination. It would introduce Buyers to Nottingham who have never thought of making a visit to the

Nottingham Business Houses before. It would be an inducement for Business Houses to place their factories within easy reach of Nottingham Air Port. From Nottingham we can re-distribute people and goods by Air, by Road, by Rail and by Water.

On 4 November 1933 the Town Clerk confirmed that the lease could be transferred to Ashworth subject to all rents and other payments due to the Corporation being up to date and the accepting of an undertaking that the terms of the lease would be strictly complied with; active steps must be taken to 'push and popularise' the airport. No record of a reply from Ashworth has been located.

On 13 and 14 November 1933 two letters were received by the Town Clerk from North Eastern Aviation of Westfield, Ashington, Northumberland. The second requested a reply be sent to Captain L.W. Hall, The Elms, Gunthorpe, Notts. The letters requested details of the conditions under which the tenancy could be transferred and said that North Eastern Aviation was negotiating with the NFS Receiver for the purchase of the assets at Tollerton. The Town Clerk met Captain Hall on 15 November and supplied details of the lease.

A further enquiry was received on 29 November 1933 from David S. F. Hunt of Alderwasley Lodge, Alderwasley, Derby who indicated that he was interested in the purchase of the lease of the aerodrome when it came up for sale in December. The Town Clerk met him on the following Saturday morning to discuss the matter.

J. J. Hall, a prominent Northumbrian and wealthy businessman in the coal mining industry and owner of North Eastern Aviation, wrote to the Town Clerk on 11 December 1933 saying:

> With reference to Capt. L.W. Hall's interviews with you, we have now received a summary of the conditions of the lease from the Receiver of NFS.
>
> We would like to go on with the proposal if satisfactory terms can be agreed with the parties concerned, and we think we should be able to give complete satisfaction all round, if we can have the support and all the assistance possible.
>
> We feel that the terms of the present lease are onerous and that we should have some modification to enable us to carry on what will certainly be an uphill job at the beginning at any rate, and hope your committee will agree to a revision or a new Lease.

In support of his case he went on to explain how his son was experienced and qualified to be in charge of the airfield operation:

> I may say that Capt. Hall, who is my son, has been resident in the Nottingham district for a good many years and was one of the original members of the Nottingham Flying Club. He is eminently suited to take charge of the Aerodrome and is probably as experienced an airman as any in the country. He was in No. 2 Squadron in France at the beginning of the War and after returning acted as

Instructor at various RAF Training Stations in this country until he retired after 10 years service. For the last 6 years he has been actively engaged in civil aviation.

In the event of our arrangements being carried out, we should also endeavour to retain the services of the present pilot.

The NFS Receivers, Whinney, Smith and Whinney of London, had previously offered the Corporation the option of buying out the remaining period of the NFS lease and the NFS effects at the aerodrome. In the light of subsequent events it can be considered that this offer should have received more serious consideration from the Corporation but its unwillingness to invest more capital in the aerodrome prevailed. The eventual purchase of the NFS effects and renegotiation of the lease were made by North Eastern Aviation. The Company sought to negotiate changes to the lease and suggested that the rent should be 5% on gross receipts, excluding the clubhouse, or £100 per annum without consideration of landing fees and it asked for the 21 year term to run from 28 March 1934 when it would take over the aerodrome. This was not acceptable to the Corporation and the rent remained at £200 per annum with the percentages of gross receipts for landing fees set at 5% in the first year of the lease term rising incrementally to 25% from the 13th to 21st years of the term.

The aerodrome company was formed as Nottingham Airport Ltd with a nominal capital of 3,000 one pound shares. The directors were Joseph J. Hall, 'Westfield', Ashington, Northumberland, Mining Engineer; Lewis W. Hall, The Elms, Gunthorpe, Nottinghamshire, Aviation Pilot; and Thomas W. Shipside, Carrington Street, Nottingham, Motor Car Agent. The Nottingham Flying Club was taken over as part of the arrangement. Captain Hall took charge of the aerodrome with his wife managing the clubhouse, and Captain R. T. Shepherd was retained as Flying Instructor.

## Nottingham Airport Ltd

Relations between the Corporation and Nottingham Airport Ltd were good in the short term but strains soon began to appear and the Corporation was to become frustrated by what it saw as a lack of impetus in developing the commercial side of the aerodrome. The Flying Club became very successful but the commercial aspects were never strong; there seemed to be a lack of willingness on the part of the Company to spend money on the commercial development of Tollerton. The Company's accounts have not been located; they would possibly have revealed a degree of undercapitalisation which could have prevented a more serious approach to commercial aviation. The Company sought financial support from the Corporation on occasions such as in March 1935 when it asked the Corporation to pay for car parking provision and stated: '... as we foresaw, we have had an uphill task in taking over the Nottingham Airport and pulling it round.' At the same time the Corporation was asked to level a ridge on the airfield which was an obstruction to aeroplanes landing from the east. On 15 March 1935 the General Purposes Committee approved the provision of the car park, the repair of the access road and levelling of the ridge.

There were further requests from the Company for the Corporation to repair the access road culminating in a letter sent to the Town Clerk on 7 August 1935 complaining that the requested work had not been undertaken and saying that many members refused to take their cars over the road. The road led from Tollerton Lane across a field to the aerodrome boundary. This complaint provoked action and Sir Bernard Wright, then Chairman of the Corporation's Aviation Sub-Committee, indicated that the pot-holes would be filled and the road top-dressed with tar which 'should be good for three to four years'. At the same time Sir Bernard said the entrance gates would be set back by three yards and the car park finished off. Some trees needed removing: three or four of them were on Council land and were not a problem to remove but others were on Lord Manvers' and Sir Albert Ball's adjacent lands. The Land Agent would only agree to remove them after the season's crops had been taken off the land. The ridge was eventually levelled by J. B. Carr, Public Works Contractor of Tettenhall, Staffordshire at a cost of £233.6s.8d; the work required covered an area of 400 yards by 20 yards.

The Town Clerk had made approaches to the Air Ministry for the establishment of customs facilities at Tollerton in 1933 when rumours were heard that Leicester would be given such a facility. The request was refused on the grounds that the Air Ministry was not satisfied that such facilities were necessary at Tollerton because the volume of air traffic was not great enough. Aerodrome operators considered that it was very important for customs facilities to exist at their aerodromes because this enhanced their standing and would allow services to and from foreign countries to operate from them. In 1935 the Town Clerk made further representation for customs facilities which led to a Customs Officer visiting the aerodrome in August 1935 to discuss the matter with the Town Clerk and Captain Hall. He was particularly interested in the siting of accommodation which Customs Officers would require. The Nottingham Chamber of Commerce was also very interested in the provision of customs facilities and corresponded with the Town Clerk on several occasions about the issue. In the end the Customs Department decided that Tollerton was not an aerodrome where they wished to supply facilities, a decision which was very disappointing to the Town Clerk.

Although the Customs Department was not interested in Tollerton the Meteorological Office was. In August 1935 it contacted the Corporation about the possibility of the aerodrome acting as an auxiliary meteorological reporting station. Their requirements were set out in a pamphlet; weather reports would need to be sent by telegram to the Met. Office at 8 a.m. and noon daily. This request was passed on to Nottingham Airport Ltd which took up the invitation to be part the scheme.

The Town Clerk remained concerned at the lack of commercial aviation at Tollerton. In a memorandum to the General Purposes Committee dated 13 August 1935 he expressed his opinion that not enough was being done by the Corporation to ensure that Tollerton was being made into an 'Important Flying Centre'. He requested that a person, either a Council member or official of the Corporation, should be made responsible for keeping in close contact with Nottingham Airport Ltd and to regularly report to the Aviation Sub-Committee on what was required 'in the interests of the City to make it a busy Airport'. This request was not granted but the Committee decided on 20 September 1935 that Tollerton matters should be placed in the hands of the Lord Mayor, who was at that time Councillor R. E. Ashworth, together with Alderman Sir Albert Atkey, Alderman Sir Albert Ball, Alderman Farr, Alderman Pollard and Councillor Braddock.

## Extensions and Other Developments

Early in 1936 discussions were being led by Alderman Farr to ascertain what land could be acquired to extend the aerodrome. Alderman Farr was an enthusiast for civil aviation and a strong proponent of the development of Tollerton as an enhancement to Nottingham's business environment. He felt that a bill being passed through Parliament supported the development of commercial aviation and that the City should seek to improve and develop the aerodrome for this purpose. The City Engineer reported that an additional 141.882 acres of land could be used to extend the aerodrome, of which 41.882 acres were already owned by the Corporation. He indicated three areas which should be sterilized from development to provide flying gaps and for the operation of blind and night landing apparatus. Certain areas should be controlled from a height of building aspect and an area of 292 acres could be reserved for industrial purposes connected with flying. He also considered that a new administrative area should be established closer to the public highway, rather than erect buildings in the vicinity of the clubhouse.

On 29 April 1936 the City Engineer and the Chairman and Vice-Chairman of the General Purposes Committee held a meeting at the aerodrome with Major Mealing of the Air Ministry to establish what developments would be desirable to improve the aerodrome for use by the larger aeroplanes then coming into airline service. On 30 April the *Guardian Journal* reported that the improvements suggested included enlarging the landing area so that the 'minimum distance from one end of the flying ground to the other, in any direction, will be 1,000 yards'. This was necessary because the landing speeds of commercial aircraft had increased substantially from when the aerodrome was first opened. Serious consideration was being given for the provision of lights to enable the aerodrome to be used at night. A Hornet Moth was to be fitted with navigation lights for testing purposes and the aerodrome would be illuminated by a new type of searchlight projector capable of throwing a beam 100 yards wide over a distance of 600 yards. The light projector was tried for the first time in late April and an air liner took off at 10.30 p.m. for Croydon, the first time a commercial flight had taken place from Tollerton in the dark. However, no evidence that this facility was made permanent has been found. In May the Air Ministry was asked to equip the aerodrome with wireless equipment to assist fog landings. This request was refused on the grounds that such equipment was strictly limited and all that was available had been allotted to other aerodromes.

Alderman Farr continued to press for development and on 2 May 1936 wrote to the Town Clerk expressing his fears that Nottingham was 'lacking enterprise'; that Leicester was forging ahead with its aerodrome developments and 'the small borough of Doncaster' was spending large sums on its recently opened airfield. By this time two commercial operators had dropped Tollerton from their schedules.

Whilst awaiting Major Mealing's official recommendations the Air Ministry indicated that there were deficiencies in the fire fighting and crash equipment at Tollerton and requested that these be urgently put right. In discussion with Captain Hall, the Corporation agreed to purchase a car chassis and a suitable body for the crash vehicle was built onto the chassis by Bennetts (Nottingham) Ltd at a cost of £75. In addition it was necessary to buy one 30 gallon foam extinguisher, six two gallon foam extinguishers, two salving hooks, asbestos gauntlets and asbestos sheeting for fire protection; asbestos was obviously not recognised as a problematic material in the 1930s. It was not considered necessary to provide an ambulance because the one stationed at West Bridgford could be at the aerodrome within minutes. The total expenditure on the safety equipment was £235.

The Air Ministry sent Major Mealing's report to the Corporation on 7 July 1936 which supported the extension of the aerodrome by the purchase of the additional land to enable a blind landing runway 1,300 yards long by 400 yards wide together with runways of 1,000 yards in all directions. The existing buildings would have to be removed and re-sited to prevent obstruction to aircraft and land outside the landing area should be purchased, or at least scheduled, to ensure that nothing outside the landing area would cause an obstruction to flying. The report stated, 'I am to add ... an excellent municipal aerodrome should evolve to serve Nottingham and the surrounded [sic] district'.

There were no problems in acquiring land owned by Sir Albert Ball's company and 321.759 acres were bought at a cost of £44 per acre totalling £14,157.7s.11d. Completion of this purchase was effected on 6 May 1937. This land was occupied by tenants, J. D. Houlbrook of Manor Farm, C. W. Kirk of Chestnut Farm, G. A. Woodward of Gamston, and there were four allotments. The District Valuer described the land as:

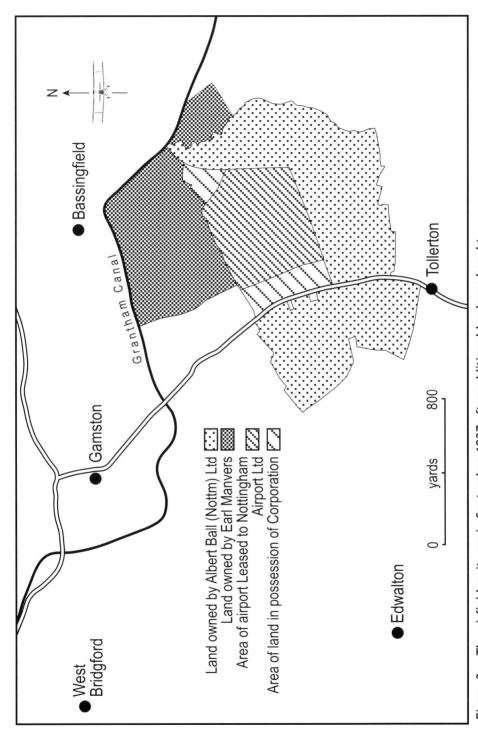

**Figure 3   The airfield as it was in September 1937 after additional land was bought.**
*Dr. Anne Tarver; Nottinghamshire County Archive Service*

A block of agricultural land adjoining the eastern, western and southern side of Tollerton aerodrome and includes mostly pasture land with some arable and a small wood … conforms to the level of the road, except a small portion on the southern boundary which rises to 6 feet above the road. The land on the eastern side of Gamston Road is practically flat, but the land on the western side falls slightly from the north and south towards the centre. Gamston road on which the land abuts contains no sewer, but water and lighting services are available.

The 165.967 acres of land belonging to Earl Manvers were made the subject of a compulsory purchase order. Tenants of this land, which mainly bordered the Grantham canal, were Dan Simpkins and John T. Hallam both of Bassingfield.

A major dispute arose between Nottingham Airport Ltd and the Corporation when the lease of the aerodrome was included in the compulsory purchase order. It is obvious that the Corporation were dissatisfied with the manner in which the aerodrome was being operated by the Company as illustrated by an undated memorandum from the Town Clerk to the General Purposes Committee:

The operation of the Airport by the lessees is not satisfactory mainly because the lessees have not done anything to promote the progress of commercial air-line operation at the Airport.

It would appear that from time to time the Corporation spend small sums at the Airport which, under the terms of the lease, are the liability of the lessees. The landing area does not appear to have been maintained in best fashion. The lessees have not complied with the obligation to collect landing fees from visiting aircraft upon which a percentage is payable to the Corporation.

It is felt that if the Airport is to be properly developed and commercial air-line traffic is to be encouraged, it is necessary to purchase further land to enlarge the landing area of the Air port and to provide lighting for night flying.

Prior to the issue of the compulsory purchase order a meeting was held on 17 September 1936 attended by Alderman Farr, the Deputy Town Clerk, Captain Hall, the Company Secretary Mr Burbidge, and the Company's solicitor Mr Jacobson of Browne, Jacobson and Hallam, when the Corporation's proposals for the aerodrome were put forward. The Company people expressed the opinion that the facilities for commercial aviation currently provided were all that were required. This suggests either that there was a financial inability to fund the improvements which were required for Tollerton to compete with the newer aerodromes in the Region or that the Company just did not know what facilities these new aerodromes were providing. The latter seems most unlikely when Club members were frequently visiting other aerodromes and it seems more probable that the directors of Nottingham Airport Ltd had no real desire to see more commercial use of their facilities. This put the Company into conflict with the Corporation which obviously held different views based on their perception of what other aerodromes were providing and what was required at Tollerton to increase commercial flights. In a letter sent to the Town Clerk on 30 September 1936, Browne Jacobson and Hallam said that the Company's Directors would have been willing to negotiate the basis of the proposals but very much resented that a Compulsory Purchase Order had been issued without notice immediately after the meeting. They said the CPO would be strenuously opposed by the Company.

The CPO had to be sent to the Air Ministry for approval and there were

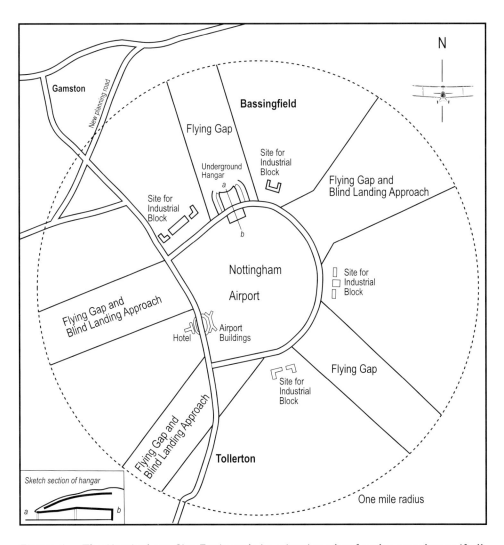

**Figure 4**     The Nottingham City Engineer's imaginative plan for the aerodrome if all the CPO land had been acquired and funds made available for construction work. *Dr. Anne Tarver; Nottinghamshire County Archive Office*

prevarications about it within the Air Ministry. Files at The National Archives show that the Air Ministry was not certain whether it could approve such a CPO under the Air Navigation Acts 1920 and 1936 and consequently delayed a decision for quite some time whilst consulting other Government agencies. The Secretary of Nottingham Airport Ltd wrote to the Air Ministry strongly objecting to the CPO on several grounds, including the opinion that the lease could not be the subject of a CPO under the quoted Acts, that the Corporation had no right to seek to recover the lease and that if it did succeed in recovering the lease the interests of the members of the Nottingham Flying Club and the Tollerton Aero Club Ltd would be prejudiced. (This is only the second reference to a Tollerton Aero Club that has been found. There were no buildings at the aerodrome which such a club could have used or any details of its activities.) The Treasury Solicitor eventually advised the Air Ministry that such a CPO was not *ultra vires* but in view of the Company's objection a local inquiry must be held. There were delays in setting up an inquiry and this resulted in several bitter letters of complaint being sent to the Air Ministry by the Town Clerk.

The Corporation was pursuing the CPO on the ground of developing civil aviation but there was a sub-plot in that they were also intending to operate an RAF Reserve Training School under Air Ministry licence. In 1936 the Government started to seriously prepare for war and expansion plans for the RAF were put in place. Recognition of the need for many more pilots than the RAF then had led to a decision to set up a civilian organisation for the training of pilots. The Corporation saw this as a way of increasing its income from the airfield by operating such a training school. Approaches were received from four companies, two of which had offered to pay £1,250 a year rent for a licence to operate a Civil Training School at Tollerton on behalf of the Air Ministry, including the erection of associated buildings. These two offers were from Airwork Ltd of Heston Airport and the Herts and Essex Aeroplane Club Ltd of Broxbourne Aerodrome. The matter was obviously of interest to the Corporation since it would provide it with an additional £1,000 a year over the rent being paid by Nottingham Airport Ltd. A third expression of interest was received from Surrey Flying Services and a later offer was received from Marshall's Flying School Ltd of Cambridge.

In view of the objections to the CPO from Nottingham Airport Ltd and the delays in the setting up of a local inquiry that part of the CPO relating to the lease of Nottingham Airport Ltd was dropped at a meeting of the full Nottingham City Council on 5 July 1937. The following day the *Nottingham Guardian* reported that the General Purposes Committee had considered that the expenditure required to develop the airfield was not justified. They thought the Air Ministry was by then more concerned with military than civil aviation and consequently circumstances had changed. This was an obvious face-saving exercise by the Corporation which had been forced to retract its position in the face of the opposition by Nottingham Airport Ltd although it was also said that a nearby airport was losing between £4,000 and £5,000 a year. The part of the order relating to Lord Manvers' land proceeded and the Secretary of State's order granting the amended CPO was signed on 31 December 1937. The Corporation did not immediately activate the CPO and it was not until the Finance and General Purposes Committee met on 31 May 1939 that it was decided to purchase the land under the order. No evidence has been found that the purchase was actually completed before war broke out.

Meanwhile, other disputes were taking place between the Airport Company and the Corporation. A small one was over the cost of licensing the fire tender at the aerodrome which the Company said was owned by the Corporation and consequently the Company should not have to pay for the licence. A more serious dispute arose over the Company's perceived failure to correctly collect landing fees which was prompted by the City Treasurer on 12 July 1937 when he asked the Town Clerk to seek appropriate fees from the Company. The Company took the view that it was not required to collect fees under the terms of the aerodrome lease but it was prepared to discuss the issue with the Corporation. On 20 March 1938 it told the Town Clerk that during 1937 the numbers of visiting aircraft were 98 commercial, 240 private owners, 217 club members and 72 RAF.

Commercial aircraft had been charged landing fees; of the private owners 25% were members of Nottingham Flying Club and of the others approximately another 25% were piloted by members of the Flying Club who were not required to pay a landing fee and none of the service machines paid a fee. There followed discussions about whether the RAF aircraft should pay fees, with the Corporation saying that the Aerodrome Owners' Association had agreed with the Air Ministry that RAF aircraft not associated with Flying Schools should pay landing fees. The Company eventually agreed to charge fees in accordance with a scale to be agreed between the Association and the Air Ministry and that from 7 May 1938 they would charge fees of:-

| | |
|---|---|
| Private Owners | 1/- |
| Visiting Clubs | 1/- |
| Commercial machines | |
| Up to 3 seats | 2/6 |
| 4 to 5 seats | 5/- |
| 6 to 8 seats | 7/6 |
| Over 8 seats | 10/- |
| RAF aircraft | |
| Up to 1500 lbs | 1/- |
| 1600 to 2500 lbs | 1/6 |
| 2600 to 3500 lbs | 2/6 |
| 3600 to 4500 lbs | 5/- |

A. 3641/39

## FORM OF REQUISITION OF LAND (AND BUILDINGS)
## FROM THE OWNER.

To   The Mayor, Aldermen and Citizens of the
                City of Nottingham.

The Owner of the land (and buildings) described in the Schedule annexed hereto.

TAKE NOTICE that in exercise of his powers under the Defence Regulations, 1939, the Secretary of State has given authority for taking possession of the land (and buildings) described in the Schedule hereto annexed, and that I, on behalf of the Secretary of State take possession of the said land (and buildings).

Date 26ᵗʰ September, 1939.

(*Signed*)

(~~Assistant~~) *Lands Officer,*
*Air Ministry, W.C.2.*

I hereby acknowledge receipt of a notice of which the above is a duplicate.

Date 29ᵗʰ September 1939

(*Owner*)

Town Clerk
Nottingham

Compensation for the lands (and buildings) requisitioned will in due course be paid on such terms as Parliament may authorise.

(393/2610A) G. 2357  2000  8/39  H & S, Ltd.  (2555)

**Plate 5:**   **The Air Ministry's requisition certificate dated 26 September 1939.**
*Nottinghamshire County Archive Service*

On 24 June 1938 the Corporation received payment of its proportion of the landing fees for 1935 to 1938 amounting to £4.11s.10d.

A twist in the tail of the lease situation occurred early in 1939 when the Company sought to surrender the remaining term of the lease to the Corporation subject to it being allowed to continue operating the Reserve Training School, the civilian flying club and the Civil Air Guard scheme. The Corporation would receive all the payments from the Air Ministry relating to the training schools and would pay the Company £200 a year for 18 years, but the Company would pay rates for its buildings at Tollerton. The Airport sub-committee decided on 19 May 1939 that they would not pay the Company £200 a year and that they would not grant an extension of seven years when the 18 year term expired. They also resolved to limit the number of aircraft free from landing fees connected to the Civil Air Guard and the civilian flying club to 10; any in excess of this number would require payment of fees to the Corporation. Although the Company wrote to the Town Clerk on 2 June 1939 agreeing to the terms for the surrender of the lease no evidence has been found that this actually took place and it can be assumed that the outbreak of war and the requisitioning of the aerodrome by the Air Ministry on 2 September 1939, confirmed on 26 September 1939, interfered with this process.

## Agricultural Tenants

The aerodrome did not encompass all the land that the Corporation acquired in 1929 and the surplus was let to local farmers. The land bought in 1929 had been held by Mr Plowright who had given notice that he was quitting the tenancy before the sale took place and, consequently, the Corporation had vacant possession when the sale was completed.

On 27 August 1929 D. G. Hutchinson of Edward Road, West Bridgford asked the Town Clerk if he could exercise horses on the aerodrome. He was a member of the Nottingham Aero Club and said he was aware that the aerodrome should be kept clear and he would, therefore, only have horses there between 5 a.m. and 8 a.m. He suggested that there was a precedent in that such use was allowed on the military aerodromes at Cranwell and Spittalgate near Grantham; his request was refused.

On 6 April 1931 Mr Kirk of The Chestnuts, Tollerton, asked that the field on the south side of the road leading to the aerodrome be fenced because his cattle and sheep were straying onto the main road when the aerodrome gates were frequently left open. The aerodrome did not extend directly up to Tollerton Lane at this time; there was a field between its boundary and the lane. The City Engineer investigated the complaint and said that the hedge on the south was not in perfect condition and cattle could push through. He considered that as the rent was only 25/- an acre the tenant should make good the defects and that the Corporation was not responsible for the gates or the hedges.

In December 1931 Kirk asked for the tenancy to be transferred to his son who had apparently taken over the grazing at the aerodrome. He was told that the lease could not be transferred but there was no objection to him sub-leasing the land to his son. In November 1933 Kirk unsuccessfully requested that his rent be reduced because he could not cover its cost due to the low price of cattle and sheep. He rented 22.807 acres of grazing land from 10 May 1930 and his annual rent was £34.4s.2d.

Another unsuccessful request for rent reduction was made by John Holbrook of Manor Farm, Tollerton, in November 1934 on the basis that he paid less per acre to Sir Albert Ball for renting land adjacent to that which he rented from the Corporation.

P. S. Woodward of Hill Farm, Gamston took the lease of land west of the aerodrome in late 1934 and said that the water supply to the land was poor. In May 1935 he asked for water to be laid on to the land because the pond there was almost dry. This request had not received attention a year later when it was mentioned by Kirk who, when paying his rent, said 'which is required very bad'.

The land bought from Albert Ball (Nottingham) Ltd in 1936 had several tenants. The main two were C. W. Kirk and J. D. Houlbrook, both of Tollerton. Kirk paid 29/- per acre for each field except one for which he paid £10.14s.8d on a yearly tenancy. Houlbrook paid 26/- an acre apart from one field where the rent was £1 per acre.

There were also allotments in the parcel whose tenants were:-

| Mr Chambers, | Tollerton | 8/- per annum |
|---|---|---|
| Mr Lane, | Tollerton | 5/- per annum |
| Mr Shaw, | Tollerton | 5/- per annum |
| Mr Orr, | Tollerton | 2/6d per annum |

Kirk was persistent in his efforts to secure a reduction in his rent and in December 1937 he asked again on the grounds that the sale of some adjacent land for building had led to inconvenience caused by cesspools draining onto his land which was very injurious to his cattle because they were constantly paddling in and drinking from it. He also said his land was mainly arable and not a good proposition at that time. He was told that no reduction could be made but the Town Clerk would write appropriately to any property owner who was causing the nuisance if he would supply their names. Kirk does not appear to have followed this up. There were two private properties on this land, one bungalow occupied by Captain Hall of Nottingham Airport Ltd and another property owned by Mrs Meakin.

Kirk tried for a rent reduction yet again in July 1938 saying that the spring had been wet and he had been unable to get onto his land to work it and therefore his crops did not produce enough money. He said the land was in need of draining and that he had two acres of summer fallow. There appears to have been an element of frustration with Kirk when the Town Clerk replied that no reduction could be given and 'there is a feeling that your land is not properly farmed and that you are not making the best use of your opportunities'. Kirk was given notice to quit 22.807 acres of his holding on 21 March 1939 because the land was required for Air Ministry developments at the aerodrome. At the same time some of Woodward's land was required for the same purpose. He was willing to give immediate possession having sold stock in anticipation of this after he had learned that Kirk had been given notice. Negotiations for both tenants were conducted by Turner Fletcher, land agents of Nottingham with agreement being reached on compensation for Woodward at £33 and Kirk £13.

Houlbrook received notice that the Air Ministry was to requisition 29.812 acres of his land and, on his behalf, Walker, Walton & Hanson of Nottingham contacted the Town Clerk. Houlbrook had a right of way across the southern boundary of the aerodrome to a bridge in the south-east corner on the east side of the brook. They requested a replacement right of way along the south boundary of a field which was to be requisitioned; if Houlbrook could not have this he would be unable to use the bridge and so could not access 40 acres of his land. The alternative would be for a bridge to be built for him closer to Tollerton village. He had also been instructed by the Air Ministry to immediately move his beasts off the requisitioned land and, having sold 16 of his 66, he would have to sell the rest unless the Air Ministry erected a fence on the new boundary to the aerodrome. The Town Clerk replied that this request should be addressed to the Air Ministry; no evidence of whether the request was granted has been found.

In April 1940 the Corporation's Estates Surveyor reported that land given up by Kirk had been re-let to Mr Hallam of Clipston-on-the-Wolds on condition that the Corporation would erect a cowshed for 10 beasts together with a small wash-house and milk store. The rent was 27/- per acre for the first half year and 32/- per acre thereafter. On 22 June 1940 Albert Ball (Nottingham) Ltd advised that Hallam was saying the land was in poor condition and had asked for a year free of rent. They said this was not justified but as he would be a good tenant a contribution towards lime and slag could be justified. They also said the previous tenant, Kirk, was 'most unsatisfactory' which supported the Corporation officials' opinion of him.

# Chapter 3

# Moving People and Goods

The development of internal air services in the United Kingdom lagged far behind its European neighbours and the USA. Great emphasis was placed on air services to the Empire, and Imperial Airways, flying out of Croydon, received support and encouragement from successive governments. There was less official enthusiasm for internal air-line development which was partly due to the lack of aerodrome facilities and partly to a lack of enthusiasm for air travel from business and general public. In addition distances between large towns and cities were much shorter than on the Continent and in the USA and there was an efficient rail network connecting large areas of the country. Sir Alan Cobham sought to raise the profile of air travel with his air pageants in the 1930s and had tried to encourage the building of aerodromes by local authorities in the mid and late 1920s by visiting many municipalities throughout the country.

Nottingham's Council was in the forefront of the establishment of municipal aerodromes and received encouragement from the Junior Chamber of Commerce and local business leaders, especially the Managing Director of William Hollins Ltd, a large textile business. However, the Council was not prepared to spend money on developing the aerodrome's infrastructure beyond making a level landing-ground and so leased the running to National Flying Services Ltd. The decision to grant National Flying Services Ltd a lease of the aerodrome was not without its critics and, particularly, the aviation correspondent of the *Nottingham Journal* who wrote several articles in 1930 and 1931 criticising the Corporation for not playing an active part in the development of Tollerton. His opinion was that the Corporation was not prepared to take a serious interest in the aerodrome. He also criticised the lack of use of facilities for air travel by Nottingham businessmen and, in particular, thought that the Junior Chamber of Commerce was not doing enough to encourage businesses to use air travel. A short quotation can summarise his attitude:

> Those cities which have efficient airports, equipped for every kind of air transport, will have a great advantage over those which have not.

He compared Nottingham City Council adversely with Leicester where the City Council and Chamber of Commerce were actively giving support to aviation at the Leicestershire Aero Club's aerodrome at Desford and, later, to a municipal aerodrome at Braunstone.

The correspondent was happy to acknowledge that the NFS Flying Club was doing a useful job, although he had some reservations about how the Company could make commercial aviation fit into its prime activities in training people to fly. He reasoned that 'NFS must pay their way and no aviation company can pay its way and develop other people's business at the same time.' This was a rather harsh comment because members of the Council's Aviation sub-committee - in particular Sir Albert Ball - were enthusiastic about the aerodrome and felt it had great potential for the business community of the city. However, it does become apparent that a lack of investment in the infrastructure of the aerodrome, coupled with an apparent lack of enthusiasm by business in the City, meant that Tollerton did not become the major airport for the region and was not used by airlines to the extent that those people who supported its opening had hoped for. Headlines in the local press to the effect that Tollerton would become the 'Croydon of the Midlands', and 'an aeroplane manufacturing centre', proved wide of the mark.

Attempts to interest local business people in aviation were made by aircraft companies and, of course, by NFS, Sir Alan Cobham and others through air pageants. On 27 November 1930 the *Nottingham Journal* reported that the Lord Mayor of Nottingham, Alderman A. Pollard, had taken his first flight in a six-seat, three-engined Westland Wessex cabin monoplane from Nottingham. This was a promotional flight by the Westland Company and the pilot was F. J. Brunton, the company's chief test pilot. Accompanying the Lord Mayor was the Chief Constable, Captain A. Popkess. Subsequent flights were made carrying businessmen from both Nottingham and Derby. After his flight Alderman Pollard said:

> We have a magnificent air port. It would be a good idea to bless it by having a municipal aeroplane. I cannot, of course, definitely commit myself to such a policy, but at the same time, any demand for such a machine would receive my fullest support. Such an aeroplane would be very useful for conducting various delegations and for survey work. It might also be used by city business men. I am convinced that air transport is going to develop rapidly and Nottingham must be well ahead.

Captain Popkess, anticipating current police practices with helicopters, said that he was anxious to have an aerial survey made of Nottingham which would enable him to quickly and easily organise patrols as well as being useful to simplify traffic problems. Sir Albert Ball backed the Lord Mayor's suggestion for a municipal aeroplane but the Council was not prepared to fund this because it saw no need for one.

A number of more or less successful small independent airlines were formed in the UK between 1932 and 1936 but none made a massive impact on air travel and some only existed for a short time. Internal air services were mainly operated in the spring, summer and autumn months and not during winter. An article in *The Aeroplane* of 18 March 1936 provided figures for the route miles covered by private airlines serving Great Britain and Northern Ireland which give a very good indication of how much flying was being undertaken by these concerns:-

| PERIOD | SUMMER MILES | WINTER MILES |
|--------|-------------|--------------|
| 1933 | 1,180 | |
| 1933-34 | | 377 |
| 1934 | 3,170 | |
| 1934-5 | | 1,605 |
| 1935 | 6,500 | |
| 1935-6 | | 2,350 |

Table 1: Route flying figures for the internal air lines, 1933 to 1936

## Air Taxi Service

An early attempt at commercial operations was made by NFS which sought to establish an air-taxi service from its seven aerodromes, including Tollerton. *Flight* of 11 July 1930 reported the establishment of this service and that the aircraft used were Desoutter two-passenger monoplanes which cruised at 95 mph. The company owned nine Desoutters, seven of which were in service at any one time with two held in reserve for emergencies. It also reported that NFS owned a total of 55 aircraft, all of which could be used for urgent air-taxi work if required. The cost of the air-taxi was one shilling a mile for a single passenger machine such as a Moth or Bluebird, and one shilling and six pence a mile for a Desoutter.

In June 1930 an NFS Desoutter was put on display for publicity purposes in the show rooms of Oscroft's, a car dealership in Nottingham.

An attempt to publicise the air-taxi service was made at the September 1930 Tollerton air pageant. An NFS owned de Havilland eight-seat air liner flew from the NFS headquarters at Hanworth to Tollerton carrying visitors to the following day's air pageant. On the morning following the Tollerton pageant the aircraft was to leave Tollerton for an NFS pageant being held at Sherburn-in-Elmet. The fare was thirty shillings, the journey was one way and passengers had to return by bus or train. They were collected by car from outside the Black Boy Hotel in central Nottingham and taken to Tollerton for the flight. Unfortunately no record was made of how many took advantage of this flight. However, the fact that it was aimed at publicity is illustrated by NFS saying it was an experiment which was aimed at businessmen who could use such a service to fly themselves or their goods to any part of the UK or the Continent.

The *Nottingham Guardian* Trade Review of 1 January 1931 reported that a Nottingham man first showed the public how useful an air-taxi could be. He arranged a flight by NFS from Hanworth to visit his dying father on the Canary

Islands. The review suggested that his example could be followed by any businessman needing a quick visit to the Continent. However, there does not seem to have been much demand for such services and the Tollerton based Desoutter had not been used by anyone according to the *Nottingham Journal* Business Review of 1 January 1931.

## Going To The Seaside

Eastern Air Transport Ltd was formed in February 1932 by G. A. Pennington of Staines and M. D. L. Scott of London. Scott had been operating an air-taxi and pleasure flight business at Skegness since 1929. He was offered the aerodrome site adjoining the North Shore Golf Club at Skegness, increased its size to 80 acres and built a clubhouse and additional hangars. His business seems to have been successful as *Flight*, in reporting the formation of Eastern Air Transport Ltd, reported that Scott's previous business had carried 10,000 passengers in the previous two years and owned a Puss Moth and two Gypsy Moths which operated daily services between Skegness and Hunstanton.

The inaugural flight of a new service between Tollerton and Skegness took place on 18 May 1932 when the Lord Mayor of Nottingham, Alderman W. Green, flew to Skegness in DH Puss Moth, G-AAXL. (This aircraft later crashed on Dog's Head Sands in the Wash on 26 May 1932 whilst on the Hunstanton service.) The flight from Skegness to Tollerton took 33 minutes, flying over Grantham, Sleaford and Boston, at an average speed of 120 mph. The pilot was Scott and the Lord Mayor was accompanied by a friend, Mrs Robert Hardy; the Lady Mayoress travelled by car. A second aircraft took Mr & Mrs Richardson to Skegness. Richardson, of the Derby Road Car Park Company in Nottingham, was joint operator of the service with Eastern Air Transport Ltd. On arrival at Skegness the party was met by the Chairman of Skegness Urban District Council and other dignitaries.

On the return trip the Lord Mayor travelled with another friend, Mrs Ireland of Beeston and, again, the Lady Mayoress returned by car. The return flight left Skegness at 5.50 p.m. and arrived at Tollerton at 6.30 p.m., the pilot having detoured to avoid a thunderstorm over Boston. It was said that the aeroplane was so warm the party did not require their overcoats or wraps.

This service was operated daily, leaving Tollerton at 10.00 a.m., with return flight leaving Skegness at 5.30 p.m. It proved popular, but was not without controversy. On 6 June 1932 Eastern Air Transport Ltd wrote to the Nottingham Town Clerk complaining that NFS were adopting an obstructive attitude to the service as well as charging six shillings landing fee. Eastern said the service was so popular that on 5 June they had flown five trips to Skegness. They felt the landing charges were forcing them to charge more than they wished for the journey. The letter was referred to NFS who said the charges were in accordance with Air Ministry rates but a small reduction had been immediately made. This was followed by a letter of 14 June from The Master of Sempill, the Managing Director of NFS, who took the opportunity of reminding the Town Clerk that the City had done nothing to help them by reducing their annual rent for the aerodrome.

The service operated during 1933 and 1934 but was taken over by Crilly Airways for 1935. In 1936 Scott disbanded his airline and closed the airfield and the associated Skegness and East Lincolnshire Aero Club.

## Further Afield

On Friday 9 February 1934, London, Scottish and Provincial Airways Ltd demonstrated aeroplanes at Tollerton to the Lord Mayor of Nottingham, the Deputy Sheriff of Nottingham, the Town Clerk, three councillors from the City, three councillors from Manchester, five business people from Derby and some staff members from Rolls-Royce Ltd of Derby.

The purpose of the day was 'to emphasise to the population of Midlands towns the vital importance of speed and to demonstrate the types of aircraft which are to be used towards gaining this end'. A booklet was supplied giving details of a proposed London to Glasgow air service, where the traveller was promised breakfast in Glasgow and lunch in Paris. Internal travelling times would be less

**Plate 6:    Passengers waiting to embark on a flight from Tollerton to Skegness.**
*Simon Woodroffe family archive*

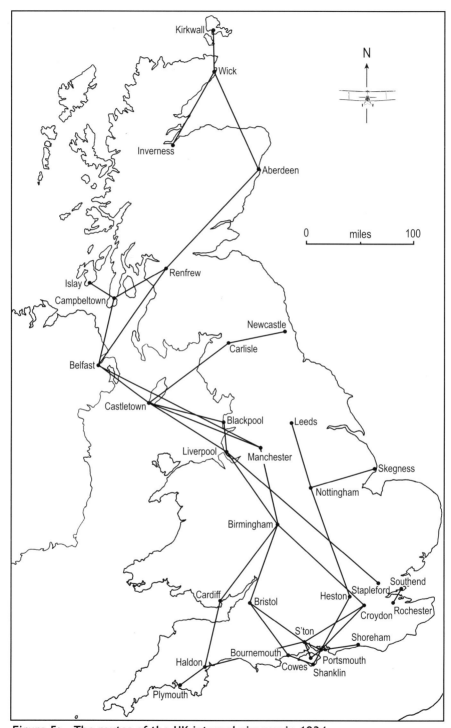

**Figure 5: The routes of the UK internal airways in 1934.**
*Dr. Anne Tarver; Nottinghamshire County Archive Service*

than half the time taken by the quickest train. The service would operate between Croydon, Derby, Manchester and Glasgow and the Company had offered to build and operate an aerodrome at Derby if the corporation there would supply the site. If Derby Corporation could not agree to this then Tollerton would be used instead, and if this was not possible then the service would go straight to Manchester.

The aeroplanes demonstrated were an Airspeed Courier with Siddeley Lynx engines and a Blackburn Seagrave with two Gipsy 11 engines. Also to be seen were the Hart and Horsley loaned to Rolls-Royce Ltd by the Air Ministry for engine testing purposes which were based at Tollerton at that time. *Flight* for 15 February 1934 indicated that the airline had ordered four Lynx IV C engined Airspeed Couriers for the service.

The service was inaugurated at the start of August 1934 operating daily from Leeds. The Airspeed Courier six-seat monoplanes departed from Tollerton at 9.35 a.m. and 3.35 p.m., were at Heston, London, less than an hour later, at Le Touquet in two hours and Paris within three hours. Flights left Paris at 9.00 a.m. and 3.00 p.m., arriving at Tollerton at 12.05 p.m. and 6.05 p.m. respectively. Connections were available to Jersey and the Isle of Wight. Passengers were collected by car from the Black Boy in Nottingham 35 minutes prior to the flight time and returned there on arrival back at Tollerton. The booking agent for Nottingham was Mr Richardson of Derby Road Car Park. The single fare from Leeds to Nottingham was £1.1s.0d and Nottingham to Paris £5.5s.0d; the return Tollerton to Paris cost £10.

Claims were made that this was the second fastest air service in the world and the fastest in the British Empire. A reporter for the *Nottingham Journal* who made the flight in September 1934 said the speedometer rarely dropped below 140 mph. *Flight* for 20 September 1934 reported that in its first week of operation the service carried nine passengers, a month later 40 had been carried including 21 on one day, and 98 per cent regularity was being achieved. The Paris sector was said to be not entirely satisfactory because facilities at Le Bourget were poor for small operators and the magazine suggested that the airline should get together with Hillman Air and Jersey Airways to pool resources, although there is no indication that this suggestion was taken up.

The same company used Tollerton as a stop on its London to Glasgow service which commenced operating on 19 March 1935 travelling via Manchester. The first flight carried three or four passengers and on landing at Tollerton the pilot did not stop his engines whilst he asked for a telegram to be sent to London. This was a Courier aircraft and, on the same day, another Courier landed at Tollerton from Manchester at 11.10 a.m. carrying two passengers. This latter aeroplane was piloted by F. Jacques, the Company's Group Superintendent, who told a *Nottingham Journal* reporter that the schedule was for an aeroplane to leave Tollerton for Glasgow at 10.20 a.m. every day and another for London at

11.10 a.m. However the London flight might be at 12.10 p.m. on alternate days until the company could have seven aeroplanes running the service. It was reported that the flight to Glasgow took three hours and, whilst crossing the border between Cumberland and Scotland it had to fly at 7,000 feet. The flight to London was less than an hour from Tollerton.

On 20 January 1935 Provincial Airways Ltd based at Croydon notified the Town Clerk that they were proposing to operate a summer service between Hull, Nottingham, Leicester, Southampton and Plymouth commencing on 1 March. There would be two services a day on the route which would connect at Plymouth with their London to Penzance service, and they expressed a hope that the service would carry mail. The timetable and fare table supplied was:

| SERVICE 1 | | SERVICE 2 | |
|---|---|---|---|
| Hull | Depart 11.55 a.m. | Plymouth | Depart 10.50 a.m. |
| Nottingham | Arrive 12.30 p.m. | Southampton | Arrive 11 50 a.m. |
| Leicester | Arrive 12.45 p.m. | Leicester | Arrive 1.40 p.m. |
| Southampton | Arrive 2.00 p.m. | Nottingham | Arrive 1.55 p.m. |
| Plymouth | Arrive 3.35 p.m. | Hull | Arrive 2.30 p.m. |

Table 2    The timetable for the route from Hull to Plymouth flown by Provincial Airways in 1935

| PLACE | SINGLE | RETURN |
|---|---|---|
| Hull – Grimsby | 5s. 0d | 9s. 0d |
| Nottingham | £1.7s. 6d | £2.12s 6d |
| Leicester | £1.12s.6d | £3.0s.0d |
| Southampton | £3.12s.6d | £6.10s.0d |
| Shanklin | £4.0s.0d | £7.12s.0d |
| Grimsby – Nottingham | £1.2s.0d | £2.2s.0d |
| Leicester | £1.7s.6d | £2.12s.0d |
| Southampton | £3.7s.6d | £6.8s.0d |
| Shanklin | £3.15s.0d | £7.2s.6d |
| Nottingham – Leicester | 10s.0d | 19s.0d |
| Southampton | £2.10s.0d | £4.15s0d |
| Shanklin | £2.17s.6d | £5.10s.0d |

Table 3:    Fares for the 1935 Provincial Airways service

| NOTTINGHAM TO | SINGLE | RETURN |
|---|---|---|
| Croydon | £3.15s.0d | £7. 2s.6d |
| Portsmouth | £3. 0s.0d | £5.15s.0d |
| Bournemouth | £3. 5s.0d | £6. 5s.0d |
| Torquay | £4.10s.0d | £8.10s.0d |
| Plymouth | £4.15s.0d | £9. 0s.0d |
| Penzance | £6. 0s.0d | £11.7s.6d |
| Newquay | £5.15s.0d | £10.17s.6d |

Table 4: Fares for the Provincial Airways Ltd service from Nottingham to Newquay, 1935.

The Company invited Nottingham's Lord Mayor to have a free passage on the inaugural flight of 1 March and promised the timetable would be adjusted to ensure his return to Tollerton before dusk but he had to decline. The inaugural date was changed to 4 March and the invitation re-issued. The Lord Mayor again declined but said he and the Town Clerk would meet the aeroplane on its arrival at Tollerton to greet those civic dignitaries from Hull who had accepted the invitation.

The Corporation agreed to place posters advertising the service on its public notice boards although this brought protest from the City Librarian to Provincial Airways who wrote a rather sharp letter to the Town Clerk:-

Perhaps your City librarian cannot see that internal airways are bringing benefit to internal cities, and that we look to cities such as Nottingham to help us whenever possible. Perhaps YOUR [sic] City librarian will know that Nottingham will shortly have a Northern Command Performance and that we hope to bring visitors to your city by air service. We do hope that the City of Nottingham can see their way to assist us in this matter of exhibiting our posters which I am sure is to our mutual advantage.

The Town Clerk smoothed the City Librarian's ruffled feathers by suggesting that because the airport was owned by the City it was, in effect, advertising its own property. This goodwill on the part of the Town Clerk did not extend to accepting an invitation from the airline to take a seat for himself and Mrs Broad on a flight from Tollerton at the Empire Day display on Saturday 25 May.

A survey published in *The Aeroplane* on 1 May 1935 showed that the service called at Grimsby only on request. The company was hardly a success from the outset and the Route Manager wrote to the Town Clerk of Nottingham on 6 August 1935 expressing concern at the lack of response from Nottingham people to the service. He gave passenger figures for July as 17 flying into Nottingham and 14 leaving compared to 16 incoming to Hull and 14 leaving with 21 incoming to Leicester and 22 leaving. The Nottingham figures included five free passengers both to and from the city together with eight people who made an evening trip. This meant the people using the regular service for Nottingham were four in and one out whereas all the Hull and Leicester people were fare-paying passengers. The Manager went on to ask whether the Corporation could do anything to help them publicise the service by ensuring that there were frequent press reports relating to the aerodrome and the airline services operating from it. This was a concern for the Town Clerk because on 13 August 1935 he wrote to the Council's General Purposes Committee explaining that Nottingham was being used commercially and was a stop on a route to Paris. He continued:

> These services are not being made use of by Nottingham people to the extent they warrant and as compared with other towns the results are disappointing. Other Airports in the Midlands and especially Leicester are doing much to foster Civil Aviation and although Tollerton Aerodrome is leased to a Company (who as far as the Town Clerk is aware is doing all that can be expected of them), the Town Clerk feels that as Tollerton Aerodrome is the property of the Corporation, it behoves the City Council to do everything that can be done to ensure that it is made an Important Flying Centre.

At this time the Deputy Lord Mayor, J. Farr, was expressing his view that the City should be seeking another site to develop as a commercial airport because he believed that Tollerton would never achieve the highest, Class A, status as an airport. He was disappointed that Broxtowe was not developed as the airport but acknowledged that probably this was a correct decision given the Council's need of sites for new housing. (Broxtowe became one of the City's largest housing developments). Alderman Farr was elected to the Municipal Aerodromes sub-committee of the Association of Municipal Corporations in October 1935 and tried to drive the interests of Nottingham Airport with enthusiasm; unfortunately he failed in this mission.

Nottingham Airport Ltd advised the Town Clerk on 16 July 1935 that Provincial Airways Ltd was operating two services from Tollerton on the Hull, Leicester, Croydon and Southampton route which went on to Le Touquet and Paris. This service linked with services to Bournemouth, Southampton, Plymouth and Penzance, carrying an average of one hundred passengers a week. In the light of complaints from air lines that they were not being supported by Nottingham people it seems most likely that this was an overall figure and not the number using the service from and to Tollerton. This view is supported by a response from the Town Clerk seeking more information. Nottingham Airport Ltd replied that the number of people booking per week on the Nottingham to France route was four with six booking from France to Nottingham. Although there was a facility to carry freight none had been carried to the knowledge of the Airport Company.

Provincial Airways Ltd failed despite a creditors' meeting of 4 October 1935 requesting the company to seek a sale as a going concern rather than close.

## An East Midlands Airline

F. Leo Crilly of London visited the Nottingham Town Clerk in November 1934 to outline his intention of forming an airline operating from Doncaster to London calling at Tollerton and Leicester where the airline was to be based.

Doncaster had built an aerodrome on land opposite the racecourse and it was equipped with all the modern aids to flying required of a first class aerodrome, including night landing equipment. It was certainly viewed as a serious competitor to Tollerton within the Nottingham City Council. One of its early successes was to attract the KLM Royal Dutch Airline to use it rather than Hull which had been used for two years as its landing base for England. Hull had been initially chosen because it was one of the early municipal aerodromes and was situated on the coast. When Doncaster opened it was more attractive due to its situation in the centre of the country with better onward communications than Hull could offer.

On 6 March 1935 Crilly wrote to the Nottingham Town Clerk indicating that he was forming an airline as discussed when he had visited in 1934. He was flying from London to Doncaster on the following Sunday in his first machine, an eight seat Dragon, and invited the Lord Mayor to accompany him to Doncaster on the following day to be greeted by the Corporation of Doncaster.

*The Aeroplane's* survey mentioned previously indicated that Crilly Airways commenced a service from Doncaster to Northampton, calling at Nottingham (Tollerton) and Leicester, which would extend to London on demand from May 1935 and, starting on 6 June 1935, a twice daily service between Leicester, Nottingham and Skegness. These services were operated by de Havilland DH 84 Dragons, initially second-hand machines previously operated by John Sword, later by two new Dragons with a Fox Moth held as a reserve aircraft.

Crilly estimated that their aircraft would run at 50% capacity but, if eight passengers were being carried, the fuel cost for a journey of 110 miles would be £1.2s.5d, running costs would average $5^1/2$d per mile and overall costs, including servicing, $7^1/2$d per mile or 62 shillings an hour. If a minimum of three passengers were carried 4d per mile covered all running and overhead costs.

The first flight from Nottingham to the new Leicester airport at Braunstone carried a full complement of passengers including the Sheriff of Nottingham, Councillor Wallis Binch who was making his first flight, Councillor E. G. Underwood, the *Journal's* air correspondent, and the Western Brothers who were appearing at the Empire theatre in Nottingham. The flight took 13 minutes and was escorted by three aircraft from the Nottingham Flying Club. At Leicester it was greeted by Mr Crilly and the Deputy Lord Mayor of Leicester. Almost immediately after it landed other aeroplanes arrived from Northampton,

Bristol and Norwich, and lunch was provided at Leicester Town Hall. After this function everyone involved in the inauguration flew to Tollerton where the Flying Club provided tea. 15 aeroplanes, including two DH Dragons and an Airspeed Envoy made this flight and, before landing, flew over Nottingham.

*The Aeroplane* reported on 7 August 1935 a new service by Crilly between Liverpool (Speke), Leicester, Norwich, Nottingham and Northampton. The inaugural flight carried civic dignitaries from the latter places to Speke in two Dragons. Nottingham was represented by the Sheriff of Nottingham. The party was greeted by the Lord and Lady Mayoress of Liverpool and conducted through the Mersey Tunnel to Birkenhead. (The tunnel was first used on 17 December 1933, officially opened on 18 July 1934, and was therefore something of a novelty.) The party returned to the Adephi Hotel in Liverpool for lunch. After lunch Mr Crilly announced a new arrangement of 1,000 mile tickets costing £10.10s.0d fully transferable between family members or a firm's employees and applying to any Crilly service. The cost equated to $2^1/2$d a mile which he said was only a little over the cost of First Class rail travel.

He presented ticket number eight to the Lord Mayor of Liverpool and said that the Prince of Wales had accepted ticket number one, with others given to the Prime Minister, the Air Minister, the Director of Civil Aviation and the Mayors of Bristol, Norwich and Leicester. No mention of the Lord Mayor of Nottingham was made in this list and it would appear he was not given a ticket. *The Aeroplane's* correspondent praised Crilly for this ticketing innovation stating:

> The sooner other Air Transport companies issue similar tickets and arrange for mutual transfer of each other's tickets over all the country, the sooner will Air Transport move forward. In the meantime all honour to F. Leo Crilly, the issuer of the first "Season" by Air in the World.

A report by Nottingham Airport Ltd to the Town Clerk dated 16 July 1935 stated that Crilly operated a daily service calling at Nottingham, Leicester, Bristol, Norwich, Northampton, Doncaster and Birmingham and that 50 passengers a week were being carried. The same caveat should be applied to this figure as to that mentioned in connection with Provincial Airways Ltd.

In common with other airlines Crilly did not operate during the winter months and dropped Tollerton from its schedule before the start of the 1936 commercial flying season. Crilly reportedly said that the facilities at Tollerton were not adequate, it was not big enough and the landing fees were too high. Crilly also dropped its service from Leicester to Paris for the 1936 season which suggests the company was not attracting a large number of passengers. A service between Leicester, Madrid and Lisbon which operated under a contract with the Portuguese Postmaster General commenced in February 1936 but did not include a Nottingham link.

# CRILLY
# AIRWAYS

FIRST AIR SERVICE TO AND FROM LEICESTER.

## DAILY SERVICES TO NORWICH, NOTTINGHAM, NORTHAMPTON, BRISTOL, with connections to all parts

| | Depart | Arrive | Single | Return |
|---|---|---|---|---|
| To BRISTOL (Through plane) | 10-20 a.m. | 11-30 a.m. | 30/- | 50/- |
| | 5-50 p.m. | 7-0 p.m. | | |
| NORWICH ... ... ... | 10-20 a.m. | 11-30 a.m. | 30/- | 50/- |
| | 5-40 p.m. | 6-50 p.m. | | |
| NOTTINGHAM ... ... | 12-40 p.m. | 12-55 p.m. | 10/- | 15/- |
| | ... ... | 5-40 p.m. | 5-55 p.m. | | |
| NORTHAMPTON ... .. | 12-40 p.m. | 1-0 p.m. | 10/- | 15/- |
| | ... .. | 5-40 p.m. | 6-0 p.m. | | |
| LIVERPOOL (After Aug. 1st) | 10-15 a.m. | 11-15 a.m. | 25/- | 40/- |
| | ... ... ... | 3-15 p.m. | 4-15 p.m. | | |

**DONCASTER & BIRMINGHAM. On Demand. Particulars at Agents.**
**Fares include conveyance to and from Aerodrome.**

*BOOKING AGENTS FROM WHOM ALL INFORMATION CAN BE OBTAINED:*

Sec., Aero Club, Braunstone Aerodrome. Tele. 88156. Grand Hotel, Tele. 5222. Midland Holiday Bureau, 53, Granby Street, Tele. 59377. Offices of "Leicester Evening Mail" 37, London Road, Tele. 20411. Highfields Garage, 16, St. Peter's Road, Tele. 5598.

## CRILLY AIRWAYS LTD.
## LEICESTER AIRPORT

Plate 7:    Crilly advert and timetable from the *Manchester Guardian*
            of 26 July 1935. *Nottinghamshire County Archive Service*

49

# Railways and Aviation

Prior to the advent of railways people who needed to travel long distances had to use the stage coach system on roads which were often very difficult to travel along when the weather was bad. Canals provided some passenger services and, of course, for cities and towns like Nottingham, navigable rivers also provided passenger services. However, the canals and rivers were mainly used for the transportation of freight. When the railways were built their owners generally financed them on the assumption that freight would be the main basis of income and they regarded the canals as competitors. Many canal companies were bought by the railway owners so that freight could be re-directed from the canals to the railway and this led to the demise of the canal system.

It would be a reasonable assumption that the development of internal airlines serving the United Kingdom would be perceived as a threat by the railway companies. In the 1930s and earlier, railways were carrying large numbers of people and the possible loss of even a small number of these passengers could be considered a source of lost income. Airlines were anxious to be used for the carriage of mail and the first aeroplane to leave Tollerton with airmail was during an exhibition in Nottingham in May and June 1934 when a letter was sent to the Post Master General arriving at Radlett, 115 miles from Nottingham, in less than an hour. Loss of the carriage of mail would certainly be a concern to the railways but, instead of seeking to smother air travel in the way the railway companies had constricted the canals, the four main railway businesses got together with a view to forming their own airline to compete with the others.

The notion of an airline jointly owned and operated by the four major railway companies, Great Western Railways, London and North Eastern Railway, Southern Railway and London, Midland and Scottish Railway, was initially raised in 1928. The government took an interest and there was a suggestion that Imperial Airways should be involved due to their experience in operating aircraft. The idea of the formation of Railway Air Services did not initially meet with universal acceptance and doubts were expressed both within government and the railway companies. Eventually agreement was reached and Railway Air Services Ltd was registered on 21 March 1934 with a nominal capital of £50,000. The chairman of the Board was Sir Harold Hartley and the other board members were representatives from Imperial Airways and the railway companies.

During 1934 the Company's aeroplanes flew about 3,000 miles over 12 routes, but only the longer distance services across water to Jersey, the Isle of Wight, Belfast and Kirkwall showed promise and only the Jersey service came close to being profitable.

On 16 July 1935 Nottingham Airport Ltd reported that daily services were using Tollerton as a stop on routes to Liverpool, Manchester, the Isle of Man, Belfast and Glasgow. Other services went to Birmingham, Cardiff, Bristol, Southampton, Portsmouth, Torquay and Plymouth connecting with Jersey

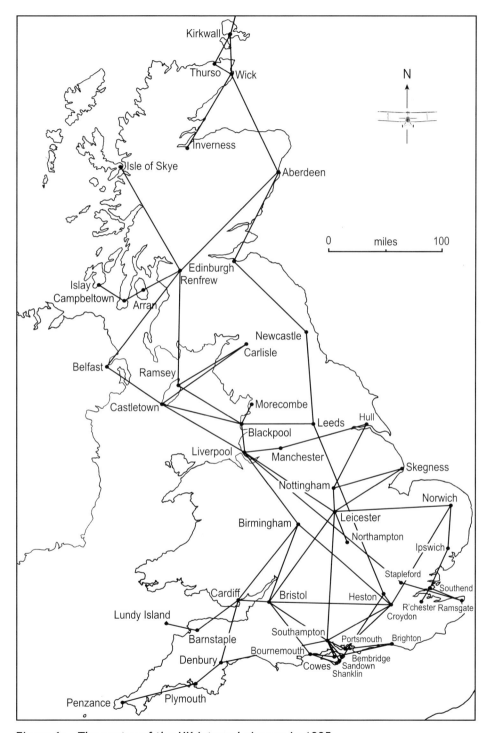

**Figure 6:    The routes of the UK internal airways in 1935.**
*Dr. Anne Tarver; Nottinghamshire County Archive Service*

Airways' service to Shanklin on the Isle of Wight and to Jersey itself. The service linked with Imperial Airways at Southampton and so 'service can be obtained to almost any part of the world'. The number of passengers from Nottingham was given as 12 a week.

The Aeroplane's survey of air services in Britain of 1 May 1935 shows Great Western Railway, as part of Railway Air Services Ltd, intending to operate a twice daily service commencing at the end of May from Nottingham to Birmingham, Cardiff, Torquay and Plymouth using DH Dragon 84 aircraft. This aeroplane could carry six passengers, each with 45 lb of luggage, and used 13 gallons of fuel per hour at a maximum speed of 109 mph.

The service ran from 27 May to 14 September on weekdays leaving Nottingham at 9 a.m. and 4.35 p.m. and arriving at Plymouth at 12.05 p.m. and 7.30 p.m. The Plymouth departures were at 9 a.m. and 4.35 p.m. reaching Tollerton at 11.55 a.m. and 7.25 p.m. There were connections to other services at all the stops on the route and all air tickets could be used for return on first class rail. Tollerton provided overnight housing and maintenance facilities for the aircraft together with accommodation for their pilots. The service did not seem to attract passengers because The Aeroplane was reporting on 27 November 1935 that:

> The West Country still does not seem to be air minded and the Plymouth-Nottingham route is the least promising [of all Railways Air Services' routes].

Railway Air Services dropped Nottingham from its 1936 schedules and, in reply to an enquiry from the Town Clerk as to the reason, said:

> When reviewing activities during last season consideration had to be given to the traffic that was carried, which, for your confidential information, amounted to 104 passengers during the period 27/5/35 to 15/9/35, of these 48 passengers were conveyed from and 56 to Nottingham.
> Having regard to the lack of support that was given to the service last year we regretfully decided to discontinue the facilities during the coming season.

*

North Eastern Airlines in 1937 were prepared to fly from Doncaster to Nottingham and other places on request. However, 1936 was in reality the end of the use of Tollerton by commercial airlines before the onset of WW2. This marked the closure of the grand ideas of those Council Members who had supported the purchase of the land and development of the aerodrome in 1928 and 1929, and those who had frequently called upon the Council to more actively pursue the aim of making Tollerton into the major aerodrome for the Midlands. The cause of the failure of the original aims was the lack of will to spend money on such a scheme, coupled with the decision to award the lease to NFS, and subsequently to Nottingham Airport Ltd, rather than take direct control of the aerodrome. Both NFS and Nottingham Airport Ltd were either unwilling or unable to invest the amount of money required to provide the facilities at Tollerton which commercial airlines increasingly required, such as night flying facilities. The Corporation always took the view that it was the lessee's duty to develop the aerodrome's facilities and not the responsibility of the Council. The success of those municipal aerodromes which were in the direct control of their Corporations, such as Leicester and Doncaster, two which were seen to be in direct competition with Tollerton, showed what could have been achieved at Tollerton with more willingness to invest on the part of Nottingham City Council or its lessees. It could, of course, be argued that those municipalities which were not in the vanguard of aerodrome development, such as Leicester and Doncaster, had been able to see what was happening at Tollerton and thereby learned lessons from it thus retaining direct control of their aerodromes with suitable investment programmes.

Certain assumptions had been made in 1928 when the development of Tollerton was being first mooted regarding the development of civil aviation in the United Kingdom. At that time the widespread view was that every major town and city should have an aerodrome and that flying would become a widely accepted form of transportation. This notion did not foresee the way aeroplanes would develop in size and efficiency nor did it take account of how relatively small the UK is compared to places like the USA where commercial flying was very successful. The Maybury Report of 1936 stated that since 1933 only those scheduled airlines which crossed some stretch of water had continued to exist in the three years to 1936. In that year a decrease in route mileage had occurred, and most airlines were operating at considerably less than 50% capacity and at a financial loss. Against this background it can be argued that had the Nottingham Corporation or the lessees of Tollerton invested large sums in the aerodrome's infrastructure it would have been wasted money because internal commercial airlines did not prove financially viable in Great Britain.

# Chapter 4

# Flying Clubs and Air Shows

Private flying in Great Britain was not allowed during the years of World War One but on 1 May 1919 the law was relaxed and people could once again take to the air in private aeroplanes. During the war the RAF and its predecessors, the RFC and RNAS, trained many men to fly. The majority left the RAF very quickly after the war ended, most returning to their civilian occupations. A few found employment where they could use their flying skills and those with the inclination and money founded flying clubs where they could pursue an interest in flying as well as meet socially with like-minded people.

The clubs bought aeroplanes, and people who could not afford an aeroplane of their own were able to fly the club-owned machines at a relatively modest cost. People could also learn to fly at the clubs. Most members were from the upper and middle classes because cost put the pursuit out of reach of the working classes. However, working class people could, and certainly did, enjoy the air displays, or pageants as they were termed in the 1930s, and tens of thousands flocked to Tollerton to witness the stunts and displays of these occasions. Opportunities to take pleasure flights were part of these events and many men who volunteered for the RAF in the lead-up to World War Two said that their interest in flying was stimulated by a flight at one of Sir Alan Cobham's air pageants.

The failure of Tollerton to retain commercial airlines was of more concern to certain members of Nottingham Corporation than to the general public and especially those members of the public who were interested in flying. The flying clubs which were formed at the aerodrome were very successful and members, whether interested in learning to fly or only in the social aspects of membership, greatly enjoyed the facilities available to them at the aerodrome.

The first Nottingham man to make a flight in Nottingham was H. A. Searby who learned to fly at Hendon in a Bleriot in 1910 when he was 18 years old. Wishing to own his own aeroplane, he designed and built one in a workshop in Hartley Road, Nottingham. The aircraft was a monoplane and Searby was assisted in building it by A. Allen. It had a wing span of 30 feet and was powered by a 25 hp four-cylinder JAP engine. Its first flight was in 1912 over the canal at Dunkirk, Nottingham. It was later exhibited on the Notts County Football Club ground at Meadow Lane from where short flights were made. Searby lost the sight in his right eye whilst testing the engine when a piece of the propeller broke off and struck him. This did not deter him because he built another aeroplane in 1914 and in 1919 yet another, although he did not fit an engine to the latter and it only flew as a glider. He built a total of nine gliders and was a founder member of the Nottingham Gliding Club.

There is a single reference, in a *Nottingham Evening Post* article of the 1960s about the King's Cup air race, to Tollerton having been used for private flying in 1922. No other reference about this or where it took place in the parish has been found.

The first flying club in Nottingham was formed as the Nottingham Aero Club on 15 November 1926 soon after Air Vice Marshall Sir Sefton Brancker, who was then the Director of Civil Aviation, made a speech to the Nottingham Rotary Club in the Mikado restaurant in Nottingham. He suggested that the City could support an aeronautical club and he was sure the Government would allow the club to use the military airfield at Hucknall. The first Council meeting of the Club was held in the United Services Club in Nottingham on 24 November 1926 when Sir Harold Bowden was invited to become President and Sir Albert Ball was made Vice-President. The club chairman was D. Rushworth and the Secretary R. Macpherson. The *Nottingham Journal* of 25 November 1926 reported that there had been many applications for membership. A DH Moth was bought for the use of members and a second one in 1928, although one was badly damaged in a forced landing shortly afterwards. Newspaper reports indicate that the club had a reasonable membership but it was never really financially sound. The facilities at Hucknall were very basic, there being no clubhouse and this is said to be the reason why women were not keen to become members.

In 1927 there were 11 aero clubs in Great Britain with around one thousand flying members. Nottingham Aero Club, together with others, received an Air Ministry subsidy of £50 whenever a trainee qualified for the 'A', or Private Pilot's, licence. The cost of tuition was 30 shillings an hour with the average cost of gaining the licence £6.10s.0d.

In 1928 the RAF decided it required Hucknall as a bomber station and the Flying Club was told that it could no longer use the aerodrome. By 11 January 1929 the club had found a new field of 40 acres situated between Ruddington and Bradmore owned by W. L. Beeby where they could use a hangar owned by Harold Ashworth adjacent to the field. The site was to be temporary as it had been agreed with Nottingham Corporation that the Club could move to the new aerodrome at Tollerton when it was ready for use. Indeed the Aero Club had offered to run the new aerodrome for the Corporation but was turned down on the grounds that it did not have the financial resources to develop it. Unfortunately, and despite gaining an Air Ministry certificate for the Bradmore site, the Club was unable to move there but was allowed to extend its stay at Hucknall until Tollerton was available. The reason for the problem at Bradmore has not been ascertained.

By March 1929 there were 13 Aero Clubs in the country. Nottingham's had 48 members. The club owned a DH 60X aeroplane G-AABA and between January and March 55 hours were flown.

As soon as the aerodrome at Tollerton became useable the Nottingham Aero Club moved there although the only facilities were two tents, one of which was used as an office. The aircraft was kept at Hucknall and flown to Tollerton daily for members to use. The Club seems to have had constant financial concerns, leading a rather hand to mouth existence, although it did employ a full-time instructor. The first instructor, in 1926, was Bernard Martin who left to become a pilot with a Canadian airline; he was followed by Flying Officer K. K. Brown who then went to the Cinque Ports Flying Club and Flight Lieutenant Bateman who left at the end of August 1929 to become instructor at the new Leicester Flying Club when the Nottingham club was absorbed into National Flying Services. The decision to merge with NFS was controversial but agreed at a meeting in the Black Boy Hotel in Nottingham on 14 August 1929 when it was reported that 'there was a very lively discussion'.

Meanwhile, in June 1928 Tollerton Hall was bought by Sir Albert Ball for £40,000 and was opened in February 1929 as a luxurious Country Club. The brochure for the Club refers to it being only a couple of fields from the new aerodrome, home to the Nottingham Aero Club which was doing important work in training pilots. Tollerton Country Club was marketed as a centre for hunting which could be enjoyed by London businessmen who could fly into the aerodrome for a day's hunting. Unfortunately the venture was not a success and in 1930 the Hall was sold to the Congregational Church to become a training establishment for the Ministry.

## The First Success

When the Nottingham Aero Club was taken over by National Flying Services it became Nottingham Flying Club Ltd which was incorporated on 30 July 1930. The nominal capital was one hundred pounds divided into one hundred shares of one pound each and its aims were stated as:

> To enter into and carry into effect ... an agreement already prepared and expressed to be made between The Nottingham Aero Club Ltd ... this Company ... to establish, form and maintain an aeroplane club in connection with the City of Nottingham.
>
>  To take on lease, purchase, or otherwise acquire the property known as Tollerton Aerodrome near the City of Nottingham, and to acquire for any estate or interest land suitable for aerodromes, landing grounds, air parks and flying clubs, and to equip the same for all purposes connected with flying or flying clubs or the running of air services.

The Club's directors were all connected with NFS apart from Sir Albert Ball of Nottingham. The company lasted for seven years and the notice of dissolution was posted in the *London Gazette* of 27 July 1937. NFS built the clubhouse to their standard pattern with a hangar alongside. The facilities were regarded as being of high quality. The hangar was completed at the end of March 1930 and the clubhouse a little later in time for the official opening on 19 June 1930. The

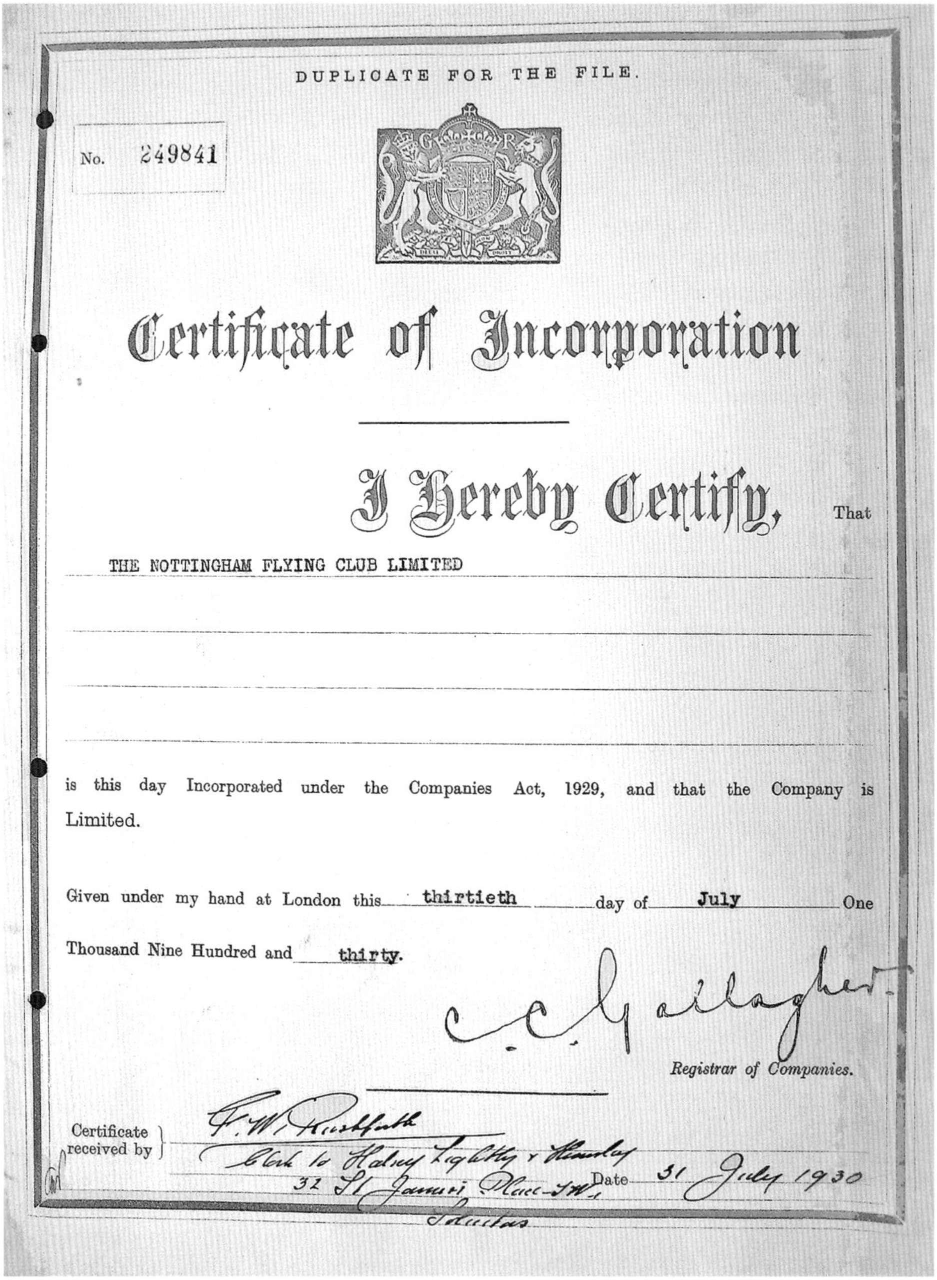

DUPLICATE FOR THE FILE.

No. 249841

# Certificate of Incorporation

## I Hereby Certify, That

THE NOTTINGHAM FLYING CLUB LIMITED

is this day Incorporated under the Companies Act, 1929, and that the Company is Limited.

Given under my hand at London this **thirtieth** day of **July** One Thousand Nine Hundred and **thirty**.

*C. C. Gallagher*

*Registrar of Companies.*

Certificate received by

Date 31 July 1930

---

**Plate 8:** The Nottingham Flying Club's Certificate of Incorporation
dated 30 July 1930 *Nottinghamshire County Archive Service*

clubhouse comprised a kitchen, lounge, bar, bedroom and separate changing rooms for men and women. There was a badminton court because it was felt at the time that badminton was a game which helped develop eye and limb co-ordination beneficial to a pilot.

In a letter published in *Flight* of 9 May 1930 Mr Donald Wynn of Derby indicated how members were looking forward with enthusiasm to using the new facilities:

> It is with pleasure one notices the progress being made at Tollerton (Nottingham) with the National Flying Services' buildings and accommodation which is nearing completion and one looks forward to the near future when the NFS machines will be permanently housed there and when more aircraft will be available for cross-country flights. Flying during the winter months at Tollerton has been difficult, owing to the state of the aerodrome, but with the present dry weather improving the surface, and the extra facilities available when the buildings are finished, one feels that this season will be one of much increased flying activity from Nottingham.

A slight sting in the tail of his letter complained that American-made petrol pumps were being installed.

Fees were initially fixed at an entrance fee of £3.3s.0d for flying and non-flying members plus an annual subscription of the same amount. Family members received a discount as did serving officers in the forces. Tuition fees were set at £2 per hour dual instruction, £1.15s.0d per hour solo under instruction, and £1.10s.0d per hour solo. Pilots who gained their 'A' licence were to have substantial reductions in flying fees. In addition to flying

Plate 9:
The Nottingham
Flying Club
members' badge.
Its colours are red,
black and silver
*Original badge loaned
by John Stafford*

instruction, pleasure-flights and air-taxi work would be undertaken. Fees were revised in December 1930 adding ten shillings to each category. There was an extra benefit of being a member of an NFS club because free use of any other NFS club was included in the membership fee.

The NFS instructor in charge of Tollerton was Captain R. (Ronnie) P. Shepherd who had 12 years service flying experience after enlisting in the Royal Flying Corps in 1916. He served in France and, after the war, in Egypt and Turkey before returning to finish his career at Biggin Hill. He then instructed at Reading Flying Club before joining NFS and coming to Tollerton. He arrived in a brand new Moth aircraft which had to be housed overnight at Hucknall until the Tollerton hangar was completed. The programme for the Tollerton Air Fete of 13 September 1930 says that the average time taken to gain the 'A' licence was between 13 and 20 hours. The minimum allowed by NFS was 8 hours dual instruction followed by 5 hours solo flying and the cost for this minimum course was £37. After qualification club aircraft could be hired at £2 an hour but on a reducing scale the more hours were flown in a year. NFS provided maintenance facilities for members with their own aircraft as well as special rates of insurance and touring information.

The *Nottingham Journal's* Air Correspondent on 6 September 1930 wrote that

**Plate 10:** **A group of NFC members in attendance for a press visit to the airfield in 1931.**
From left to right: Gilbert Thorpe, Dawson, Ashworth, Bradley, Smith, Seely-Whitby, Lovesey, Soil and Thompson.
*Nottinghamshire County Library Service Local Studies Department*

Captain Shepherd's remarkable ability has a great deal to do with the success of those whom he teaches. The instructor sat in the front cockpit and communication between him and the pupil was by way of headphones and speaking tubes. Initially the pupil followed the instructor's movements on the dual controls but was quickly being allowed to fly the aircraft under voice tuition and, even on a first lesson, landed the aircraft.

The club made steady progress and *Flight* was reporting on 10 April 1931 that there were 71 flying members with 31 holding the 'A' licence of whom 17 were trained in 1930. Despite very bad weather average flying of ten hours a day was achieved in February 1931. The Club's AGM held in February 1931 was told that in 1930 a total of 685 hours and 25 minutes flying time was made.

To create publicity on 12 April 1931 every journalist in Nottingham was invited, together with 'wives and wives-to-be' to visit the aerodrome and take a flight. The club aircraft were augmented by those of members, and the Club Chairman, G. G. Thorpe, said the day would be part of a series of similar events involving leading city institutions with a view to increasing 'air-mindedness', a phrase which was in common use at that time. The day was rounded off with tea in the 'extremely cosy' clubhouse. Members of Nottingham Rotary Club were similarly entertained on 20 July 1931. The press also used the club's aircraft on occasions as in May 1932 when the *Nottingham Guardian* undertook an aerial survey of extensive flooding from the River Trent.

An interesting event took place in March 1931 when a glider designer, Lowe Wylde, visited to demonstrate his gliders and his method of launching them by being towed by a car. A large crowd attended the event and several people were able to try gliding and take the 'A' gliding licence, one of whom was Captain Shepherd who gained the licence at his first flight in a glider. A slight mishap occurred when one pilot trying for the licence undershot the aerodrome and slightly damaged the machine. The Nottingham Gliding Club had been founded in 1930 but was not based at Tollerton; it initially used facilities provided by Captain Sherbrook at Oxton.

*Flight* of 26 February 1932 reported that the Club's membership was 110 with flying members very much in the majority and 45 holding 'A' licences. Club members had flown two thousand hours during 1931 of which the two Club aircraft had flown 950 hours. Members were very keen on cross-country flying and one member had flown to Dublin and back. In the same issue The Master of Sempill is quoted as saying that the cost of flying was the same as using a 20 hp car at between 4d and $4^{1}/2$d a mile.

Visits to the aerodrome and club were made by pilots from other clubs and by individuals. One noted visitor was the Prince of Wales who flew in his Puss Moth to Tollerton on several occasions when visiting Grove Farm in Lenton, Nottingham, which he had bought in 1927. Rumour has it that he mainly used the farm as a pied-à-terre for entertaining lady friends. The farm now forms

part of the playing fields of Nottingham University. It was said that, on one occasion, the Prince's chauffeur lost his way when travelling back to Tollerton and not long afterwards a signpost was erected on Trent Bridge to indicate the way to the airfield.

On 28 August 1932 Hull Aero Club created a record by becoming the first club to visit another en masse, some members by flying; 58 others arrived by car. After lunch the afternoon was devoted to inter-club aeronautics, a landing competition, a motor gymkhana and other sporting events.

In 1931 the *Nottingham Journal* presented a trophy for an annual Efficiency comp-etition. The final of the 1932 event was held on Sunday 2 October and the Director of Civil Aviation visited Tollerton to

**Plate 11: The signpost erected at Trent Bridge indicating the route to Nottingham Aerodrome.** *Roy Bonser collection*

**Plate 12:    NFC members preparing to leave Tollerton for a visit to the club  at Hull in 1931.** Left to right: Hall, Lovesey, Thorpe (in the aircraft) and Thompson
*Nottinghamshire County Library Service, Local Studies Department*

present the trophy to the winner. Contestants had to write a 750 word essay about the value of light aeroplane clubs, fly 25 miles to a pin-point, execute two figures of eight above Tollerton at an altitude of 600 feet and then land on the circle from an altitude of 1,000 feet. The winner was Donald Wynn of Derby who had also won the previous year. In 1933 there were 14 entries including Mrs Richardson of the Nottingham Club and pilots from the Leicestershire and Skegness Aero Clubs. The winner was Tom Bradford of Nottingham Flying Club with second place going to H. J. V. Ashworth of Nottingham and third to R. C. Winn of the Leicester Club; Mrs Richardson was sixth.

On Sunday 17 September 1933 a competition was held for the NEMO Cup presented by an anonymous person in 1931 but not competed for in 1932. Any 'A' pilot of the Nottingham Flying Club could enter and all flights had to have an instructor on board who was to deduct points for poor and dangerous flying. The 19 competitors were required to climb to 1,000 feet, switch off the engine and land over a tape set five feet above the ground, the winner being the pilot who finished closest to the tape. On this occasion the winner was Donald Wynn. Fourteen of the entrants, including Mrs Richardson, were disqualified, mainly due to the strong wind blowing on the day which caused them to strike the tape. These competitions were very popular and hotly contested.

The *Nottingham Journal* reported on 13 June 1933 that the youngest person to fly from Tollerton was Robert Peter Shepherd the son of the Pilot Instructor

**Plate 13:** **Club and some members' aircraft at Tollerton in 1933.**

At the rear - NFC's DH60X Moth G-EBXG.

Next row - Batchelor's DH60G Gipsy Moth G-AAWR, Shipside's DH60G Gipsy Moth G-AAEF, NFC's DH60X Moth G-AAPW

Third row - Ashworth's DH60G Gipsy Moth G-ABLN, Lovesey's DH60G Gipsy Moth Coupe G-AAEE.

Front row - Granger's Archaeopteryx, Mrs Greenall's DH80A Puss Moth G-ABLC

*Nottinghamshire County Library Service Local Studies library*

Captain Shepherd, the occasion being his first birthday; Captain Shepherd piloted the Hon Mrs Edward Greenall's Puss Moth and the boy was accompanied by his mother to 'show him the sights'.

When NFS passed into the hands of the receiver and its assets sold, the Nottingham Flying Club Ltd was one of those assets at Tollerton and passed, with the clubhouse, hangar and lease, to the Halls.

Mr Hall bought the NFS assets at Tollerton; his son, Captain L. W. Hall, took over the running of the aerodrome; and his daughter-in-law managed the clubhouse. Captain Shepherd continued as instructor until he was offered the position of Test Pilot for Rolls-Royce for whom he had been doing engine test flying from Tollerton. There is no doubt that the Halls improved the Flying Club and made it a great success both from flying and social perspectives. However, to the chagrin of some members of Nottingham City Council, they did not make a success of the commercial aspects of the aerodrome.

The clubhouse was improved in 1934 with the addition of a verandah and an office was built between the clubhouse and hangar for the use of time-keepers.

In January 1935 the Nottingham Flying Club had 280 members of whom 88 were flying members. 350 hours had been flown between March 1934 and the end of the year which represented a 66% increase over the same period in the previous year. On the social side badminton was a popular sport and regular tournaments between the Nottingham and Leicester Clubs featured in the

Plate 14:   The lounge of the clubhouse.

programme. There was a children's Christmas Party to which Santa Claus arrived by aeroplane, followed by a dinner and dance at which Captain Shepherd and M Purnall, who had been the Ground Engineer, were presented with gold watches in appreciation of their services to mark their departure from the Club to take up full time employment with Rolls-Royce Ltd. The clubhouse was extended by adding three bedrooms and enlarging the lounge and bar. It was especially noted that the bar stock was being increased! The extensions were officially opened on 28 March 1935 by the Lord Mayor of Nottingham when it was reported that 300 members and guests attended the event.

Regular reports in *The Aeroplane* in its club feature reveal the number of hours flown per week and special visitors to the club. From these notes it can be seen that there was regular social interchange with the Leicestershire Aero Club, a few of whose members were regular Sunday lunch diners at Tollerton. Several members flew their aircraft to attend race meetings such as the Grand National. Notable cross-country trips were flown to Holland, Carlisle, Brooklands and Farnborough. A garden party on 22 June 1935 was attended by visitors from other clubs. Other social events were monthly dances held through the winter months, a themed party on bonfire night and an Annual Dinner at the Mikado Café in Nottingham.

On 20 March 1935 the Assistant Instructor, Roxborough, was replaced by Captain Cudemore MC DFC. Captain Hall had assumed the position of Chief Instructor on the departure of Captain Shepherd. The engineering staff was increased in July 1935 when Tom Graves, who had gained his qualification certificate at Brooklands in 1912 on a Bristol biplane, was appointed.

Flying competitions continued to be held. The *Nottingham Journal* always carried detailed reports on the Journal Efficiency Cup. That for June 1935 was

Plate 15: The dining room of the clubhouse.

held in conjunction with the annual Garden Party and members of other clubs, including from London, attended. The competition winner was Roy Winn of Leicester, flying a Puss Moth, the first time the cup had been won by a non-Nottingham club member.

In 1937 the club operated four aircraft, two Moth Majors, a Hornet Moth and a BA Swallow. At this time there was no entrance fee to the club and the annual subscription for Flying members was £3.3s.0d and Associate, or non-flying, members £2.2s.0d Dual flying cost £2.0s.0d an hour and solo flying between £1.10s.0d and £1.16s.0d an hour depending on experience. The club facilities included tennis, badminton, squash and horse riding. There was a tennis court at the rear of the clubhouse and the badminton court was marked out on the hangar floor.

The company of Nottingham Flying Club Limited was dissolved by notice under the Companies Acts in the London Gazette dated 27 July 1937. Why this was done is not known but the Club continued and it has to be presumed it was as a private club operated by Nottingham Airport Ltd with a committee drawn from the membership but subject to overall supervision by the directors of the Company. No reference to this change has been found in local newspapers.

The minute book of the Nottingham Flying Club, dating from its first Annual General Meeting held on 19 September 1935 and extending to 5 March 1963, provides interesting information for the pre-war years although there are no minutes for 1936 or 1937. In December 1938 the committee was split into two, a Flying Committee and a Social Committee with six members elected to each. At this meeting complaints were voiced that no aircraft were available for private flying because all the club's aircraft were in use for the Civil Air Guard. It was said in response that additional aircraft were to be purchased, one of which would be allocated solely for private flying. Badminton was to be played on Thursday and Sunday evenings at a charge of 2/6d and the radiogram in the clubhouse was to be overhauled. There would be a New Year's Eve Dance and the Annual Dinner would be at the Black Boy Hotel in Nottingham.

A committee meeting of 16 July 1939 decided that alterations to the clubhouse should be made to include extending the dining room, the bottom lounge converted into a bar-lounge with minor alterations to doors and windows. Additional tube heaters and furniture were to be purchased and the kitchen would be modernised. All this would call for a high expenditure which suggests a Club with healthy bank balances.

There was co-operation between the Flying Club and other users of the airfield as shown by the comment of Flight Lieutenant West, the manager of the aerodrome, at a meeting a week later; he said that the building used as a mess for the Volunteer School was temporarily out of use. It was agreed that the Club dining room could be used for the volunteers but non-Club members would not be allowed into the bar unless buying drinks to accompany a meal.

After the aerodrome was requisitioned by the Air Ministry the committee decided that all the Club's trophies should remain with their present holders and the committee members should remain the same until civil flying was once again permitted.

## Personalities and Recollections

It is clear that members greatly enjoyed the facilities at the Flying Club and that the Club had a strong social side which attracted members from those levels of society which could afford the fees. Membership was by application and if an applicant was not proposed by an existing member then it was necessary to undergo an interview with one or more members of the committee. There was therefore an element of elitism involved in membership.

An attempt to form an Artisan's Flying Club at Tollerton in 1932 received publicity in the local newspapers and the Lord Mayor lent his support. The idea was that, because normal working people could not afford the fees charged by Nottingham Flying Club, if a sufficient number of artisans could be found to join a club, the costs involved could be substantially reduced and therefore flying made affordable. Although Nottingham Airport Ltd gave permission for the erection of a clubhouse and hangar for an Artisans' Club this did not come to fruition.

The *Nottingham Journal* offered scholarships for one of its readers to learn to fly at no cost in 1935 and 1936 with reduced cost tuition to the second and third placed applicants. Applicants had to pay one pound for a half hour lesson and the winner would be the person judged by the instructors to have shown the most aptitude for flying.

An indication of how people felt about the Flying Club is expressed by Mrs Chris Wing of Carrington, Nottingham; her son had been a member of the Club but had died in an air crash at Cotgrave in 1930. Mrs Wing donated the tennis court at the clubhouse and ten pounds a year in his memory to be used for some purpose in connection with the aircraft. Her letter of 16 November 1937 includes the following:

> I want to thank you the more than I can express on paper or in words for the lovely flowers you sent my beloved boy on "his anniversary". He would love to look down – as he would – and see them there – the remembrance and his Club which he loved in his heart – and like I do in mine.

In 1971 Maisie Don, who worked for the Flying Club for several years and became its Secretary in the late 1930s, wrote some notes which give an excellent picture of the Club and its activities. She wrote that the staff had to work long hours: hers were from 10 a.m. to 11 p.m. six days a week including Sunday and her pay was £3.10s.0d a week. She said that if she had her days over again she would willingly return under the same conditions because she felt part of a happy family at the aerodrome. Her memories include the parties, dawn patrols, display days, and particularly drinking champagne out of the King's Cup when Alec Henshaw won it. She remembered visits by famous aviators such as Amy Johnson with her husband Jim Mollison, Tommy Rose, Sir Sefton Brancker, Sir Alan Cobham and the Duchess of Bedford who was known as 'The Flying Duchess'. Maisie recalled that the *Nottingham Journal's* air correspondent, Jim Hall, was a member of the Club. In 1939 the membership was over 400 of which half were regular flying members. A particular memory was gathering mushrooms from around the concrete letters spelling out 'Nottingham' which were situated in the middle of the aerodrome and which were removed at the outbreak of war.

She told how the Club's Spartan 3-seat aircraft was used on several occasions to carry small children with whooping cough to a height of 5,000 feet where they were told to take deep breaths: but she had no knowledge of any recorded cures! The Spartan was used at weekends to give 5/- and 10/- pleasure flights to members of the public for which there was a good demand.

Maisie recalled the use of Tollerton by air advertising operators and her description of how they undertook the work is most interesting:

> Air Publicity Ltd had a kind of goalposts laid across the airfield to which a banner was attached (a long roll of metal netting with big canvas letters fastened to it). The pilot would then take off, fly around until the right moment, and then fly between the posts and took up the banner fitting on his tail-skid, his wings just clearing the ground. He then did an almost vertical climb and the banner unrolled behind him and by the time he was over the city it was fully extended (usually reading "Bile Beans nightly keep you fit").

Plate 16:   The crash at Cotgrave in which Ronald Leslie Wing died
*Nottingham Guardian 11 November 1930*

68

. . . Equally, if not more skilled, in aerial advertising was Mr Sidney St. Barbe, who advertised for Players. He used a different method, but even more spectacular and this was done with a heavy vapour carried in a container under the fuselage of a specially constructed, fully aerobatic monoplane. The day had to be exactly right, little wind and a clear patch of blue sky with no cloud. He would then climb to his correct height and by a series of wonderful aerobatics, release the vapour and write "Players Please" right across the patch of blue sky ... Mr St. Barbe would spend many hours working out all the minute details of his sky-writing as he of course could not see what he was doing.

Another person with memories of the social life of the Club is Joyce Cartlidge whose first memory of aircraft is being taken to Bill Shipside's private airfield by her parents who had been invited for a 'flip'. She says she was puzzled by her mother wearing riding breeches and boots for the occasion but this was because it was an open cockpit plane. Her three year old brother later asked their mother what she did when the aircraft got so little in the sky! Her father, Reg Burton, was bitten by the flying bug and joined the Nottingham Flying Club, first flying solo in 1936. Her first flight was sitting on her father's lap in a Tiger Moth. Her parents were friendly with Lewis and Maud Hall and so she and her brother were left with the Hall's children in the bungalow opposite the end of the aerodrome entrance road in the care of 'Nana', whilst the Halls and Burtons were at the aerodrome.

Joyce remembers events to which the children were invited and especially the Christmas Party when Santa arrived by air. Maisie Don had been given £3 with which to buy presents for the 50 children who attended and says it was sufficient to buy quality presents. Joyce also remembers the fuss which was raised in 1938 or 1939 when a member and his German wife were listening to Hitler's radio broadcasts on the Club's radio with the volume turned to loud. She recalls feeling

**Plate 17:    The Club's Spartan 3-seater awaiting pleasure flight customers.**
The pilot is named as Captain Hall. *Roy Bonser collection*

Plate: 18    A group including the two Shipside children waving goodbye as Mr & Mrs
Shipside take-off from Tollerton on their holiday to Egypt.
*Ken Shipside collection*

Plate 19    A page from Mr. Shipside's log book showing a North African
leg of the journey. *Ken Shipside collection*

threatened by Hitler's voice even though she could not understand the words. She also says that when the aerodrome was allowed private flying after WW2 Lewis Hall had died and his widow emigrated to Kenya with their three children.

An early and long-standing member of the Flying Clubs at Tollerton was T. W. Shipside of the well known car dealership in Nottingham, a director of Nottingham Airport Ltd who had been an RFC pilot in WW1. His son, Ken, has made his father's flight log books available and it is clear that quite long journeys were being made by members of the flying clubs. Mr Shipside visited Ostende, Rotterdam and Amsterdam as well as many places in Great Britain. In 1938 he and his wife flew Leopard Moth G-ACTJ on an exciting holiday to Egypt. The log-book for the journey shows the route out and return with comments about the conditions such as:

| | |
|---|---|
| Lyon-Pisa | Tail wind at first lousy after coast |
| Palermo-Tunis | Poor half way after good |
| Sirte-Benghazi | Lousy sand storms |

**Plate 20:** The Archaeopteryx at Hucknall in 1929.
*Nottingham County Library Service, Local Studies Library*

**Plate 21:** The Archaeopteryx in flight at Tollerton.
*Dave Birch collection*

Members were not averse to building their own aircraft and Francis and John Granger of Attenborough designed, built and flew an unusual aircraft which they named 'Archaeopteryx'. The machine first flew in 1930 and in subsequent years they redesigned and modified the aeroplane. The design was for a high wing monoplane of wingspan 27 feet 5 inches, powered by a Bristol Cherub 29.4 hp engine capable of cruising at 75 mph with fuel consumption of 45 miles per gallon. There was no effective tail and the design was called 'tail-less' and it was said to be the smallest and lightest aircraft in the world. Maisie Don refers affectionately to the machine as 'Archie'.

Someone else who built an aircraft was T. H. Foulds, a Derby member of the Club, who built a 'Flying Flea' aircraft, the invention of a Frenchman, M. Mignet, who demonstrated his machine before a crowd of 3,000 people at Tollerton on 6 September 1935. The Flying Flea cost £70 and it was said that it could be built by an amateur builder in 300 hours. M. Mignet made two flights on his visit to Tollerton and in the crowd were the Lord and Lady Mayoress of Nottingham.

Muriel Robinson was the first woman to become a member of the Nottingham Flying Club and she was the first woman to gain a pilot's licence at Tollerton and

**Plate 22:
Muriel Robinson's
pilot's licences.**
*Mary-Rose Vandervord*

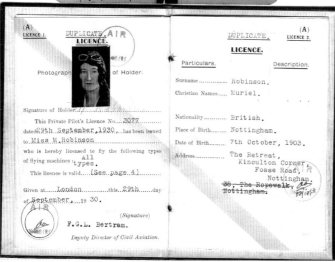

also the first in Nottinghamshire. Muriel took her first solo flight in a Puss Moth on 7 November 1929 after only eight hours dual instruction and passed the test for her pilot's licence on 1 July 1930 at 27 years old. Her daughter, Mary-Rose Vandervord of New Zealand has provided us with some of her mother's items which give an insight into this woman who Mary-Rose describes as a great character.

Prior to Charles Lindbergh returning to America after his solo flight across the Atlantic in 1927 he was given a reception at which Muriel was present and shook Lindbergh's hand. On that occasion her brother, who was also present, told her that he would buy her an aeroplane as soon as she could fly solo. After her solo flight she told the *Nottingham Evening Post* that she would use the aircraft to fly to the Continent in connection with her business and gave her opinion that flying was far safer than motoring.

The test for the pilot's licence at that time required, amongst other things, the making of five figure-8s within an allotted area over the airfield and an ascent to 7,000 feet followed by a descent, with the engine switched off, to a marked place on the aerodrome.

Muriel was chosen to represent the youth of Nottingham at a special luncheon, held at the Savoy Hotel, London in August 1930, in honour of Amy Johnson, who had flown solo from London to Australia.

The oldest flying members of the club were the Reverend J. W. Pyddock, who made his first solo flight on 26 March 1930 aged 60, and his wife, of Pleasley.

Plate 23:    **Muriel Robinson on the occasion of her first solo flight.** To her left is Captain Shepherd and to her right the Nottingham Flying club's Ground Engineer. *Mary-Rose Vandervord*

Both Mr and Mrs Pyddock gained their 'A' licences in February 1931 on the occasion of their silver wedding anniversary at which time she was 52 and he was 61. Mrs Pyddock took part in flying events, especially the Efficiency Flying Cup, but was never placed. She seems to have enjoyed fancy dress because she figures in the reports about the winners of various fancy dress events at dances in the clubhouse.

## Crashes and Fatalities

Flying in the light aircraft of the pre WW2 period was by no means without its dangers. It required a great deal of skill on the part of the pilot who had few instruments to assist and forced landings in ordinary fields were not uncommon. Mechanical reliability was generally good but things could and did go wrong. It was not uncommon for propellers to break and if that happened in the air it would cause difficulties. The aerodromes were grass surfaced and few had landing aids other than a wind-sock. It is perhaps surprising that there were not more serious crashes.

Whilst still based at Hucknall the DH Moth which was the Nottingham Aero Club's first aircraft crashed almost immediately after take off. It climbed to about 400 feet, started to turn and seemed to stall, hitting the ground and bursting into flames. The pilot, Robert Arthur Blake of Edwalton and passenger Lieutenant William Richardson RAOC of Nottingham were both burned to death.

Plate 24:   The wreck of the Moth which crashed at Sheffield. *Mary-Rose Vandervord*

On 19 June 1930 H. Andrews of Southampton was more fortunate. Flying home after competing in an air race at the Tollerton Air Pageant he crashed at Ratby from unknown causes but only sustained shock and minor cuts.

The first crash involving a Tollerton aeroplane was a DH Moth flown by Captain Shepherd who was instructing T. W. Shipside. They were making a training flight from Tollerton to Leeds on 27 March 1930 and came down in a field at Intake, Sheffield, owing to poor visibility in order to ascertain where exactly they were. The crash occurred on take off when, despite ample room, the aeroplane would not lift off. Heading directly towards a stone wall Captain Shepherd tried to turn right to pass through a gap into the next field. He almost made it, just a wing tip striking the wall causing the aircraft to overturn, pinning the occupants underneath. Although a petrol pipe broke in the incident there was no fire and the two men were able to crawl out without injury.

Mention has already been made of Mrs Wing's donations to the Nottingham Flying Club in memory of her son. Ronald Leslie Wing, who was 20 years old, died in a crash near Cotgrave at about 4 p.m. on Sunday 9 November 1930 whilst flying the Club's DH 60X Cirrus Moth G-AAMT from Tollerton. The official report of the Air Ministry Inspector in The National Archives says that the crash occurred when the aircraft went into a spin at about 1,000 feet. After four complete turns it came out of the spin, started to climb but fell over to the left and nose-dived into the ground. The cause of the original spin is not given: perhaps the age and relative inexperience of the pilot contributed to it.

The chairman of the Flying Club, E. F. Winser, escaped injury on 22 February 1932 when he was taking off from Tollerton. A connecting rod in the engine broke and the engine stopped. Mr Winser tried to make an emergency landing on the far side of the Grantham canal which runs close to the aerodrome boundary but his undercarriage struck the canal bank and collapsed. Fortunately the pilot was unhurt.

Another lucky escape is recorded in the *Nottingham Journal* for 24 September 1936 which carried a picture and report of a crash involving a Flying Club aeroplane between the aerodrome and Edwalton. Wilfred Clarke of Hucknall was the pilot and had been putting the Moth Major through some aerobatic manoeuvres when he crashed. Fortunately he sustained relatively mild injuries but was detained in Nottingham General Hospital for a few days.

In November 1938, however, Edward Thomas aged 22 of Nottingham was another fatality when his Miles Magister crashed into the Old Rectory Field at Holme Pierrepont during a flight from Tollerton. Edward was a civilian trainee at the RAF Elementary Training School based at Tollerton and the inquest was told that his aeroplane had spun out of control and hit the ground at about 200 mph. As in the case of Ronald Wing, the exact cause was not ascertained.

On 5 June 1939 an Avro Cadet belonging to the Flying Club crash-landed at Dunkirk, Nottingham, and overturned. The pilot, Ernest Gudgeon, escaped with a badly lacerated scalp. It seemed that an engine fault caused it to stop requiring a forced landing which resulted in the crash. It was reported that hundreds of people went to look at the damaged aircraft.

Later that summer a rather macabre incident involved two RAF aircraft in a collision over the Meadows District of Nottingham on 6 August. The observer in one of the aircraft, Sergeant R. J. Williams, was decapitated and his head fell onto housing. Both aircraft landed safely, one on Holme Lane, Radcliffe-on-Trent, and the one with the body of the observer at Tollerton aerodrome. The aircraft had been part of a flight of three from 103 Squadron carrying out an exercise when one rose too quickly and struck the other.

## Thrills and Spills

We are bound to wonder what the people of the Nottingham area made of the intrusion into their lives created by the airfield. People living in Nottingham and the surrounding towns and villages could not help but be aware of the aerodrome at Tollerton. The local papers carried frequent reports about the activities at the aerodrome and those living nearby were well aware of the aircraft using the airfield. It comes as no surprise that not everyone was happy about it. On 10 September 1938 West Bridgford Urban District Council discussed a complaint from a local resident that the noise from aeroplanes disturbed the Sunday enjoyment of his garden. The Chairman of the UDC was in sympathy with the man and his complaint was reported to the police in case low flying regulations were being breached. No report of the outcome has been found but Sunday flying was in no way abated.

However, the advent of the airfield and its activities did intrigue and delight many people. The main way in which the general public of the East Midlands would know about Tollerton aerodrome was the holding of air races and especially air displays. These were put on to entertain the public and thousands flocked to Tollerton to attend them, seeking thrills from the aerobatics and stunts which the airmen performed.

Mention has already been made of the trophies for which the members of the Nottingham Flying Club and other flying clubs competed annually throughout the 1930s at Tollerton, particularly the Nottingham Guardian Efficiency Cup and the Nemo trophy.

The main race of National importance which occasionally used Tollerton as a turning point was the King's Cup Air Race. In 1927 the King's Cup race actually started and finished at Hucknall. The following year the aerodrome was used as a control point where the competitors had to land. Bernard Martin, the Instructor of the Nottingham Aero Club, took part in this race flying the Club's aeroplane.

Tollerton's first connection with the race was as a turning point in the 1931 race on 25 July when it started and finished at Heston, London. After stopping at the Norwich control point the competitors flew to Tollerton and turned there to head for Brough. The turning point was marked by a white cross with a bell tent erected close to it. Turns had to be executed no more than 500 feet high and within 300 feet of the cross which had to be on the right of the aircraft. A further Tollerton connection with this race was the entry of Nottingham Flying Club member T. W. Shipside with his navigator H. Seely Whitby Jnr. in the former's Gypsy 1 Moth G-AAEF. Unfortunately the race was flown in adverse weather conditions and the Nottingham aeroplane was forced to retire without finishing the course. Spectators could watch from inside the aerodrome at an entrance fee of 6d.

The race did not schedule Tollerton again until 1936 when it used Tollerton as its northernmost turning point for a race which started and finished at Hatfield. Tollerton was again the turning point after Norwich, a leg of 103 miles following which was a flight of 121 miles to Bristol. *The Aeroplane* described the Norwich to Tollerton leg :

This leg is just as open and carefree as the first, considered merely as terrain over which to fly low down and flat out. ... Tollerton ... is not a particularly easy

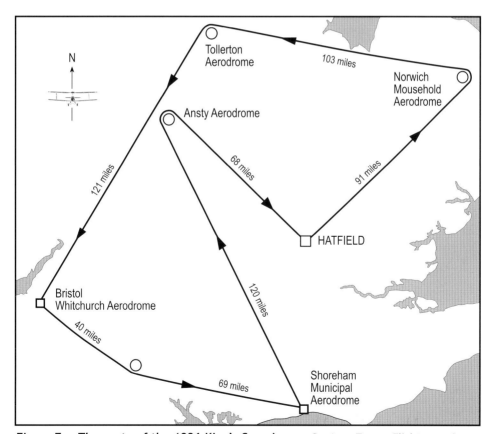

**Figure 7:   The route of the 1936 King's Cup air race** *Dr. Anne Tarver; Flight magazine*

aerodrome to find when flying low and fast. Four miles before reaching it one crosses a canal, which then winds along between a mile and half a mile on the right until the aerodrome is reached. The white cross must again be left on the inside of a left-hand turn.

Tollerton was not used again for the race in the pre-war years.

## Air Displays and Pageants

Annual displays and pageants were held at Tollerton between 1929 and 1938. Some were organised by the aerodrome lessees and others by national organisations like that of Sir Alan Cobham. They all took the same pattern although the nationally organised ones used participants who became household names because of the dare-devil nature of their stunts. Some stunts were regarded as so dangerous that, for example, wing walking was banned by the government in 1933 which deprived the spectators of at least one of the thrills of the event. Thousands turned up to watch the events and Cobham estimated that over all his display years some three million people paid to see his shows and that the same number enjoyed them without paying! Some 990,000 people also paid for a pleasure flight at his events.

Plate 25:
Advert for the Air Pageant of 13 September 1930
*Nottinghamshire County Archive Service*

The first Tollerton Pageant was held on 19 June 1930 on the occasion of the official opening of the aerodrome under the NFS regime already described. In the same year the Nottingham Flying Club organised an Air Fete on Saturday 13 September.

Special bus services were laid on to the aerodrome and the entrance fees were one shilling and two shillings and six pence dependent upon which enclosure was chosen. Car parking was one shilling and for charabancs two shillings and six pence. On the following Monday the *Nottingham Journal's* report was headlined 'Hair-Raising "Stunts" at Tollerton Pageant'. The report indicates that the event was held in the rain and lasted for about two hours. The displays involved various aerobatics; a parachute jump by John Tranum had to be cancelled due to the conditions but he compensated the spectators by a display of wing-walking during which he climbed down from the wing onto the undercarriage, back up to just behind the engine cowling and raised his arms to show he was not holding on to anything. There was a race between the Autogiro and dirt-track motor bike riders which the latter won, a gliding display by Nottingham Gliding Club members, and the finale was a spectacular bombing of an oil depot which was said to have 'flared magnificently'. After the display members of the public could take pleasure flights in a Giant Moth and Desoutter.

The display scheduled for Whit Sunday 1931 proved somewhat controversial. The Town Clerk of Nottingham received letters of protest from several

Plate 26: This poor quality photograph shows the enthusiasm of the crowd at the Pageant as they watch a wing-walking display. *Roy Bonser collection*

clergymen and religious organisations, including the Nottingham Ruridecanal Conference and the Nottingham Free Church Council. The latter's protest said:

> On behalf of the Nottingham Free Church Council I respectfully protest against the proposal to hold an Air Pageant at Tollerton on Whit Sunday. To hold such a Pageant on the Lord's Day is a gross affront to the deepest and most cherished convictions of the Christian people of this City.
> It tends to secularise and to commercialise the Lord's Day, and to invade its wonted quiet with noise and disorder.

In all, five religious protests were received about this event to which the Town Clerk replied that the aerodrome was leased to NFS and the Council had no say in the matter. Perhaps the protesters found some satisfaction that the weather was so bad that a postponement to the following Tuesday was required. *Flight* reported that the event was very well organised and that it was fortunate that Whit Tuesday was a customary holiday in the East Midlands. The magazine commented about the parachute jump:

> Readers will know that we do not agree with parachutes being used for such shows, but this does not in any way detract from Capt. Stewart's excellent judgement.

**Plate 27:    The air park at the 1930 pageant; the aircraft show the distances people travelled to the event.**

G-EBQP is a DH63 Humming Bird owned by Robert Somerset of Plymouth, G-EBEQ is a Boulton and Paul P9 owned by Hugh Kennedy of Stag Lane, London and G-EBIY is a Westland Woodpigeon of unknown ownership. *Roy Bonser collection*

Shortly afterwards on Sunday 7 June 1931 Captain Barnard's Aerial Circus gave a display at Tollerton which included his famous Fokker 'Spider' monoplane in which he had created records for flying to India and back. *Nottingham Journal* readers were given a chance to fly with Barnard by entering a draw for 20 places on a free flight. The programme was much the same as the earlier displays but on this occasion the speedway rider who raced against the Autogiro was Fred Strecker, a well known Nottingham rider.

1932 was the year of the first visit by Sir Alan Cobham's National Aviation Day display on Thursday 12 May. Sir Alan had a personal mission to popularise flying in what he termed developing 'air-mindedness' in the general public. His air displays were the means he chose to achieve this but at the same time they also had to make him a living. He employed the best pilots and stunt men and women in his team and travelled the length and breadth of the country with a cavalcade of motor transport. He undoubtedly gave employment to several hundred people at a time when the country was in the throes of depression. As has already been mentioned many members of the public had their first experience of flight in his Airspeed Ferry aircraft 'Youth of Britain'. Cobham's displays also visited Tollerton in 1933, 1934 and 1935 after which year his display company was disbanded and he concentrated his work on his air refuelling company.

The Nottingham Flying Club held a Pageant on 18 June 1932 which attracted 5,000 spectators and included a formation flying display by No. 504 County of Nottingham Squadron's bombers based at Hucknall and a demonstration of the Lockheed Vega which had made a record flight to The Cape. There were demonstrations of the latest aircraft, both civil and military, and a comic stunt where a man pretended he had never seen an aeroplane and didn't know what it did.

An opportunity for the public to visit RAF stations and civilian aerodromes was given when they were opened for the public to visit on Empire Air Day, first celebrated in 1935. There was the usual pleasure flying but the public was also able to see the latest RAF aircraft of the particular station they were visiting. Both Hucknall and Tollerton were open to the public at no charge on these days.

The Jubilee Air Display held at Tollerton on 16 June 1935 was distinguished by displays from Lieutenant Owen Cathcart-Jones and T. Campbell-Black who had established record flights to Australia and back to England. The Granger brothers also demonstrated their Archaeopteryx. This event had two displays, one in the afternoon and one in the evening and several thousand people visited to watch them.

Air displays of this period created their own legends and heroes. In 1936 60,000 people visited the exhibition given by Clem Sohn, an American billed as 'The Bird Man', as part of T. Campbell-Black's Air Circus on 16 May. There was traffic chaos on all the roads surrounding the aerodrome, backing up to Trent Bridge and 'in some places three deep'. Strong and gusty winds prevented Sohn from making his display until 6 p.m. but he then flew to 10,000 feet in a DH Dragon before launching himself out of it. The *Nottingham Journal* described his descent:

> The machine climbed steadily to a height of 10,000 feet, and as it flew directly over the aerodrome, so high that it looked no bigger than a pin, the spectators craned their necks and watched expectantly.
>
> Suddenly a small white object was seen to leave the aeroplane. As he dived head-first from the machine the "Birdman" had exploded a smoke bomb to indicate his position to the crowd below.
>
> After a 300 feet drop he spread his wings and began to fly like a bird, his movements being in perfect control. Swooping and circling until within about 1,000 feet of the ground, Sohn then pulled the rip cord of his parachute and made a perfect landing on the aerodrome about 100 yards from the airport buildings.

Sohn was killed whilst performing at Vincennes, France, on 25 April 1937 when he was just 26 years old.

Tom Grant of Quadring in Lincolnshire remembers being taken by his uncle to see Clem Sohn's display and photographing the famous daredevil in the hangar at Tollerton. He recalls Sohn's jump and what he thought was flour from a canister on Sohn's leg leaving a white trail to mark his position before the wings unfolded. Sohn then swooped about the sky until eventually his parachute opened and he descended to the ground. Tom was ten when his uncle, Sid

**Plate 28:** Gloster Gladiators flying a formation display at the Tollerton air display in September, 1938. *Nottingham Guardian*

Grant, started taking him to Tollerton airfield five or six times a year for two or three years, starting in 1936. The Grants were farmers at Swineshead in Lincolnshire but Sid and his friends, Austin Monks, the famous motor cycle racer and TT winner, and Alec Henshall, the King's Cup winner and holder of the record from Britain to Cape Town and return, were members of The Nottingham Flying Club. Tom was taken for flights by either his uncle or uncle's friends and thoroughly enjoyed the experience. It was always in a two-cockpit aeroplane where communication was through a speaking tube. He kept his leather flying helmet for many years. Most of the aeroplanes at Tollerton were biplanes but Henshall flew a monoplane and, on one occasion, he took Tom for a flight to demonstrate the variable pitch propeller which he had just fitted to the machine, during which he flew some aerobatics which slightly alarmed Tom.

Tom was a scholar at Sleaford Grammar School and his school friends, including some whose fathers were with the RAF at nearby Cranwell, were somewhat jealous of his connection with Monks and Henshall. This was especially so when, on an occasion when Henshall was shooting on Tom's father's farm, Tom collected expired cartridge cases from Henshall's gun and took them into school. Another shooter on that occasion, who was later to become famous as an RAF pilot, was 'Sailor' Malan. Tom says that Alec Henshall was a very nice man, always kind to him, and he felt the same about Captain Hall of Tollerton.

The last air display at Tollerton prior to war was held in September 1938 when it is said that 10,000 people attended the event which included a 'realistic' A.R.P. [Air Raid Precaution] demonstration. The attendance figures at these displays show how popular they were with the general public.

# Chapter 5

# Industry and the Military

At the outset Tollerton was intended to be a civilian aerodrome for the use of commercial flying and a flying club. There was never any intention in the minds of its founding councillors that there would be any future military use although the suspicion was voiced at a Council meeting when the proposal was discussed, that the Air Ministry's encouragement of municipal aerodromes was militarily based. It must be borne in mind that after the first World War the RAF had been deliberately run down by successive governments. There was no apparent governmental enthusiasm to expand the service until the mid 1930s.

An element of military use at Tollerton emerged when Rolls-Royce Ltd of Derby entered into an agreement with NFS to use the aerodrome to flight test engines and to house their two test aircraft in the NFS hangar. The main military use, however, followed from a government decision to expand the RAF in 1935/6 and the realisation that, in the event of war, a large number of new pilots and other aircrew would be required by the RAF. The result was the opening of civilian training schools and Elementary RAF Training Schools in various parts of the country.

In 1938 the Air Ministry leased some land at Tollerton aerodrome on which to build facilities for Rollason Aircraft Services Ltd to establish a factory and for an Elementary Training School.

## Rolls-Royce Ltd

Rolls-Royce Ltd became involved in the provision of engines for aeroplanes quite early in the development of powered flight, but it did not install the engines in the aircraft, this being the responsibility of the aeroplane manufacturers. In 1927 the company decided that they needed to have more direct control over how their engines were being used because they realised that many engine failures were due to incorrect installation rather than engine defects. A poorly designed or installed radiator, for example, would eventually lead to overheating and consequent engine failure, as would a badly designed engine mounting lead to vibration and engine damage.

The Bristol Aeroplane Company was already controlling its engine installations and Rolls-Royce decided they must do likewise. An old WW1 DH9a was bought and had an 'FX' engine, later designated 'Kestrel', installed and de Havillands agreed to service the aeroplane at their Stag Lane airfield. This aircraft was used for testing until May 1928 when it was decided that it was too old, but the Company was convinced by the results of the tests that it had to undertake its own flight testing.

Stag Lane was inconvenient being in London and far from the Rolls-Royce factory at Derby and so an airfield closer to home was sought. Hucknall was initially considered but there was no hangar available and the Company then looked at Tollerton which proved suitable. The Rolls-Royce development engineer, Cyril Lovesey, was a member of the Nottingham Aero Club and the Chairman of NFS, the lessee at Tollerton, was Colonel The Master of Sempill who had been a premium apprentice at Rolls-Royce. There was, therefore, no difficulty in securing agreement with NFS for the Company to use the aerodrome for its testing work and space was made available for the Rolls-Royce aircraft in the hangar.

The Air Ministry loaned aircraft for the tests, all of which were carried out under Air Ministry contracts on service type aircraft. The first aircraft to arrive at Tollerton in October 1931 was a Buzzard-powered Hawker Horsley, followed by a Kestrel-powered Fairey 111F. The Fairey was later replaced by a Hawker Hart. Much of the test work undertaken by these aircraft involved the development of radiators and cooling systems. The Hart was used to test glycol instead of water as the cooling agent. The fourth aircraft to be used for these tests at Tollerton was a Gloster Gnatsnapper, which had an evaporative cooling system.

The test pilot involved was the Nottingham Flying Club's Chief Instructor Captain Ronald Shepherd. The ground engineers Frank Purnell and Jack Hall undertook the servicing. A Rolls-Royce engineer, Ronnie Harker, was a private pilot and he also undertook some test flying at Tollerton and became the first Company-employed test pilot. The testing regime was a success and the Company began to consider that they required a permanent base for the work, having concerns that Tollerton, being a public airfield, was not fully suited for use on government test development work for military aircraft. A new base was

**Plate 29:** The Rolls-Royce Hawker Horsley at Tollerton in October 1931
*Dave Birch collection*

sought and because two hangars had become available at Hucknall the Company moved there in February 1935. At the same time Captain Shepherd became the full-time Rolls-Royce test pilot and the ground engineer, Frank Purnell, also became a full time Rolls-Royce employee. At the end of his career Ronnie Shepherd was the test pilot for the Flying Bedstead which was a vertical take-off and landing machine in the early 1950s.

## Rollason Aircraft Services Ltd

Rollason Aircraft Services Ltd was formed in 1933 by Captain Bill Rollason and Freddie Kent to service and maintain aircraft from a base at Croydon Airport. The company became associated with British Continental Airways in 1936 to service their aircraft and when BCA merged with British Airways in 1937 this work continued. British Airways became part of the British Overseas Airways Corporation (BOAC) in 1939. Rollason handled the servicing of aircraft owned by well known personalities such as the band-leader Billy Cotton and famous pilots of the time such as Jim and Amy Mollison, Kingsford-Smith and Jean Batten. It had contracts with the Austin Motor Co to manufacture airframes, with Vickers, Hawker Aircraft and, most importantly for the story of Tollerton, the Air Ministry. The Company was experienced in the modification of aircraft such as the Westland Wessex conversion to dual control for Imperial Airways, Airspeed Ferry engine changes and the conversion of Avro 642 passenger aircraft to freight use.

In 1938 Hunting and Son Ltd bought shares in Rollason and in early 1939 gained full control of the business which had its name changed to Field Consolidated Aircraft Services in 1941. Early in 1939 two subsidiary companies were formed, one at Croydon and one at Tollerton: the latter was named Tollerton Aircraft Services Ltd and was formed to operate one of four Civil Aircraft Repair Units under the auspices of the Air Ministry.

The Air Ministry negotiated with Nottingham City Council for the lease of land at Tollerton adjoining Tollerton Lane on which to erect a hangar and offices for Rollason's use at a rent of £120 a year. Rollason engaged Fairweather & Co to erect and fit out the hangar, the contract for the work being signed on 6 May 1939. It was necessary to build a cesspool and, to ensure an adequate supply of electricity, a transformer house. A clinker pathway was made to connect the hangar to the landing-ground. This hangar is the one which is still in existence at Tollerton, at present used by a vehicle recovery company for the storage of accident-recovered vehicles and generally known as the Main Hangar.

In order to staff the Tollerton operation 25 key personnel were moved from Croydon; about 250 local workers were engaged and the Company started its work at Tollerton in August 1939.

# The Civil Air Guard

An important role which developed for Tollerton was the training of civilian pilots for potential military service. The earliest organisation to undertake this work was the Civil Air Guard. The CAG, as it was known, has to be distinguished from the Royal Air Force Volunteer Reserve, although both bodies had the aim of training pilots who could be called upon by the RAF at the outbreak of war. However, they were distinct bodies with their own regulations, recruitment and administration. The main differences between CAG and RAFVR were the age range accepted by CAG and the fact that its trainees had to pay a contribution towards their training. RAFVR recruits made no contribution to their training and received payments from the Air Ministry during the training period.

The CAG was officially formed in 1938 as a joint venture between the Air Ministry and private flying clubs. Its roots extend back to the late 1920s when the then Director of Civil Aviation, Sir Sefton Brancker, persuaded the Air Ministry to offer a subsidy to approved non-commercial organisations for each pupil they trained to Amateur Pilot Licence level. In effect this meant subsidising private flying clubs. The subsidy was reduced in 1934 which hit the clubs' finances quite hard and so they welcomed the scheme introduced in 1938 as a source of increased income.

In spring 1938 Sir Kingsley Wood was appointed as Secretary of State for Air, and Captain Harold Balfour, MP became Under-Secretary. Shortly after these appointments there was a meeting between Captain Balfour and representatives of the flying clubs at which the Civil Air Guard was outlined. Agreement between the clubs and the Air Ministry was quickly achieved and Lord Londonderry was appointed to head the scheme.

The CAG accepted trainees of either sex between 18 and 50 years of age, subject only to their passing a medical examination at the standard required for an 'A' pilot licence. They had to make an honourable agreement to enter the RAF if required. The cost to the trainees was 2/6d per lesson which was a large reduction on the normal cost of a lesson at that time which was:

|                            |                             |
| -------------------------- | --------------------------- |
| Normal training aeroplanes | 10/- per hour at weekends   |
|                            | 5/- per hour on weekdays    |
| Lighter type of aircraft   | 5/- per hour at weekends    |
|                            | 2/6d per hour on weekdays   |

The scheme was an immediate success nationally. Thirty-three thousand applicants came forward in the first three months, of whom half were found suitable for training. By October 1938, four thousand were either in training or had achieved the 'A' licence; by November 1938 this figure had increased by eight hundred. Of these numbers ninety per cent were men and ten per cent women and the men's figures were further broken down by age:

| 18-30 years | 55.67% |
| 30-40 years | 36.61% |
| 40-50 years | 8.02% |

The figures indicate that the CAG was of interest to a higher proportion of women than might have been supposed and, of the men, there was a good spread of ages with, as would be expected, younger men predominating. As war approached training for over 32 year-olds was ended on 29 August 1939.

The 'A' licence was achieved by flying 12 dual and four solo hours followed by ten practice hours a year to the following syllabus:

First Year

| Flying an accurate compass course | $\frac{1}{2}$ hour dual; $\frac{1}{2}$ hour solo; $\frac{1}{2}$ hour test |
| Forced landing practice | $\frac{1}{2}$ hour dual; $\frac{1}{2}$ hour solo; $\frac{1}{2}$ hour test |
| Map reading | 1 hour solo; $\frac{1}{2}$ hour test |
| Cross country flying | 3 hours solo |
| Aerobatics | 1 hour dual; 1 hour solo; $\frac{1}{2}$ hour test |

Second Year

| Flying an accurate compass course | 1 hour solo |
| Forced landing practice | 1 hour solo |
| Cross country flying | $7\frac{1}{2}$ hours solo |
| Aerobatics | $\frac{1}{2}$ hour solo |

In addition, trainees who achieved the 'A' licence were identified as belonging to one of three classes: those who were likely to become service pilots or instructors; those who would be more suited to other flying duties such as observers, air-gunners or wireless operators; and those men, and all women, more suited to being Ferry or Ambulance pilots. Each class received further training, often alongside the RAFVR pilots appropriate to their classification.

Nationally, sixty clubs took part in the scheme, including Nottingham Flying Club at Tollerton. A variety of aircraft were used, not all of which were used at Tollerton. The 'Normal' or 'Standard' types of aircraft were typically the Tiger Moth, Moth Minor, Avro Cadet and Swallow. Others were the Taylorcraft, Cygnet and Tipsy.

At Tollerton in 1938 the CAG used five aircraft, three Swallows and two Cadets. 480 individuals applied and 250 were accepted for training before the success of the scheme made closure of applications necessary. The Nottingham Unit Leader was George Simkin and the five flight leaders were T. Bullens, G. Marshall, C. J. Williams, E. J. Wilson and D. Wynn. The women's section leader was Mrs Goldberg.

The scheme started on 1 September 1938 and in its issue of 7 September *The Aeroplane* reported on those clubs which had already commenced their training work. It said that at Tollerton 70 applicants were either flying or about to start flying. The members were divided into squadrons and flights under the direction of an experienced licensed pilot. Apart from the flying there were lectures of a good standard twice weekly which involved talks and the showing of films. Those with no flying experience and who could only attend at week-ends were not to have their flying training commenced until spring 1939. Anyone with some flying experience or who could attend at any time was to be given intensive training.

## The Royal Air Force Volunteer Reserve

Flying training was also provided by the Royal Air Force Volunteer Reserve which was organised on a different basis to the CAG. The RAFVR school was started at Tollerton on 24 June 1938 under the command of Flight Lieutenant West whose nickname, according to *The Aeroplane*, was 'Knocker'. This organisation was quite distinct from the standard RAF Reserve whose trainees were intended to become RAF officers and who were trained at RAF operated flying schools on a

Plate 30:   A cartoonist's version of typical CAG personnel.
*The Aeroplane 12 October 1938*

ten month course, although in 1935 elementary training could be at a civil flying school followed by advanced training at an RAF flying school. The RAFVR was intended to train civilians who continued with their normal occupations and received the RAF training in their spare time.

The RAF Volunteer Reserve was instituted on 27 August 1936 and recruiting started in December of that year. All entrants were ranked as Airman Pilot, made a commitment for a five year term and undertook to enter the RAF in the event of war. The motive for its formation was a recognition in the RAF and Government that a readiness for war would require large reserves and a war training organisation and that the RAF in wartime would need a much greater number of pilots than were entering as regulars. In addition it became a requirement in April 1937 that all heavy aircraft had to carry two pilots rather than a pilot and an observer which put a further strain on pilot resources.

The RAFVR was controlled by the Air Ministry although training would be at civilian flying schools. Each Reserve centre would have a city-centre base with an aerodrome nearby. Ground instruction was given at the city-centre accommodation. These places were managed by retired or Reserve officers and the airfields by competent firms. In Tollerton's case Nottingham Airport Ltd was such a firm. By the end of 1937 there were to be 23 centres and another ten to be added in 1938. There were initial starting delays due to a lack of suitable instructors and no town centre arrangements had been started before June 1937. However, by the end of 1937 845 recruits were being trained at 19 centres.

After two years training a recruit would move onto service training by being attached to a service squadron. Pilots had to do 60 hours flying a year, 29 hours at weekends, 12 on summer evenings and 20 during a fortnight annual training period. After reaching a required standard of efficiency a volunteer received an annual retaining fee of £25 and if called up for service or when carrying out continuous training was paid at standard RAF pay rates of:

| | |
|---|---|
| Aircraftman second class | 3s. 3d a day |
| Sergeant under pilot training | 10s. 6d a day |
| Sergeant Pilot | 12s. 6d a day. |

Travelling expenses were also paid and 1/- per hour was paid for training at weekends and weekdays.

Not all recruits would be trained as pilots: some would become observers and others air-gunners but they were all under the same requirements.

In order to accommodate the school at Tollerton the Air Ministry leased land from the City Council on which to build a Bellman hangar and erect a building for the accommodation of the trainees whilst attending the school. This building contained a lounge, pupils' canteen, instructors' mess, kitchen, and a clothing, armament and parachute store. There was also a workshop building, motor transport garage and a building to contain a Link trainer. The cost of erecting all these buildings, including the hangar, was £14,000. Initially the school was to be a category 'A' centre limited to 50 pupils but it was expected that it would quickly move to category 'B' which allowed for 100 pupils and this was achieved in August 1938. The Air Ministry paid the Corporation £50 a year for the lease, but required improvements to the landing ground where there were ridges across it and also that the area of the aerodrome be extended by 95 acres.

Applications to join were invited from men between 18 and 25 years and the first Selection Board was held at the aerodrome on 21 June 1938. In addition to training at the aerodrome, pupils were required to attend other training at a centre on Carrington Street, Nottingham, which opened on 30 March 1939 and for drill at Redhill Lodge, Arnold, Nottingham.

The unit at Nottingham was designated No. 27 Elementary and Reserve Training School, shortened to No. 27 ERFTS. By the end of December 1938 there were 66 trainees at the school and by 1 May 1939 its capacity was for 100 pilots and 100 other aircrew with the actual strength being 110 pilots and 36 aircrew. The aircraft in use were six Elementary type aircraft: Tiger Moth, Miles Magister and Blackburn B2, for what was called 'ab initio' training. More advanced

Plate 31:   Tollerton airfield in 1938 looking south-east from 3,000 feet. The newly built hangar for the RAFVR can be seen on the left.
*Roy Bonser collection*

training was given on Service type aircraft: Hart, Hind, Audax and Demon. Aircrew other than pilots were trained on three Avro Ansons. The *Nottingham Journal* for 14 January 1939 reported that the Elementary School had at that time six Harts and six Magisters but it was to be expanded within three months by the addition of six Avro Ansons and within the next six months six Fairey Battles and that, by the end of the year there would be 27 Harts. The same paper for 27 May 1939 reported that the fleet of aircraft would eventually reach 51 and that three dual control Ansons and three Fairey Battles were to be at the school within a week. It also suggested that three Hurricanes would arrive for use by July. No confirmatory evidence has been found that all of these aircraft actually arrived at Tollerton but some certainly did. No-one with memories of the RAFVR at Tollerton recalls any Hurricanes being there.

At the end of its first year the School had produced 31 fully trained pilots and there were 82 pilots in training together with 40 observers and 25 air gunners.

Jim Flint of Keyworth recalls his time at the Nottingham RAFVR School. He recounts how he completed his application forms and then had a medical before being interviewed at Tollerton by five RAF officers. He had no particular motivation to join other than that it sounded a good idea when a friend mentioned it to him at a cricket match. When he drew his kit he and other recruits were allowed half an hour to learn how to put it on. His first flying experience was with 'Knocker' West who took him up to 'show me one or two things'. Jim had a motoring accident one night when he was passenger in a friend's car leaving the aerodrome in which he sustained concussion and had to attend for medicals in London before he was allowed to fly again. Apparently this was standard practice but consequently Jim says he was not as advanced as he could have been when war broke out.

Jim's training was done on Magisters which he thought 'a nice little

**Plate 32:** A Hawker Hind of RAFVR at Tollerton undergoing maintenance.
*Ron Birch collection*

aeroplane', and his night flying was on a Tiger Moth. He also enjoyed the camaraderie of his fellow recruits and talks about the parties they enjoyed. He says there was no formal training format and that pilot recruits were passed as proficient when they were deemed fit to fly solo. He took about 15 hours to achieve this. There was pressure on aircraft use and recruits did not necessarily fly every time they attended the school. At the outbreak of war he was posted to the RAF Training School at Cambridge with 25 other Tollerton RAFVR recruits and he went on to have a distinguished career in the wartime RAF.

Ron Bramley of Nottingham joined the RAFVR at Tollerton in June 1939 but says he did not believe at that time that he would actually have to go to war. At the time he worked for Forman's the printers and three of his colleagues became recruits at the same time as he did. Ron trained as a wireless operator and air-gunner and describes attending upstairs training rooms in Carrington Street, Nottingham, on two evenings a week for training in the theory of wireless and to learn the Morse code. He received no gunnery training whilst at the Elementary School; for this he had to wait until he was called up into the RAF. His air experience was gained at Tollerton where he flew in either a Hart or a Hind with a pilot instructor called Hargreaves who would take the recruits over Nottingham to look at their homes from the air. To get from his home to Tollerton he borrowed his father's car and was paid expenses for using it. He thinks there were about 150 recruits at the aerodrome on a Sunday and the

Plate 33:   Members of the RAFVR, Tollerton at their first annual dinner held at the Black Boy Hotel, Nottingham in 1939.
Standing from left to right are: Flight Lieutenant N A West, Air Commodore E L Gerrard, R S Day, Wing-Commander J L M de C Hughes-Chamberlain, J M Birkin, Air-Commodore S W Smith, Wing-Commander G H P Padley, F H Holmes, Major A L Ashwell and T Birkett. *Ken Shipside collection.*

lucky ones were taken for a flight. On some Sundays the recruits had to attend at Redhill Lodge, Arnold, Nottingham in uniform for marching drill practice. Ron enjoyed the company of his fellow recruits and says that the Forman's lads got on well with a group from Boots, and that there were ten of them in the group who were all called up to the RAF together.

Stanley Hibbert of Keyworth joined the RAFVR when he was 19 years old in early 1939. Some friends joined at the same time and they all did so because they thought it was a good way to learn to fly and be paid for learning. At the time he was living with his parents in Lenton, Nottingham, and to get to Tollerton he had to catch a bus to Trent Bridge and then walk the three miles to the aerodrome. Stanley learned to fly in Miles Magisters, had 30 lessons, and went solo after nine hours.

The Elementary Training School was effectively closed at the outbreak of war although a plaque fixed to a pill-box at the airfield shows dates of 1937-1945.

Maisie Don, whose reminiscences were quoted in Chapter 4, said that alongside the happy memories of her years working at Tollerton, she also had sad memories of 'all the wonderful young men from both Club and VR School who went off so cheerfully to the war and never returned.' She gained some small solace in the thought that at least they had happy times at Tollerton before war broke out.

**Plate 34:  Plaque sited at Tollerton airfield celebrating No. 27 E & R F T S.**
*Nigel Morley*

# PART II: WARTIME – 1939 to 1945

## Chapter 6

# War Is Declared

At 11.00 a.m. on Sunday 3 September 1939 the British Prime Minister, Neville Chamberlain, announced over the radio that war had been declared on Nazi Germany. That statement would affect millions of persons throughout Great Britain, the British Empire, and the rest of the world. The British way of life would be affected in a myriad of ways, not only over the following six years, but also for years to come. The war would touch people in all walks of life, all classes, and all ages. Rationing of food, clothing, furniture and other essential commodities would become a feature of everyday life for the entire population. Families would be split up for months, and even years, at a time; husbands were separated from wives, parents from children. Many people would have to carry the burden of bereavement, as they had done in the Great War: a new generation would know what it was like to lose fathers, mothers, brothers, sisters, friends and relatives.

That Great Britain and Nazi Germany would eventually go to war seemed, somehow, an inevitable outcome of the deteriorating international situation caused by the aggressive and expansionist foreign policy of Nazi Germany and her allies in the years leading up to September 1939. What neither country had planned for was that war would come as early as it did. Thus, when war did finally break out, neither country was fully prepared for the conflict that would ensue. It would not be unreasonable though to suggest that the German army was far better prepared than Great Britain's for war, but neither the Luftwaffe or the Kreigsmarine enjoyed the same degree of supremacy. Indeed the Royal Navy was more than a match for the German Kreigsmarine whilst the RAF was equipped with fighter aircraft and radar that were at the least the equal of their German opponents although the Luftwaffe was numerically superior to the RAF.

As for Great Britain, since the mid 1930s a major rearmament programme had been taking place. Whilst the government had been trying to avoid a war via negotiation, diplomacy, and appeasement, plans had nevertheless been ongoing so that in the event of a war Great Britain would be capable of defending herself. The desire to avoid another full-scale confrontation with Germany was only natural, bearing in mind that memories of the horrors of The Great War were still very fresh. The flower of a generation's youth had been sacrificed in 'the war to end all wars' and no one wished to see a repeat performance of such a colossal tragedy. However, circumstances dictated otherwise, and once again, for the second time in a generation, the people of Great Britain and her Empire found themselves involved in a war against Germany. How that war would affect

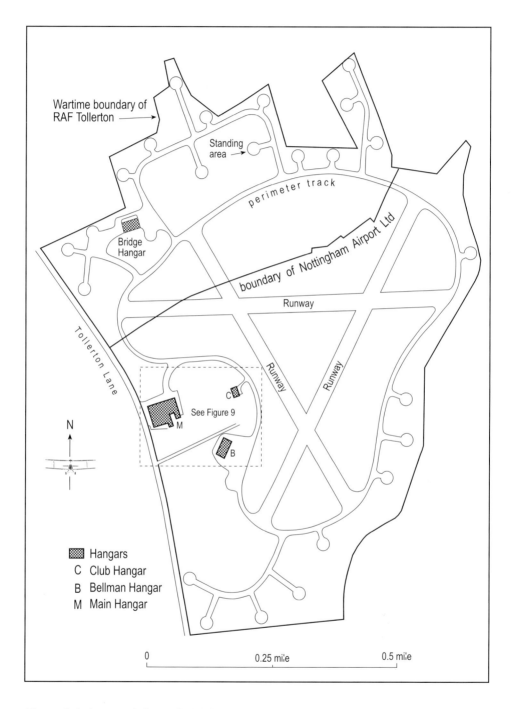

**Figure 8: A map of the airfield showing the Increased area of land occupied by the Royal Air Force.** *Dr. Anne Tarver; Nottinghamshire County Archive Service*

Tollerton airfield and some of the people associated with it is the subject of this section of our book.

Tollerton airfield, in keeping with other airfields throughout the country, would feel the dramatic effects that war would cause. With the outbreak of war the Air Ministry requisitioned all civilian airfields for possible use by the RAF. From 1 September 1939 all civilian flying was banned in the United Kingdom; this included the flying clubs that were located at Tollerton, both military and civilian. The Elementary & Reserve Flying Training School (which trained pilots for the Royal Air Force Voluntary Reserve) and the Civil Air Guard Scheme (which trained civilian pilots) were both disbanded immediately when war was declared. The transformation of Tollerton from a civilian to a military airfield was officially signalled on 26 September 1939 when its name changed from Tollerton Airfield, or Nottingham Airport, as it was also known, to RAF Tollerton. A small enough change on paper but the implications of that change would be considerable in the ensuing months and years of the war.

The next six years would see huge changes. Not only was the airfield requisitioned by the Air Ministry for military use by the RAF, the site was also developed into a major centre for the assembly, modification, overhaul and repair of military aircraft, which at its peak would employ over 700 personnel. This involved a transformation from a grass airfield with relatively few facilities used mainly for private and pleasure flying, to an RAF station with concrete runways, a perimeter track and hard-standing for approximately two dozen aircraft, and all the new buildings to work in and live in that were required by a huge influx of personnel. Coupled with this expansion was the development of the civilian facilities to enable large numbers of people to be employed assembling, servicing, modifying and repairing a range of military aircraft.

The contribution made at Tollerton to the war effort falls into two distinct categories. Firstly, there is the military role, mainly in the training of aircrew for the RAF; and secondly, there is the part played by private companies engaged in the assembly, modification and repair of military aircraft for the RAF. Each of these two operations, military and civilian, was conducted on separate parts of the airfield with only minimal interaction between them. Both, however, played their part and made a significant and worthwhile contribution to the war effort.

It was logical that when war was declared Tollerton, with its existing airfield, would immediately be brought into action. Whilst it would be fair to say that Tollerton was never destined to be one of the 'star' airfields like Scampton, Biggin Hill, Waddington, or Tangmere, it would still have an important role to play in the eventual defeat of Nazi Germany.

## The Royal Air Force Arrives at Tollerton

For Tollerton the months leading up to the outbreak of war had seen considerable activity at the airfield. Both the RAFVR and the CAG schemes (described in chapter 5) had ensured that it was used extensively for training purposes. However, when war was declared both of these schemes were immediately abandoned. In keeping with Government policy Tollerton airfield was requisitioned by the Air Ministry for possible future use by the RAF. At this early stage of the war the RAF had only a partial understanding of how it could best utilize the resources at its disposal or what its future requirements were likely to be in order to continue fighting the war.

As early as 16 January 1939 the RAF had identified Tollerton, along with other airfields at Grimsby, Norwich and Ipswich, as a possible candidate to be used as a satellite airfield to an operational Bomber Command airfield. It was RAF policy to nominate certain airfields as 'satellites' to a 'parent' airfield. The satellite airfield would fulfil certain functions for its parent airfield. These functions could include, amongst many others, any or all of the following roles:

1. A 'scatter' field where aircraft could be dispersed to make them less vulnerable to enemy attack.
2. An emergency landing ground for times when it may not be possible for aircraft to land at their parent airfield.
3. A place where aircrew can be 'stood down' for periods of rest and relaxation.
4. A place where routine maintenance of aircraft from a parent airfield may be carried out.
5. A place where aircrew could undertake practice and training flights.

One of the criteria used to select an airfield to be used as a satellite station was that it must be no more than 10 miles from the airfield that it was to serve. By March 1939 it had been decided that Tollerton was unsuitable for such use as Bomber Command thought that it was too distant from suitable operational airfields. However, by October 1939 the Air Ministry had had yet another change of mind and decided that Tollerton would, after all, be scheduled for possible future use as a satellite airfield.

One immediate result of war being declared was that Tollerton was officially declared a 'scatter field' for use by other operational RAF airfields. A scatter field is, as its name implies, an airfield to which aircraft may be dispersed from other airfields in order that large concentrations of aircraft on the ground may be avoided, thus making them less vulnerable to enemy attack. The Government had seen how the Polish air force had rapidly been all but destroyed on the ground when the country was overrun by Nazi Germany. Not wishing to offer the Luftwaffe an easy target of valuable aircraft it made sound military sense to disperse aircraft wherever possible to scatter fields. As a result of this policy, Handley Page Hampdens of 44 and 50 Squadrons, which were normally based at RAF Waddington, used RAF Tollerton as a scatter field on several occasions during the first months of the war. The first time that Tollerton was used in this capacity occurred on 1 September 1939 when, due to the imminent threat of war, eight

Hampdens of 44 Squadron flew into the airfield (seven in the morning and one in the afternoon). However, by late afternoon the order was reversed and at 1750 hrs the aircraft were recalled to Waddington, arriving there at 1900 hrs.

At various times during September, October and November, aircraft from 44 and 50 Squadrons used RAF Tollerton as a scatter field whenever it was felt to be operationally desirable. Also during this period, when serviceable aircraft from these two squadrons were standing down, some aircrew and their aircraft were sent to Tollerton so that the men might be afforded some rest and relaxation away from the pressures associated with life on an operational airfield. One repercussion of this was that Nottingham became a magnet for off-duty airmen. Establishments such as the Black Boy Hotel, the Flying Horse, the Palais de Dance, the Locarno dance hall, and the Empire music hall all became sought-after venues where the 'boys in blue' could let their hair down and have a good time. At that time Nottingham was known as 'The Queen of the Midlands' due to the high proportion of young women in its population - an imbalance accentuated by the conscription of many of Nottingham's young men into the Armed Forces. In today's military jargon, Nottingham became a 'target rich' environment for aircrew looking for female company!

In September the first contingent of the RAFVR aircrew that had completed their training at the airfield were posted to commence their careers in the RAF. The names of the airmen involved are recorded in the table on page 102:

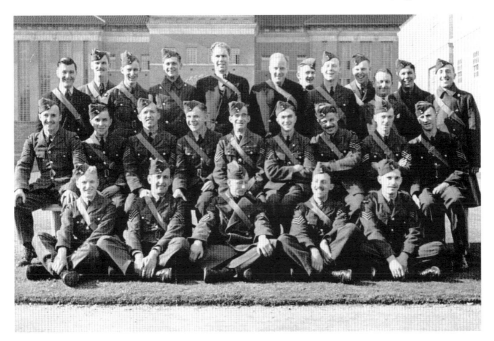

Plate 35:  The first contingent of Tollerton trained RAFVR airmen to enter service with the RAF in 1939. *Jim Flint Collection.*

| | From | The Town Commandant. | To | Headquarters |
|---|---|---|---|---|

From     The Town Commandant.     To     Headquarters
RAF Volunteer Reserve              Reserve Command
Nottingham District.             Royal Air Force

Date       18th September 1939

Ref. No.     NTC/57/Air

Subject:-     Posting of 25 Airman Pilots to R.A.F.V.R u/t

Herewith Nominal Roll of 25 Airman Pilots under training posted today to No.1 Initial Training School, Cambridge in accordance with Officer I/C Records Postagram S/140621/324 dated 14/9/39.

| Name | Rank | Service Number |
|---|---|---|
| Allen J.W. | Sergeant | 742911 |
| Caunt A.S. | Sergeant | 745015 |
| Chester S.C. | Sergeant | 742952 |
| Flint J. | Sergeant | 741968 |
| French H.A. | Sergeant | 745954 |
| Forbes D.L. | Sergeant | 742502 |
| Garton J.F. | Sergeant | 742973 |
| Hickling P.F. | Sergeant | 745012 |
| Howitt J.P. | Sergeant | 745757 |
| Hutchinson D.S. | Sergeant | 745129 |
| Knighton T.H. | Sergeant | 745273 |
| Lang K.C. | Sergeant | 745486 |
| Morley R.D. | Sergeant | 745266 |
| McCubbings I.N. | Sergeant | 745265 |
| McKenzie K.A. | Sergeant | 745274 |
| Pearson J. | Sergeant | 745267 |
| Richards K.C. | Sergeant | 745011 |
| Rowe P. | Sergeant | 745268 |
| Ruxton T.R. | Sergeant | 745276 |
| Sellors J.F. | Sergeant | 745277 |
| Travell W. | Sergeant | 745270 |
| Turner J.W. | Sergeant | 745271 |
| ???????? | Sergeant | 745093 |
| Whitfield D.G. | Sergeant | 745010 |
| Wollatt A.G. | Sergeant | 745009 |

W E A Scott. Fl/Lt. Town Commandant, RAFVR, Nottm. District

**Table 5:**     **Extracts from Correspondence Relating to the First Posting of RAFVR Personnel from Tollerton**

With war though comes danger and on 21 October 1939 an incident occurred at Tollerton to remind everyone that flying in wartime has its hazards. A Hampden (L4077) piloted by 580291 Sgt Wild struck a dummy gun emplacement in the centre of the airfield causing the death of 4963932 Sgt C. Fretwell and injuring 1474701 Gunner G. Wardle of the 53$^{rd}$ Light Anti-Aircraft Battery. Unfortunately there would be other incidents during the course of the war that would cost the lives of more aircrew and ground personnel.

This phase of activity at Tollerton, however, was short-lived. When the aircraft from 50 Squadron were sent to the Scottish town of Wick in late November 1939, RAF Tollerton lost its status as a scatter field. There then followed a relatively quiet period at Tollerton during which little appeared to be happening as far as the war was concerned. In some respects, even in the world beyond Tollerton, it was hard to imagine that a war was taking place. It was true that Britain's armed forces were being mobilized on a massive scale and that incidents occurred to remind people that the nation was at war. One of the most significant in 1939 was the sinking of the German 'pocket-battleship' *Admiral Graf Spee* in the Battle of the River Plate. This action captured the imagination of the British public and reinforced the image of invincibility that the Royal Navy presented. However, this was a fairly isolated incident and because of the overall lack of military activity this period became known as 'The Phoney War'. The policy of both Great Britain and France at this stage was to avoid armed confrontation with Germany on her western borders and leave Hitler with a free hand to pursue his expansionist policies in Eastern Europe. The Phoney War came to an end when Hitler launched an invasion of Denmark and Norway in April 1940.

However, the apparent inactivity during the Phoney War period was a godsend: it provided Great Britain and her Empire with an invaluable breathing space in which to organize defences and build up fighting capability. RAF Tollerton and those people associated with the airfield would soon feel the effects of this mobilization. In the meantime, the apparently peaceful atmosphere that prevailed in the country was merely the calm before the storm that would break once Britain's ally France had been invaded and defeated. The fall of France heralded the attempt by Germany to invade England. Before that invasion could be successfully contemplated the Luftwaffe needed to achieve mastery of the skies over England. That necessitated the defeat of the RAF as a fighting force. The result of this was the Battle of Britain, followed by the Blitz. With Great Britain now engaged in a full-scale conflict the pace of life at Tollerton would increase dramatically.

In mid 1941 the airfield became a training base for Polish airmen but prior to that Tollerton continued to be used for other purposes. In January 1941 RAF Binbrook, Lincolnshire, was the home of 12 Squadron but considerable difficulties were being experienced there due to heavy rain flooding parts of the airfield. It was decided to relocate 'A' and 'B' Flights of that squadron to

Tollerton where they could continue to train in their Vickers Wellington aircraft. Consequently, on 9 January 1941 Wing Commander Lowe visited Tollerton to inspect the airfield and ascertain if it was indeed a suitable site for his aircraft. Satisfied that it was suitable, 'A' Flight of 12 Squadron flew into Tollerton on 16 January 1941 and continued with their training schedule until 24 January 1941 when they returned to Binbrook. On the same day they were replaced by 'B' Flight of 12 Squadron, under the command of Squadron Leader Lawrence, and they too continued with their training programme.

It was during one of these training exercises on 8 February 1941 that one of the squadron's Wellington bombers crashed near Tollerton with tragic results. The Wellington (W5365), piloted by Squadron Leader Lawrence, stalled and crashed whilst attempting to land at the airfield. The aircraft crashed into the ground close to the village of Cotgrave with the loss of seven lives. A plaque at the airfield commemorates the sad event. The names on the plaque, however, present something of a mystery. Seven aircrew are reported killed although a Wellington usually only carried a crew of six. In the book *Bomber Command Losses of the Second World War 1941* by W R Chorley there is no mention

Plate 36: **The Plaque commemorating the tragic accident, involving the Wellington Bomber (W5365) on 8 February 1941.**
The plaque is attached to the side of a pillbox close to the airfield control tower. *Nigel Morley*

whatsoever of two injured aircrew. Chorley mentions that on the day that the Wellington crashed AC1 J D Boxall of 12 Squadron lost his life. It is conjectured that he may have been a passenger on the aircraft although his name does not appear on the plaque. Perhaps the 'extra' crew were also passengers (travelling either officially or unofficially). Whatever the true explanation, the fact remains that the tragedy involved the greatest loss of life in a single incident at Tollerton for the whole duration of the war.

However, life must go on and 12 Squadron continued with their training, mainly in the form of cross country flying, feathering airscrew tests (i.e. flying on only one of the aircraft's two engines) and practice firing with the guns on the aircraft. A minor diversion from the squadron's training programme occurred on 19 February 1941 when the flight was treated to a lecture from a member of Nottingham University on 'Causes of the War'. The brief tenure of 12 Squadron at Tollerton came to an end on 5 March 1941 when it was decided to return the squadron to Binbrook. Nevertheless, it would not be many months before a completely different group of airmen would be calling Tollerton 'home'. However, before the arrival of the Polish aircrew there was to be a significant event in the history of the airfield. That event was the installation of the concrete runways, perimeter track and hard-standings that resulted in the transformation of the airfield into the site that we recognize today.

## From Grass to Concrete Runways

In mid 1940 RAF Tollerton was again designated as a satellite airfield, this time to serve RAF Newton, situated on the Fosse Way near Bingham. RAF Newton, like RAF Tollerton, only had grass runways, which for an operational airfield could be a severe handicap if the ground became waterlogged. To resolve this problem at RAF Tollerton the decision was taken to install concrete runways, perimeter track and hard-standings for around two-dozen aircraft. Strangely, especially as it was an operational airfield, no such improvements were ever made at RAF Newton, which continued to be a grass airfield until it closed in November 2000.

The concrete runways at Tollerton were laid down in 1941 and conformed to the, by then, standard 'A' pattern layout. The three runways were respectively 1,118 yds, 1,146 yds, and 1,033 yds in length; all three were 50 yds in width. The perimeter track was 11,108 yds long and 50 ft wide. However, these runways were not of sufficient length for the airfield to be considered for operational duties. By 1942 the Air Ministry had decided that it was desirable that all operational Bomber Command stations should have three runways, preferably set at 60 degrees to each other (thus forming a triangular pattern); the main strip was to be 2,000 yds long by 50 yds wide, while the remaining two strips were to be 1,400 yds long by 50 yds wide. Airfields that met these criteria were classified as 'A' Class airfields and were thus suitable for operational use. It can be seen that RAF Tollerton did not meet these criteria and, as such, was not suitable for Bomber Command to use in an operational capacity. The main runway was simply too short for a fully loaded bomber to take off safely. Likewise, a badly damaged bomber would quite probably need a longer distance in which to land. The relative shortness of Tollerton's runways could explain why, during the research into this book, no documentary evidence has been discovered that Bomber Command ever used the airfield operationally at any time for the whole duration of the war.

It may be of interest to offer a general explanation as to why the transition from grass to concrete runways came about.

Airline passengers of today take it for granted that the flight that they are embarking on will begin and (hopefully) end safely on a runway with a hard surface such as concrete or tarmac. In 1939 airfields with such runways were few and far between. The adoption of concrete and tarmac for the construction of airfield runways was brought about by practical, operational experience during the early years of the war.

When war broke out the RAF possessed only nine airfields in the whole of the country that had concrete or tarmac covered runways. Prior to 1939 grass had been the accepted surface for airfield use for a number of reasons, the principal one being that such airfields were relatively inexpensive to build and maintain.

**Plate 37:**   **An aerial view of the airfield showing the newly laid runways.**
*Nottingham Evening Post*

Grass was also a very suitable environment for the aircraft of the day to operate on. At a time when aircraft did not weigh very much and had relatively low take-off and landing speeds grass was a perfectly acceptable surface to use. Aircraft tyres were relatively large and were not inflated to a very high pressure, so there was little, if any, wear and tear on the grass surfaces during everyday use. The main problem encountered with grass airfields occurred during wet weather. During periods of prolonged heavy rain, particularly if there were problems with drainage, an airfield may become waterlogged. When this did happen, flying was simply abandoned. This may have been tolerable in peacetime but it would not be acceptable in wartime.

Serious concerns about the all-weather serviceability of airfields had begun to arise in the mid 1930s. In a letter written during 1937, Hugh Dowding, the head of Fighter Command, wrote to the Secretary of State at the Air Ministry voicing his concerns at the large number of his airfields which were unserviceable because of bad weather. During the winter months of 1936/7 the majority had been out of action for weeks and even months at a time because the ground was either waterlogged or covered in snow. This would clearly be a highly unsatisfactory situation in the event of war.

Another problem was that aircraft were changing. The aircraft then being delivered to the RAF were causing new problems. A new feature with aircraft such as the Spitfire and Hurricane was that they had brakes on their landing wheels. Pilots used these brakes when taxiing in order to steer. On wet ground in particular this was creating potholes where, during a turning manoeuvre, the inside wheel had dug into the ground. Furrows and ridges could develop and present a serious danger to aircraft that were taxiing, taking off or landing. The weight of aircraft was also increasing, as were take-off and landing speeds; tyre pressures, too, were increasing; and added to this was the problem caused by service vehicles being driven over the grass to and from the aircraft.

All of these factors contributed to a very unsatisfactory situation as far as the serviceability of grass airfields was concerned given the deteriorating international situation. Should war break out it was imperative that the RAF's airfields should remain fully operational at all times irrespective of the weather and other problems. The Director of Works at the Air Ministry was ordered by the government to investigate the situation and present some suitable solutions.

Within days the Director of Works, Colonel J. Turner, began visiting all the fighter stations around London and interviewing each of the station commanders to sound out their views on the issue. Once this had been done a conference was called at Adastral House (RAF Headquarters) in London in June 1937. The initial view of the Director of Works was that putting down a prepared surface on an airfield was not desirable, for two main reasons. Firstly, whilst no one had yet formulated any definitive standards for the configuration of runways or materials to be used, he was certain that the cost to the Treasury would be 'prodigious'; secondly, airfields would lose the natural camouflage that grass provided. All this time it was only the problems that faced Fighter Command that were being addressed. Oddly, given that the bombers were significantly heavier than the fighters and would thus, theoretically, present a larger problem, Bomber Command at that time seemed strangely unconcerned by the whole issue.

Further meetings were convened and evidence gathered on which to base future policy. Most of the discussions were of a sound technical nature but one eccentric proposal was the use of catapults to assist with take-off (presumably along similar lines to those used on board warships). The thinking was that with a catapult the size of aerodromes (and consequently their costs) could be significantly reduced. While this may have addressed the problems associated with runway lengths for take-off, what about when those same aircraft came in to land? (Were arrester hooks envisaged as also used on aircraft carriers?)

When an aircraft takes off or lands it does so 'into the wind' to increase the 'lift' on the wings. On a grass airfield pilots simply checked which way the windsock was blowing and altered their take-off or landing positioning accordingly. To surface the whole airfield with concrete or tarmac would not be a practical option (quite apart from the astronomical cost). The solution to that particular problem was to lay down three runways at sixty degrees to each other in the classic 'A' pattern. With these three runways a pilot could always take-off and land more or less into the wind. In keeping with practice at virtually all RAF airfields, this was the configuration adopted at RAF Tollerton when the concrete runways were installed in 1941.

By June 1939 a reluctant Treasury had been persuaded to finance the building of prepared surfaces at thirteen airfields, of which eight belonged to Fighter Command. Coastal Command had two of the other airfields and the remaining three belonged to Bomber Command. By January 1940, and with the war only just over four months old, government policy was changed radically. The harsh realities of war soon brought about a rapid reappraisal of what was required at an RAF airfield and the cost of installing runways with a concrete or tarmac surface very rapidly became of secondary importance. The over-riding criterion was that the airfields needed to be available for operational use at all possible times, and to this end new runways and perimeter and service tracks were to be installed wherever it was felt operationally necessary, irrespective of the costs involved.

The implications of this new approach were far-reaching. Once it became apparent what the war required, a massive programme of airfield construction was launched. During the years 1939 to 1945, some 444 airfields with paved runways, perimeter tracks and hard standing were constructed for the RAF at a cost of over £200,000,000 (excluding any buildings that were also constructed on them). In addition, major extensions were undertaken at a further 63 existing RAF stations.

The peak year for airfield construction was 1942, the year after the runways were laid down at Tollerton. So intense was the building activity during 1942 that new airfields were being opened at a rate of one every three days. To achieve this, a colossal amount of planning and manual work needed to be undertaken. During 1942 a labour force of about 127,000 men was employed on building and civil engineering works for the RAF, of whom approximately 60,000 were employed exclusively on the civil engineering task of airfield and runway construction. Since most of this intense building activity tended to be in quiet, rural areas the public at large remained in relative ignorance of the huge effort that was taking place. By 1942 the average cost of constructing one of these new bomber airfields, exclusive of any buildings or services, was around £500,000. With the extra cost of the additional buildings that were required on the average airfield that sum would rise significantly.

Who would build these new airfields? At that time the total manpower available for the building industry was approximately 400,000 men. Thus, the Works Directorate (which organized the supply of labour throughout the country) allocated nearly one third of the country's total available labour force to the Air Ministry for constructional work for the RAF. This was a staggering proportion of the country's resources being employed in the colossal expansion of the RAF's fighting capabilities. After the fall of France in 1940 and the British army's evacuation from Dunkirk large numbers of soldiers from the Pioneer Companies of the Royal Engineers became available to assist the RAF. However, at the beginning of 1941 the War Office informed the Air Ministry that it must withdraw the Pioneer Companies from repairing airfields, as they were required for other military duties and further training.

This presented the Air Ministry with a severe problem: how could they continue to ensure that damaged airfields were rapidly repaired? To replace the Pioneers they decided to form RAF units called 'Works Squadrons', originally divided into headquarters units with an attachment of ten works flights. A Warrant Officer commanded each flight of approximately eighty men, which included some tradesmen but a majority of unskilled workers.

Some of the facts and figures for this construction work are hugely impressive. For instance, from 1939 to 1945, 175,000,000 square yards of concrete, tarmacadam or other hard surfacing material were laid in paved runways, perimeter and connecting tracks at various airfields throughout the United Kingdom. To achieve this level of construction new machines had to be developed specifically for the purpose. A vital requirement for the construction of these runways, hard-standings and perimeter tracks was a constant supply of good quality hardcore as the foundation for the concrete or tarmac surfaces. Initially this vital ingredient was in desperately short supply; however, somewhat ironically it was the Germans themselves who provided the solution to the problem. The massive bomb damage being inflicted by the Luftwaffe on London and other provincial cities was creating a serious problem with regard to the disposal of the brick and masonry rubble that was generated. It was decided that this rubble could be used for airfield construction work and a network was set up using road, rail and canal to distribute the hardcore to those sites where it was required. So the rubble created by the German bombing, quite literally, laid the foundations for the runways that the RAF would later fly from, when, in 1943, 1944 and 1945 Bomber Command took the air battle to Germany with such devastating effect.

As the war progressed airfields underwent a dramatic change. In 1939 the RAF's nine airfields with concrete or tarmac runways had maximum dimensions of 1,000 yds long by 50 yds wide, designed to take the load of the heaviest bombers then in service which were the Vickers Wellington and the Armstrong Whitworth Whitley both with an all-up weight of between 30,000 to 35,000lbs and tyre pressures of 45 lb per square inch. By 1945 runways at selected bomber airfields were 3,000 yds long by 100 yds wide, constructed of high grade concrete 12 inches thick and designed to take aircraft with a gross weight of 140,000 lbs and tyre pressures of 85 lb per square inch.

At Tollerton airfield the changes were dramatic. From a grass airfield with relatively few facilities in 1939 it had expanded by 1945 into an airfield with three concrete runways, perimeter tracks, hard-standing for 28 aircraft, four hangars, and many other outbuildings where a workforce of over 700 personnel could make their contribution to the war effort.

However, although many people were interviewed during research on this project, no one could recall the runways being built. Given the work involved and the huge numbers of lorry deliveries that must have been made over several months to bring in the materials required, this seems very odd indeed. A constant stream of lorries must have been seen on the local roads; but no one could recall them!

## A Schoolboy's Wartime Memories

The feelings that a war can stir cover the whole range of human emotions. Surprisingly, for some people such a horrendous occurrence as a world war can be the source of considerable pleasure and excitement. One such person was West Bridgford schoolboy Tom Myall. For him the war could not have occurred at a better time.

Tom's father ran a garage in West Bridgford and during the war he managed to obtain a contract for servicing Ministry of Defence vehicles. This gave him reserved occupation status and, as such, he was not liable to conscription. Tom, therefore, unlike a great many other children of the day, was lucky in that he saw his father throughout the war.

When war was declared in 1939 Tom was just a twelve-year old schoolboy. Tom's father had served in the Royal Flying Corps (RFC) in the First World War and his love of aviation had rubbed off on his young son, as had his love of photography. Tom remembers going to airshows at Tollerton and Hucknall with his father before the war and being thrilled by what he saw there. One particular event that Tom recalls was seeing two Armstrong-Whitworth Siskin bi-planes tied together and flying in formation!

As he lived in West Bridgford, the airfield at Tollerton wasn't too far away. In those days Tom could walk pretty well in a straight line through empty fields from his house to the airfield and watch the aircraft taking off and landing. Armed with his camera, and sometimes accompanied by a friend, Tom spent many happy hours watching activities at Tollerton and taking occasional photographs of the aircraft there. He would then take the photographs to the local Boots the Chemists for developing and printing.

Unfortunately Tom did not enjoy the best of health as a schoolboy. He was plagued by asthma, and this resulted in a weak chest, which in turn led to many weeks off school. Indeed, Tom thinks that around half of his schooldays were lost due to absence through illness. Every cloud has a silver lining though, and the time spent off school gave Tom ample opportunities to wander over to Tollerton and indulge his two favourite pastimes: watching and photographing aircraft.

The advent of war brought about considerable changes at the airfield; nearly all for the better as far as Tom was concerned. There was a dramatic increase in the number and variety of aircraft that used the airfield. While it was true that photography became a great deal more difficult during the war years, that

**Plate 38:   Lancaster bombers at Tollerton in 1944.** A common sight on the airfield
once TAS had acquired the contract to work on the legendary bomber.
*Tom Myall Collection*

drawback was more than offset for Tom by all the new types of aircraft that he could now witness using the airfield. He even managed to continue taking photographs, though now he had to develop and print the photographs himself (though he cannot recall from where he obtained the film, chemicals and photographic paper). Photographing military airfields and their aircraft was strictly prohibited during wartime, and going into the local Boots with a roll of photographs of military aircraft taken at the local RAF airfield would be a certain way to invite a call from representatives of His Majesty's Nottinghamshire Constabulary!

One would suppose that security at wartime airfields would be tight and that this would place severe restrictions on Tom's activities. This was not the case at Tollerton. Whilst it was true that coils of barbed wire had been placed around the airfield perimeter there were still gaps through which a determined schoolboy could wriggle. The lack of guards patrolling the perimeter also helped. Although the perimeter was also protected by a series of pillboxes, Tom has no recollection of seeing them being manned on a regular basis.

So it was that at various times Tom would make his way along the Grantham Canal to a quiet part of the airfield to see what was occurring there. A break in the barbed wire allowed him access to the site and he could then look at the aircraft at his leisure. He kept a sharp lookout, he was well aware that if he was caught he would be in hot water, with both the authorities and his parents. The risks were well worthwhile though. The part of the airfield that he visited was used for parking aircraft prior to work being carried out or when they were ready to be flown out. The variety of aircraft was immense; there were few wartime aircraft that flew with the RAF that Tom wasn't lucky enough to see at close quarters at one time or another during 1943 and 1944. But not only did he look at them; he photographed them too!

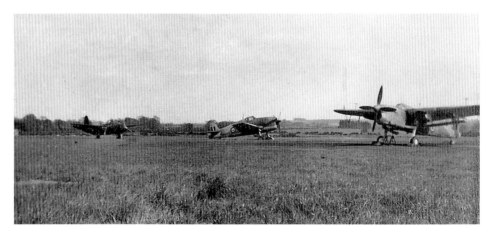

**Plate 39:  Boston, Hellcat and Barracuda at Tollerton in 1944.** At various times throughout the war a considerable variety of aircraft could be seen at the airfield. *Tom Myall Collection*

The high-water mark of Tom's trespassing activities must surely have been achieved one day in 1944 when, having negotiated the barbed wire, he and his cousin found a Grumman Hellcat fighter aircraft parked near the edge of the airfield close to the Grantham Canal. The cousin found the external button that operated the electrically controlled cockpit cover and - Hey Presto! - the aircraft cockpit was open to their further inspection. Tom's cousin climbed into the pilot's seat, where Tom took a photograph of him; then it was Tom's turn to do the same, though he didn't manage to have his photo taken. Both boys played with the joystick and pretended to fly the machine shooting down imaginary Germans: great sport. The temptation to press the Hellcat's firing button was almost too much to overcome; however, since neither boy had the faintest idea as to whether or not the aircraft's guns were armed, discretion fortunately won the day. (Usual RAF practice was that all ammunition was removed from aircraft before being flown into such places as Tollerton so it is highly unlikely that the guns were armed.) Had it not been for the photograph that Tom took of this exploit then this tale might well be put down to schoolboy exaggeration: as it is, the photograph (plate 40) is evidence of Tom's veracity.

For Tom, all in all, the war years were a time of adventures, excitement, and memorable experiences. True, there were shortages from rationing and all that that entailed, and there was Tom's poor health. But he says money could not buy the huge enjoyment that he was fortunate enough to derive from living through such an epoch-making time in our history. If only the same could be said for all those other poor souls for whom the war was nothing like the same.

**Plate 40:  A wartime schoolboy's dream come true?** Tom Myall's cousin in the cockpit of the Grumman Hellcat fighter aircraft in 1944. *Tom Myall Collection*

# Chapter 7

# The Polish Connection

In 1941 it was decided to base No 16 (Polish) Service Flying Training School at RAF Newton. As RAF Tollerton was officially designated as a satellite of RAF Newton this meant that it would be used on a regular basis by the new arrivals. Thus from 15 July 1941 No 16 (Polish) Service Flying Training School commenced using RAF Tollerton airfield on a regular basis for training purposes.

The route from raw recruit to operational flying with an RAF squadron usually followed a set pattern. Trainee pilots would first attend an Initial Training School. It was here that, amongst other things, the raw recruits would have their first taste of 'square bashing' - learning to march in step, rifle drill, etc. Upon satisfactorily completing that course they would then go to an Elementary Flying Training School where they would be taught the rudiments of flying. If they completed that course satisfactorily they would then be posted to a Service Flying Training School, which was the final stage of their training. After that, provided that they completed the course to the satisfaction of their instructors, they were deemed ready to be posted to an operational RAF unit.

The Polish pilots training at RAF Tollerton had already received their basic flying training at RAF Hucknall before being transferred to RAF Newton for more advanced training in Fairey Battle aircraft, Airspeed Oxfords and Miles Masters. RAF Tollerton was used mainly for take-off and landing practice, or, in RAF jargon, 'circuits and bumps'. One of the principal reasons for using RAF Tollerton was that, by the time the Polish pilots arrived, concrete runways had been laid down. Because RAF Newton was a grass airfield there were frequent times when the landing area was waterlogged and unsuitable for flying. Then the concrete runways at Tollerton proved invaluable in allowing training of the Polish airmen to continue uninterrupted.

From July 1941 until the end of the war RAF Tollerton was host to a succession of trainee Polish airmen as new recruits arrived to undergo their training there. These airmen had come to England prepared to risk their lives by throwing their lot in with Great Britain in the struggle to defeat Nazi Germany. Why should this be so? It may be of interest to examine why a small village in rural Nottingham-shire, with no obvious connection to Poland, should have become home to these foreign airmen, stationed so far from their native lands and loved ones.

## The Defeat of Poland

On 31 March 1939, the British Government promised to support Poland in the event of an attack from another nation. The Germans, wrongly surmising that Great Britain would not keep this promise, took a huge gamble and at 0445 hrs on the morning of 1 September 1939 began the invasion of Poland. Hitler was however correct in his assessment that neither Great Britain nor France would become embroiled in a land war on Germany's Western borders.

Germany had refined a new method of warfare called 'Blitzkrieg' (lightning war), which was unleashed on Poland on that fateful September morning in 1939. The success of this new form of warfare took both Poland, and the Germans themselves, completely by surprise. Within a month Poland was defeated. To add to Poland's troubles, while Germany was attacking from the west, the Soviet Union invaded and attacked from the east. Poland was in the unfortunate predicament of being occupied by two invading armies. Whilst the actions of the Soviet Union appear to be opportunist, in fact there was a sound military logic to their actions. Had Germany managed to occupy the whole of Poland, then, when they eventually invaded the Soviet Union in 1941 their forces would have been poised on the Polish/Soviet border. Interestingly, although Great Britain and France declared war on Germany for their invasion of Poland, they did not declare war on the Soviet Union for committing the same act of aggression.

On 2 September 1939, the British Government issued an ultimatum stating that unless German aggression against Poland ceased and a withdrawal of German troops began by 11 a.m. on 3 September, a state of war would exist between the two countries. The ultimatum was ignored, and war was declared.

Before the war Hitler's vision for Nazi Germany saw the country expanding eastwards to occupy countries such as Poland and gain what he termed 'lebensraum' (living space) for the German nation. This new land would become a part of a Greater Germany. A person's race would dictate where they would fit in the new scheme of things. A large proportion of the populations in the Eastern European countries were of Slavonic descent. The majority of people living in these captured countries would either become servants of the Greater German State or be exterminated. Hence, when Poland was defeated the treatment of her military and civilian populations was brutal in the extreme. By the end of the war, whilst approximately 120,000 of Poland's military personnel had died, a staggering total of over 5,300,000 of her civilian population would have perished, many of these in the death camps at such infamous places as Auschwitz and Treblinka.

Poland's air force at the time of the German invasion was both numerically and technologically inferior to that of her opponents. While Germany had over 1,200 aircraft at its disposal, the Poles could muster fewer than 400. Much of Poland's air force was destroyed on the ground in the opening days of the war, when German bombers and dive-bombers mounted surprise attacks against Polish airfields. Thus, while the bulk of Poland's aircraft were destroyed, the aircrews survived. Poland may have been defeated; but there were significant numbers of her military personnel who were determined to continue the fight. By one means or another a large number of these Polish airmen found their way to England.

The following quotations are from an article in *Flight* magazine dated 21 December 1939:

**Polish Airmen Will Play Their Part**

Somewhere in England, as announced by the Secretary of State for Air in the House of Commons recently, the first detachment of the Polish Air Force is already training with enthusiasm to form itself into the first of several squadrons that will soon become part of the RAF. ... Many of the officers and men arrived in the country after alarming experiences, with practically no money and very little clothing. ... By the end of this week, the first detachment will be wearing with pride the uniform of the RAF. The only distinguishing marks will be the difference in the cap badge and the Polish eagle in gold on the left pocket of the tunic.

One officer said, 'Those who have arrived so far are a magnificent body of men. All have plenty of actual flying experience and they are full of enthusiasm, yet show a quiet determination to get on with their job as quickly as possible.'

These Polish squadrons will be self-supporting, i.e. pilots, observers, gunners and wireless operators will form aircrews and maintenance will also be undertaken by Polish personnel. ... Several of them speak English already, but others are working to get a smattering of our language. Owing to the fact that so few can speak English, they do not leave camp unless they are accompanied by an English officer, or in the case of the airmen, by a RAF non-commissioned officer.

Thus, from the early days of the war there was a steady stream of Polish airmen finding their way to England, desperate to continue their fight against Germany. Quite often the journey to England that these airmen undertook involved considerable personal risk; capture could well mean death. Jan Krupa was such a person. He explained how he made the hazardous journey from Poland to England, and finally to RAF Newton and RAF Tollerton.

## One Polish Man's Experience

Before the war Jan Krupa had enlisted in the Polish Air Force as a trainee pilot but, unfortunately, failed to make the required grade. As a result, instead of fulfilling his ambition to be a pilot he became an airframe-fitter/mechanic. With the German invasion of Poland Jan was involved in the desperate rearguard action that culminated with the defeat of Poland. Once the situation was lost Jan, along with another Polish pilot whom he had encountered during the retreat, decided to escape from Poland and head for safety.

The pair of airmen eventually managed to cross the border into Hungary. There they were taken to a camp where the authorities gave them something to eat and a bed for the night in a tent. In this camp Jan became involved in the smuggling of such items as civilian clothing, false passports, and tickets for officers and first-line pilots who used the forged documents to travel to Paris on that most famous of trains, The Orient Express. Once in Paris they hoped to be able to join General Sikorski, the Polish patriot, who was trying to regroup Polish forces there in order to continue the fight against Germany. After a few weeks in the camp Jan and his friend managed to obtain the necessary documentation that would enable them to make the journey themselves. However, Lady Luck did not smile kindly on their joint enterprise and the train on which they were travelling was stopped at the border. Jan and his friend were arrested and taken to Budapest, where they were thrown in the prison known as The Citadel.

Fortunately, security at The Citadel was on the lax side and after a fortnight or so the two men managed to escape and made their way across the River Danube via the Elizabeth Bridge. From there they went to the Polish Mission at Barcz on the Yugoslav border where they were able to obtain new documents. It was then necessary to cross the river into Rumania. They obtained the services of a local boatman who was engaged in the lucrative business of smuggling escapees across the river in his rowing boat. They paid the boatman the necessary fare and began their river crossing. It was a foggy night. After being rowed for twenty minutes or so a riverbank appeared out of the gloom. The intrepid pair left the boat and scrambled up the bank. They then began walking but to their utter amazement found themselves back in Barcz. They had been duped: the boatman had taken their money and then rowed around in a circle in the fog before landing them further down the river on the same bank!

**Plate 41:  Tollerton RAF ground crew working on a Miles Master trainer in 1943.**
*Charles Loakes*

Now their only viable option was to swim across. They did, quite literally, take the plunge and swam across the freezing cold river to make good their escape. Once safely away from the riverbank they made their way to a small railway station where they received free tickets to Zagreb. With the aid of another free ticket they reached Split on the Adriatic coast. After ten difficult and fraught days in hiding they managed to board a boat, the *Patris*, which was already listing alarmingly as it was loaded well beyond its permitted capacity with refugees wanting to escape from the Germans. Conditions aboard the vessel were pretty grim: there was no food, little water, and a crew that did not inspire confidence. However, despite all these shortcomings the *Patris* managed to reach Marseilles after a journey that lasted 36 hours.

The French authorities gave the two airmen accommodation in a warehouse along with other Polish serviceman. After several unpleasant and dangerous experiences the Polish Air Force personnel were sent to Lyon to join the French Air Force there. They were duly enrolled as airmen in the French Air Force, provided with a pay-book and uniform, and given the rank of sergeant. After undergoing a course on aircraft recognition Jan was detailed to work on aircraft maintenance. However, it was not long before France capitulated and once again Jan found himself on the move. This time he made his way to Biarritz, which was in one of the safer parts of France. It was there that he heard Winston Churchill on the wireless urging ships to pick up any allied forces trying to get to England. After sleeping on a beach for a few nights passage was secured aboard a ship, the *Andora*, which brought him safely to Liverpool. During the voyage the only available food was oranges, supplemented with an occasional piece of bread, and some water.

From Liverpool Jan and some other Polish personnel were marched, under an escort of British soldiers, to a holding camp at Kirby. During this march sympathetic local people threw chocolates, sweets, and Woodbine cigarettes at the refugees. Jan, mistaking this show of goodwill as an insult, told his party to leave the gifts on the ground: a mistake that he has always regretted. At Kirby the refugees were given a meal of rich soup and bread. This proved too much for most of the party to digest since they had not had a proper meal to eat in ages. The consequence was that most of the poor souls finished up vomiting. After three further days in the temporary camp the necessary formalities had been attended to and Jan was enlisted into the Royal Air Force. What particularly impressed Jan was the amount of detailed information that the military authorities possessed relating to Polish refugees - even all of the Polish names were spelt correctly! To this day Jan has never been able to understand how it was that the British authorities were in possession of such detailed information. Now, in less than a year, Jan had been a serving airman in the air forces of three different countries.

From Kirby Jan was sent to the RAF camp at Kirkham, near Blackpool, and exchanged his Polish uniform for that of the RAF. He was also given his new service number (784946) and posted to 17 OTU (Operational Training Unit) at Upwood, near Peterborough. He was again given the rank of sergeant and examined in his trade as a fitter. This proving satisfactory he then underwent training on the maintenance of the Bristol Blenheim bomber. After four months he was posted to 25 FTS (Flying Training School) at RAF Hucknall, and then on to 16 (Polish) FSTS (Flying Service Training School) at RAF Newton in Nottinghamshire.

Jan was destined to spend the remainder of the war at RAF Newton. There were occasions, however, when his skills were required at Tollerton and on those occasions he and his crew would come over to the airfield by bus or lorry and carry out whatever maintenance duties or repairs were necessary. Virtually all of this work was undertaken outdoors – pleasant enough in fine weather but a real trial when the conditions were particularly inclement or cold.

However inclement the weather might be, visits to Tollerton acquired a new attraction to Jan when he discovered a particular young woman who worked in the offices, adjacent to the Main Hangar, of Tollerton Air Services. Her name was Alice May Simpson. A romance developed and after the war, on 26 July 1947, the couple were married. They went on to share many happy years together before the sad death of Alice in October 2000. Jan settled permanently in England, his new adopted country, but he always remembered his Polish roots.

Plate 42: **The happy ending to a wartime romance.** Jan Krupa and his wife Alice on their wedding day on 26 July 1947. *Jan Krupa*

# The Arrival of Polish Airmen at Tollerton

Thus it was that in the summer of 1941 a group of Polish airmen found themselves posted to 16 (Polish) SFTS (Service Flying Training School). They had been stationed at Hucknall but on 13 July 1941 they made the relatively short journey to their new quarters at RAF Newton. At the same time the control of RAF Newton was moved from Bomber Command to Training Command. Squadron Leader S. Skarzynski was the Polish Station Commander of the airfield and with Group Captain E.B. Grenfell set about the training of the new pupil pilots.

Upon arrival at RAF Newton two squadrons of trainee pilots were established. No 1 squadron trained in Airspeed Oxfords whilst No 2 squadron trained in Fairey Battles. No 1 squadron concentrated their flying at RAF Newton whilst No 2 squadron used Tollerton airfield. Miles Master III, de Havilland 60 Moth, and de Havilland Moth Minor aircraft were also available for the pilots to train in. July 1941 saw the commencement of night-flying training in the Airspeed Oxfords. By February 1942 Miles Master aircraft had completely replaced the inadequate Fairey Battles. Early in 1943 Miles Magister and Avro Anson aircraft also began to arrive at RAF Tollerton for training purposes.

## Training and Equipment

A Bomber Command conference in March 1940 was cautious about the quality of the new, ex-Polish Air Force pilots. A statement issued after the conference declared that 'on the whole their flying was safe, but not up to RAF standards. Their navigation was extremely weak, whilst their instrument flying was average. Their night-flying skills were negligible and they had a strongly marked lack of flying discipline.' It was felt that the Polish pilots would need at least 12 weeks training to reach the necessary operational standard. Elementary training courses were established and in April 1940 it was decided that RAF Hucknall would be one of the training bases. Twenty-two Fairey Battles were allocated there for the pilots to train in.

The training aircraft available at the time were mainly the Airspeed Oxford and the obsolete Fairey Battle. The Fairey Battle had been designated a light bomber when on operational service with the RAF, while the Oxford was an advanced, twin-engine trainer. By the time 16 SFTS was using the Battle it had long been withdrawn from front-line use, but it was an aircraft with an interesting history.

When Great Britain went to war in 1939 much of the equipment at its disposal was inadequate for the tasks that it would be required to perform. This was particularly so in the case of the RAF. With the notable exceptions of the Spitfire, Hurricane, Wellington, Sunderland and Avro Anson, many of the aircraft then in operational use were simply not up to the job. The headlong rush that had taken place in the 1930s to re-equip the RAF in readiness for a possible war had been made without any real idea as to how that war would be conducted and what the operational requirements of the aircraft would be. The Fairey Battle was one such example of this lack of foresight.

The Battle was designated a 'Light Bomber' and first flew in March 1936. By December of that same year the Chief of the Air Staff of the Royal Air Force, Sir Edward Ellington, had already stated that no more Battles should be produced, but unfortunately his decision was not enforced. In those desperate days before war broke out it was a case of anything being better than nothing, and by the time production ceased over 2,000 of the aircraft had been manufactured.

A single engine powered the Battle. It is ironic that this engine should be none other than the famous Rolls-Royce Merlin, which would find lasting fame as the provider of power for the Spitfire, Hurricane, and Lancaster. When it was introduced it was rated at 1,020 hp, which made it the most powerful aero engine in the world at that time. In the Battle, however, it proved to be underpowered for its role. The aircraft also lacked defensive armament. It was fitted with a single Browning machine gun firing forward and a single Vickers 'K' gun at the rear of the cockpit to fire aft. The original Air Ministry specification called for an aircraft that was capable of flying at 200 mph with a 1,000 lb bomb load a distance of 1,000 miles. Although the prototype managed to exceed these criteria the whole concept of the light bomber was flawed, and this would be brought into sharp focus when if finally went into action against the Luftwaffe.

The Battle was expected to operate in daylight, unescorted by fighter protection, in enemy territory, against an opponent equipped with excellent

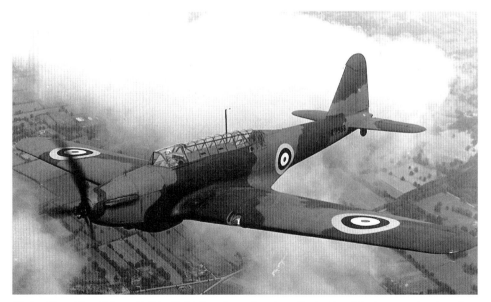

**Plate 43:    The Fairey Battle light bomber.** An aircraft destined to have a short and inglorious career.

fighter aircraft. For bombing accuracy the Battle would also often have to bomb from a relatively low altitude against ground targets that were quite possibly well defended. Without a massive fighter escort to provide protection it was a sitting duck for its German fighter opponents. As early as 30 September 1939, during an unescorted reconnaissance operation by 150 Squadron over the Saarland, German Messerschmitt fighters shot down four of the five Battles despatched on the sortie.

The acid test for the aircraft however came during the Battle for France. It was too slow to escape from its German adversaries and lacked the necessary manoeuvrability and armament to defend itself adequately when caught. Day after day the operational losses mounted. Losses of 25% and higher on bombing sorties were not unusual. The final straw came on 14 May 1940 when 35 out of

**Plate 44:** **The Fairey Battle trainer.** Obsolete Battles were converted to training aircraft by modifying the fuselage to include a second cockpit and flying controls. Even in this role the Battle's career was relatively short-lived.

**Plate 45:** **A Miles Master trainer at Tollerton.** The Master enjoyed a successful career with the RAF and proved to be an excellent aircraft for trainee pilots. *Tom Myall collection*

63 Battles failed to return from their mission. It was simply impossible to send aircrew on operations that were verging on suicide missions. The Battle was ignominiously withdrawn from front line use after one of the shortest operational lives of any RAF plane. The problem then arose as to what should be done with the surviving aircraft, which were still relatively new. Many were converted to dual-control and used as advanced trainers. Some of these were sent to RAF Hucknall and RAF Newton and it was in these aircraft that the Polish aircrew at RAF Tollerton would continue with their training. However, within a relatively short period of time even that role was denied to the lacklustre Battle and it disappeared from the scene.

By June 1943 RAF Tollerton could boast the following assortment of vehicles for use on the airfield; a heavy ambulance, two coaches, a 3-ton tender, a 30 cwt tender, a fire-crash tender, a 5 – 10 cwt van, a trailer carrying floodlights, and a beacon trailer. Unfortunately, as we shall see, these vehicles would see no shortage of use as a constant flow of incidents necessitated their presence.

## Accidents & Incidents

The training of pilots necessarily involves an element of danger and throughout their time at Tollerton there was a succession of accidents and incidents involving the Polish contingent as well as other personnel.

The following article from the *Nottingham Evening Post* of 7 October 2005 graphically illustrates the type of accident that was, sadly, a familiar occurrence at a training establishment such as RAF Tollerton.

On a June afternoon in 1944 two young Polish airmen from 16 (Polish) Service Flying Training School at Tollerton were undergoing tuition in a Miles Master II training aircraft. The trainee pilots were nearing the end of their course and it would not be too long before they would gain their 'wings' and be posted to an operational squadron. AC2 Grejcium, aged 20, and AC2 Punarowicz, aged 22, were on a one-hour familiarization flight in the training aircraft. Grejcium was the pupil pilot whilst Punarowicz was acting in the role of safety pilot.

Shortly after take-off the aircraft was seen to be performing a series of aerobatic manoeuvres over the city of Nottingham. Polish pilots of the Second World War gained themselves something of a reputation for being cavalier, exuberant and fearless fliers. On this particular afternoon however, whilst performing a series of stunts, things went tragically wrong for the young fliers. The aircraft was seen to perform a number of rolls, which brought it dangerously close to the ground. In attempting to gain some height and retrieve the situation the pilot took the aircraft into a steep climb using full power. At that critical time the engine died, there was no time for any remedial action to be taken, and the aircraft crashed into the ground.

The Master II crashed at the junction of Nuthall Road and Whitemoor Avenue in

Bobbers Mill, Nottingham with such force that parts of the aircraft embedded themselves up to ten feet into the ground. On impact a great ball of flame erupted from impact with the ground and both of the young Polish pilots were killed instantly. Miraculously no one on the ground was killed, though a few people sustained minor injuries including a six-year-old girl who suffered burns to her arms due to being splashed by burning petrol from the crash. Shortly before it crashed the Miles Master clipped the chimney of a house in Whitemoor Avenue and a part of the aircraft's wing landed in the garden there. Luckily, no one was in the garden at the time.

The resultant Court of Inquiry found that the cause of the crash was due to 'the pilot carrying out unauthorized aerobatics resulting in a spin with insufficient height to correct the resultant dive'. This, unfortunately, was far from being an isolated incident. Other such incidents involving 16 (Polish) SFTS are shown in the table on page 126. These incidents are taken from the squadron's official Log Book and are representative of the type of events that were occurring on a regular basis not only at Tollerton but also at RAF airfields throughout the country.

Also taken from the Operations Book is the following programme for Christmas 1944:

**December 25th**

| | |
|---|---|
| 1200 hrs | Airmen and Airwoman's dinner at Tollerton. The C/O will attend the dinner at Tollerton at approximately 1200 hrs returning to Newton at 1230hrs. |
| 1500hrs | Films at Station cinema. |
| 1700hrs | Tea. |
| 1800hrs | Films in Station cinema. |
| 2100hrs | Station Fancy Dress Dance in NAAFI. All cinema performances on Christmas Day will be free. Transport will be arranged to bring personnel from Tollerton to Newton after tea for the cinema and dance, returning to Tollerton after the dance. |

**December 30th**

| | |
|---|---|
| 1530hrs to 1830hrs | Christmas Party in the Officers' Mess for children up to 14 years of age of both British and Polish personnel of all ranks. Personnel wishing their children to attend should submit particulars as to name, sex, age and address to their respective station Adjutants as soon as possible. |

| Date | Name | Aircraft Type | Details |
|---|---|---|---|
| 26-08-42 | Forrester | | Struck on the back by the propeller of a taxiing aircraft whilst driving a tractor. Died later that day from a fractured spine. |
| 12-12-42 | Lackraus 793822 | | Killed night flying from Tollerton. |
| 12-02-42 | A/C Fisch 703000 | Miles Master | Hit by a propeller and killed instantly. |
| 05-05-43 | S. Schmidt | Miles Master III W.8730 | Killed when aircraft crashed at Tollerton. |
| 27-05-43 | | Miles Master III DL.607 | Crashed at an anti-aircraft site at Ruddington whilst flying from Tollerton. |
| 14-01-44 | W/O Popek 782474 | | Killed whilst sitting in cockpit of aeroplane standing on runway, (performing cockpit drill), struck by the undercarriage of a machine taking off. |
| 25-02-44 | LAC M. Szierzega | Miles Master III DM.283 | Whilst operating from Tollerton, crashed at Stapleford. Pupil pilot, LAC M. Szierzega was killed whilst flying solo during night-flying training. A Court of Inquiry found that the accident was due to the pilot flying too low and striking overhead, high-tension cables. |
| 11-07-44 | A/C2 Lusinski 705524 | Miles Master II DL 277 | Aircraft landed with undercarriage not locked in 'Down' position. Category 'A' damage to aircraft. Pilot to blame. No disciplinary action taken. |
| 12-07-44 | A/C 2 Adamowicz 704854 A/C2 W. Flieszer | Miles Master II DM.437 and Miles Master II W.9021 | At 12.10   Master II DM 437. Collided with Master II W 9021 whilst in the air during final approach to land, both aircraft damaged. Master DM 437 Cat "B". W 9021. No casualties. Accident considered due to pupil pilot in Master DM 347 704854 AC2 Adamowicz joining circuit too soon and pupil of Master W 9021 AC2 Flieszer failing to keep sufficient look out and ensuring his line of approach was clear. |
| 16-07-44 | A/C2 Fabisiak 704851 | Miles Master II DM.428 | At 11.05 Master II DM 428. Pilot stalled on landing, extensively damaged fuselage. Accident due to error of judgement on the part of the pupil pilot 704851 AC2 Fabisiak who was uninjured. |
| 25-09-44 | W/O J. Budzinski 780665 | Miles Master II DL.894 | Instructor pilot W/O J. Budzinski. 780665. Pupil pilot swung to the left when landing and ran off the runway. Instructor pilot W/O Budzinski took over control but was unable to avoid collision with two stationary aircraft. Accident due to officer in charge Night Flying allowing parking of aircraft too near runway in use |
| 12-10-44 | A/C Maciula 704930 | Miles Master II DM.424 | Aircraft caught fire in cockpit after carrying out "overshoot" at Tollerton and dived into the ground for reasons unknown killing the pupil pilot 704930 Maciula instantly. Accident investigated by S/Ldr. D.G. Allison ARC, No 21 Group. The body was taken to the mortuary at Newton. |
| 02-02-45 | P/O Wujastyk P.2103 | Harvard II.B KF.148 | At 11.00 Pilot (pupil) P/O Wujastyk (P2103) collided with a flock of birds whilst carrying out low flying exercises. Pilot uninjured. |
| 14-06-45 | Lt M. Krwawicz A/C2 Dabrowski 706454 | Airspeed Oxford I HN.378 And Airspeed Oxford I NM.419 | At 18.33 Oxford I HN 378. U/t pilot Lt M. Krwawicz collided with Oxford I NM 419 u/t pilot AC2 J. Dabrwaski 706454 whilst formation flying. Lt. Krwawicz killed and both aircraft completely wrecked. Investigation held. This occurred near Kinoulton and AC Dabrowski baled out and was admitted to SSQ. Discharged 15 June. Funeral of Lt. Krwawicz held 16 June. |

**Table 6:    Incidents Recorded in 16 (Polish) FSTS Operations Book**

126

Although the war in Europe ended in May 1945 the training of Polish airmen at Tollerton continued until later in the year. However on 14 November 1945 No 16 (Polish) Service Flying Training School was disbanded and replaced by a new unit, No 16 (Polish) Flying Training School. It became Air Ministry policy to train sufficient Polish aircrew to maintain the existing force at peace-time casualty rates only. As a result of this decision the number of aircrew being trained dropped to 56 pilots per year. These pilots were to undergo basic training on de Havilland Tiger Moth aircraft and service training on Airspeed Oxfords, all of which was to be carried out at RAF Newton. Thus a chapter in Tollerton's history closed with the departure of the Polish airmen.

## Local People Welcome the Polish Airmen

The training courses undoubtedly were stressful times for the Polish airmen and while it would seem that life was never dull, they naturally welcomed the opportunity to unwind when not on duty. It was then that they had the opportunity to meet people from Tollerton and the surrounding villages. One such person was Jenny Phimister, who lived in Plumtree.

Jenny Phimister was born in Plumtree and, at the age of sixteen in 1939, had lived there all her life. She was another one of the lucky people for whom the war was an exciting and enjoyable time. Village life, especially in a small community such as Plumtree was in those days, offered only limited opportunities for young people to socialize and to go out and enjoy themselves. All that would change as the war progressed, due in part to the huge increase in the number of people that were employed at Tollerton airfield.

Jenny first became involved with the social scene at Tollerton during 1941. The City of Nottingham was an obvious attraction for the service personnel who had been stationed at RAF Tollerton, but the local villages also held attractions of their own. It was natural that public houses such as The Griffin at Plumtree should seize the opportunity to attract some of these potential new customers. At the same time it would be an appropriate gesture to extend the hand of friendship and encourage these new arrivals from the airfield to take part in the life of the village. As a result dances began to be organized on a Saturday evening and Jenny had a hand in setting them up. They became a regular event and went down well with the airmen from RAF Tollerton as well as the village youngsters.

As time went by friendships were formed and it was not unusual for individual airmen to be invited to the homes of the villagers for a cup of tea or a meal. This particularly applied when the Polish personnel began to arrive in the summer of 1941. Every effort was made to make them welcome. For the Poles England was a strange new place, and their command of the language was, by and large, poor. And they were a long way from their homes and families - that is, if they were lucky enough to have a home or family still left in Poland.

The service personnel (but particularly the Polish contingent) were grateful for this warm hospitality and to show their appreciation they began to organize their own socials at the airfield. So it came about that on a Wednesday evening at around 7 p.m. there might well be up to twenty or thirty teenagers from Keyworth and Plumtree walking along the road to a dance at Tollerton airfield. Even though it was a military airfield getting into the site presented no problems: they simply walked past the guards posted at the entrance - Jenny could not recollect being challenged on a single occasion. So much for security on a wartime airfield!

Music was provided on a gramophone. The girls particularly had great fun teaching the Polish airmen to dance. Anything up to around a hundred people would be involved. Free food was provided by the airmen, along with cigarettes that came, again free of charge, from a special fund set up by the Lord Mayor of Nottingham to give 'comforts' to the troops. Later, live bands would come over from the base at RAF Newton, but that was still in the future. When that happened the girls made a special effort, and donned their long dresses!

Strangely, given that it was wartime and the gatherings were on a military airfield there were no particular plans for what to do in the event of an air raid. Jenny cannot recall any air-raid shelters; if the alarm went off it would seem that the best policy was to get out of the building as quickly as possible and hide in the surrounding fields. Fortunately that was never necessary, as the airfield was never attacked whilst she was there.

Language presented no problems either. Jenny remembers the young airmen as bright and well-educated people who were eager to learn English. There was no alcohol available at these functions; squash was the order of the day. When they were not dancing they would drink and chat. By and large, though, the Polish airmen did not talk about their pre-war lives in Poland. Many of them had undergone terrible experiences to get to England and they tended to keep their feelings very much to themselves. Jenny remembers that some of those who did talk had harrowing tales to tell.

As the war progressed so did the popularity of the dances. Personnel from RAF Newton got to hear of them and they too became visitors to the socials. This, however, brought with it some of the grim realities of war, realities that Jenny had not previously experienced. Serious accidents at RAF Tollerton were, thankfully, rare; but once in a while there would be incidents that cost the lives of the young Polish airmen. Every now and again a face or faces would be missing from the usual gathering on a Saturday or Wednesday evening. Someone with whom you had been dancing for the last few weeks no longer appeared. It was very sad, but no questions were ever asked, though Jenny had a good idea of what had happened.

Because RAF Tollerton was a training establishment there was always a turnover of personnel. The opportunity to make new friends constantly presented itself, but the friendships were of a transitory nature. Once the airmen had finished their training their postings took them away from RAF Tollerton and they disappeared from the scene forever. Jenny didn't keep in touch with any of them. In Jenny's experience romances between the aircrew and local girls were the exception rather than the rule: virtually all the friendships were of a platonic nature.

It tended to be the younger generation that mixed socially with the personnel from RAF Tollerton on a regular basis. The older members of the community were more likely to have family commitments, and, since everyone tended to be working long hours, often on shifts, spare time was at a premium. It was the young folk, without these personal commitments, who had the time and the inclination to get out, meet new people, and enjoy themselves. However, quite often airmen would be invited back home for a meal with the rest of the family. This was greatly appreciated by the airmen, particularly at Christmas, which must have been a terrible time for the Polish contingent.

Not all of the socials were held at the Griffin or the airfield. Jenny was also involved with the Women's Voluntary Service (WVS), which ran a canteen at Tollerton Hall. During the war Tollerton Hall was used by a variety of organizations. Like most large houses it had been requisitioned by the government for military use when war broke out. According to Jenny's recollections the first people billeted there were a contingent of the Lincolnshire Regiment who took possession of the Hall at the beginning of the war. They were followed by No 1 Bomb Disposal and later, in the early spring of 1944, the American forces arrived in preparation for the forthcoming D-Day Invasion of Europe.

The arrival of American forces was something of a special event. The first hint that something unusual was afoot came when large lorries were seen travelling in convoy down Bradmore Lane. This signalled the arrival of American engineers whose job it was to prepare the Hall for its new tenants. One of their first jobs was to construct a new camp in the woods surrounding the Hall in preparation for the forthcoming GIs. The village children were highly pleased with these new arrivals, perhaps due to the fact that the Americans were very generous, often giving the youngsters sweets and chewing gum. One thing that Jenny remembered particularly was the multi-racial mixture of the American personnel. Black faces were rarely, if ever, seen in Tollerton, so their appearance was something of a novelty. Jenny went to a few social gatherings organized for American troops in the Rectory Rooms in Tollerton, but airmen from RAF Tollerton were not invited - perhaps the Americans didn't want any competition for the company of the young women!

When the war in Europe came to an end on 8 May 1945 special VE Day (Victory in Europe Day) parties were organized nationally to celebrate the momentous occasion. RAF Tollerton was no exception. Once again Jenny and her friends from Keyworth and Plumtree took a hand in organizing the event. Naturally, on this occasion, a special effort was made to make the party truly memorable.

Not only did the usual group of youngsters from Keyworth and Plumtree attend the party: on this occasion many of their parents joined in the fun as well. The Americans from Tollerton Hall were invited, too, and a grand time was had by all! Jenny particularly remembers the huge pots of coffee that the Americans provided and the beautiful food - all free of charge of course. This was a real treat, given the years of rationing that people had become used to (and which would still last for several years to come even though the war was practically over).

The VE Day party not only marked the end of the war in Europe, it also marked the end of most of the dances and socials that had become such a way of life for Jenny and her friends. These Wednesday and Saturday evening occasions had been eagerly looked forward to and there would be little to take their place now that hostilities were at an end. A mass exodus of the personnel stationed at both RAF Tollerton and Tollerton Hall inevitably led to the end of such gatherings.

Looking back on that time in her life Jenny is grateful to have been a part of what, for her, was a thrilling time. To be a teenager in the early 1940s, living through such momentous times, was a memorable experience. Jenny feels that she played her own small part by making new arrivals at RAF Tollerton welcome. There was inevitably great sadness at times when airmen were injured or killed; but, by and large, Jenny's overall memory is one of being involved, albeit in a very small way, in something truly epoch making.

## Blind Approach Training Flight

One specific activity that brought Polish pilots to Tollerton was 'blind approach' and 'beam approach' training. What exactly were the blind approach and beam approach training flights? The following explanation may be of some help in understanding the subject.

For much of the war Bomber Command conducted the bombing offensive against enemy targets during the hours of darkness, simply because it was too dangerous for unprotected, relatively slow, heavily laden bombers to fly over enemy-occupied Europe in daylight. Consequently take-off times were often scheduled just before dusk so that by the time that the bombers entered enemy airspace they had whatever cover darkness could provide. During the long nights of winter it was possible that the aircraft would also be returning to their bases in darkness. As long as visibility was good when an aircraft returned to its home airfield then landing should not present a great problem. If the weather had deteriorated during the night's operation, however, then the situation could be very different. Adverse weather conditions could pose as many problems for RAF aircrew as enemy action. For example, on 17 October 1940 when 73 bombers, having carried out attacks in occupied Europe, returned to a fog-covered England, 14 of them crashed whilst attempting to land. The Prime

Minister, Winston Churchill, was so concerned that on the following day he wrote to the Secretary of State for Air and enquired: 'What arrangements have we got for blind landing our aircraft? How many aircraft are so fitted? It ought to be possible to guide them down safely as commercial aircraft have done before the war in spite of fog. Let me have full particulars. The accidents last night are very serious.' No satisfactory solution was provided and the problem of how to get an aircraft back to its own airfield and land safely in adverse weather conditions continued to tax the minds of scientists for the duration of the war. On 17 December 1943, after a raid against Berlin, Bomber Command had lost 25 aircraft during the raid itself, but a further 30 aircraft crashed on their return to the United Kingdom because of bad visibility.

Even before the outbreak of war the Air Ministry had realized that it would be of vital operational importance for the RAF to be able to fly its aircraft as often as possible at any time of the day or night and in all weathers. During a meeting at the Air Ministry in the mid 1930s it had been observed that 'any airforce which cannot operate in inclement weather will be severely hampered'.

Discounting enemy action the two most dangerous parts of a flight occur during take off and landing. At those times, due to a lack of airspeed and altitude, a pilot will find his options for remedial action severely limited should any problems present themselves. When an aircraft, particularly a heavy bomber, comes in to land, the pilot begins his descent and approach to the runway from as far away as ten miles. The runway at most operational airfields was only 50 yards wide, so accuracy in the approach to landing was paramount if an accident was to be avoided. There are three vital pieces of information that a pilot must have when preparing to land, namely: (1) Is the aircraft lined up with the centre of the runway? (2) How far is the aircraft from the beginning of the runway? (3) Is the aircraft at the correct height given the distance to the runway?

During the early years of the war the few technological aids that were available to provide this vital information were neither sufficiently accurate nor reliable.

The main methods in use involved sending radio signals from a location on or near the airfield in the form of a radio beam, much like a beam of light from a torch. One such method involved the transmission, from the end of an airfield runway, of a radio beam that was split into two: one half of the beam transmitted a series of 'dots'; the other transmitted 'dashes'. An approaching aircraft would attempt to pick up the signal from this beam and fly along it. When the aircraft was flying to one side of the beam, an onboard receiver would pick up a signal of either dots or dashes; when it was flying down the centre of the beam the two signals cancelled each other out and made a continuous noise and the pilot then knew that his aircraft was correctly lined up with the runway. The concept was straightforward in theory but difficult to operate reliably in practice with current technology. One problem was that the radio waves were susceptible to being 'bent' – by such things as church steeples, water towers, other aircraft, large metal objects, or even the topography of the local countryside. However, the greatest shortcoming of the system was that in really bad weather a pilot still had no idea of his distance from the airfield or his altitude.

Furthermore, when the system was first developed in the mid 1930s virtually all airfields had been of grass with landing strips perhaps 1,400 yards long and anything up to 100 yards or more wide; but new class 'A' runways were 2,000 yards long by only 50 yards wide, and narrower runways made the accuracy of the equipment much more critical. A further complication was that usually only one runway was fitted with the necessary ground equipment, but the new airfield layout was configured in the shape of an 'A' with three runways.

The Air Ministry had conducted trials with several systems to find an effective and reliable Semi Blind Approach (SBA) landing system, none of which proved to be really satisfactory. At this point the British company Standard Telephones and Cables (STC) of New Southgate, London, stepped in with a proposal that the Air Ministry simply could not turn down. STC's German sister company, C. Lorenz AG, was manufacturing a radio beam approach system that STC would supply free of charge for the Air Ministry to evaluate. The trials were reasonably successful and in March 1937 the Air Ministry gave a contract to STC worth £340,000 to begin implementing the new system. However, the original German equipment was redesigned to use components manufactured in Great Britain. Once this had been done installation of the new system, renamed Standard Beam Approach (SBA), began at RAF Scampton in September 1937.

The SBA system was dependent on two sets of equipment, one on the ground and one in the aircraft. Both sets proved to have serious technological shortcomings and the system was destined never to become as effective as had been hoped. By December 1940 the situation was so bad that thousands of the radio receivers installed in aircraft had to be considerably modified to meet operational requirements. But still problems continued to mount. By the middle of 1942 confidence in the system was at such a low ebb that the Air Ministry announced that the SBA system 'in its present form, does not work'. Despite huge amounts of time, money and effort being devoted to SBA's problems the system never achieved what had been hoped for.

In 1942 Air Marshall Sir Edgar Ludlow-Hewitt, the Inspector General at the Air Ministry, produced a twelve page report on SBA which concluded: 'Despite an enormous amount of money and time which has been expended on the system, it was rarely used, it was unreliable, and pilots had little confidence in it ... SBA was not considered to be a blind landing system ... it is now in the melting pot.'

On 15 July 1943 Air Vice-Marshall Lywood sent a memo to the Commander-in-Chief Bomber Command, and the Secretary of State for Air in which he stated: 'Owing to conflicting instructions from the Air Ministry my whole programme of work is being reduced to chaos.' The final straw came on 4 November 1943 when the decision was taken to abandon the SBA programme completely.

One of SBA's problems was that the technology being used was over ten years old and out of date. Fortunately, in the meantime a new technology had been developed which could supply the vital elements necessary to make a blind landing system work. In the years just prior to the outbreak of war scientists had been working, in great secrecy, on a new system for detecting enemy aircraft at long range, irrespective of the weather. Once detected aircraft of the RAF could then be sent to attack the enemy aircraft. This new early warning system was called 'Chain Home'; but once the general public knew about it, it was simply called 'Radar' (an acronym for Radio Detection and Ranging). This new technology became a vital weapon in the RAF's fight to defend England and played a crucial role in securing victory in the Battle of Britain.

Apart from getting aircraft safely back onto the ground, another major problem that had vexed the RAF for the duration of the war was the location of enemy targets at night and in poor visibility. Earlier in the war one method often used to navigate to a target was known as 'dead reckoning'. This required the aircraft's navigator to plot the course of his aircraft with great accuracy, and to take account of speed, compass bearing, length of time on that course, and wind speed at the altitude at which the aircraft is flying. Small errors in any of these calculations made 'dead reckoning' calculations unreliable. Concerns regarding the RAF's ability to successfully locate and bomb enemy targets by using 'dead reckoning' alone had become the subject of much debate and controversy. So it was that in early August 1941 Churchill, asked D.M.B. Butt of the War Cabinet to conduct a statistical investigation into the results that Bomber Command was achieving against enemy targets. Butt examined 650 photographs taken on 48 nights between 2 June and 25 July 1941. His report made very unpleasant reading and contained some shocking statistics. The following are some of the report's conclusions:

1 Of those aircraft recorded as attacking their target, only one in three dropped their bombs within five miles of the target.
2 Over Germany as a whole the proportion was one aircraft in four, over the Ruhr, one in five.
3 During periods of the new moon it was only one aircraft in fifteen.
4 Only one aircraft in fifteen if the target is covered by thick haze.
5 Only two thirds of those aircraft despatched to attack a target actually did attack the designated target.

The Butt Report concluded that most of the bombs dropped by Bomber Command on enemy targets were actually falling harmlessly in open countryside, nowhere near the actual target itself – a colossal waste of manpower, materials and resources.

However, in 1942 a new piece of equipment known as H2S began to be installed in Bomber Command aircraft and this, inadvertently, would provide an answer to the problem of 'blind landing'. H2S was a navigational radar system that, by scanning the ground beneath an aircraft with very powerful radar pulses, built up a representation of the landscape on a screen inside the aircraft. Water, in particular, produced a very clear image on the H2S operator's screen, making targets in such locations much easier to identify.

During the war there had been many clandestine operations into occupied territory – those involving the French Resistance for example – that required an aircraft to land and take off again in remote parts of the countryside, usually during the hours of darkness. A system was developed called Rebecca/Eureka/Lucero that made it possible to locate allied agents on the ground, and thus be able to land and take off again in the correct vicinity. It was soon realized that with this new technology, which used a ground homing beacon (named Rebecca), the essential components were now available to create a new blind landing system that could replace the unreliable SBA. At selected airfields, ground transmitters were installed at the end of the two most used runways, which acted as the beacons for aircraft to home in on. If it proved necessary to use one of the secondary runways at an airfield then portable systems were also available that could be set up in approximately an hour. The equipment sited at the airfield was known as 'BABS', and developed into the most effective blind landing system that the RAF possessed during the war.

Unfortunately, it has not been possible to ascertain whether BABS was ever used at Tollerton during the war for training purposes. What we do know, however, is that some Polish airmen did blind approach training there, presumably using the old SBA system that proved so ineffective and unreliable. On 6 June 1943, 1524 Blind Approach Training Flight joined 16 (Polish) SFTS at RAF Newton. Later, on 3 January 1944, 1524 Beam Approach Training Flight arrived from Bottesford with its six Airspeed Oxford aircraft (1524 Beam Approach Training Flight had been formed at Bottesford in October 1941). These aircraft were used to give the Polish airmen experience in using the SBA system. By June 1944 the number of training courses either completed or still ongoing numbered 31. At any one time this could involve anything up to two hundred pupils. The flight remained at Newton until it was disbanded on 9 January 1945.

# Chapter 8

# The Civilian Repair Organization

The RAF was not the only occupant of Tollerton airfield for the duration of the Second World War. Sharing the airfield with their military neighbours was a large civilian workforce employed to repair, modify, maintain, and assemble aircraft as directed by the Air Ministry.

At the outbreak of war there were already aircraft repair and maintenance facilities at Tollerton, but with the suspension of all civilian flying and the disbanding of the RAF Volunteer Reserve and CAG schemes, demand for these facilities disappeared. However it would not be long before the facilities would be put to good use towards the war effort. By early 1940 arrangements were in place to ensure that the potential of Tollerton's repair and maintenance facilities was not wasted.

Prior to the outbreak of hostilities the Air Ministry's belief was that RAF Maintenance Units (MUs) would be able to deal with all airframe repairs and that any arrangements for repair by aircraft constructors would be a temporary expedient only. Consequently the only provision that had been made especially for the repair of RAF aircraft by contractors was the organisation of three 'fringe firm units' built and equipped at Air Ministry expense specifically for that purpose. Just how inadequate this arrangement was became apparent very quickly. The tremendous strain that the war would place on British industry soon exposed the shortcomings in such a policy. Aircraft manufacturers would need all their capacity, and a great deal more as the war progressed, to produce the new machines vital for the successful prosecution of the war. It was of paramount importance to produce as many aircraft as the war effort required; it was equally vital that damaged aircraft should be repaired quickly to maintain the fighting strength of the RAF at its highest possible level.

A way out of this dilemma was the creation of a new organization called the Civilian Repair Organization (CRO). The CRO would issue contracts to specific companies, designated by the Air Ministry, who would then be responsible for carrying out this essential work. Initially three companies or 'fringe firm units' were so designated: Rollason Aircraft Services at Tollerton was one of them. The Ministry of Aircraft Production advanced a payment of £25,000 for a 'repair hangar and plant for general airframe repairs'. A floor area of 36,000 square feet thus became available for work to be conducted on around 20 aircraft of three varieties: Hampdens, Herefords, and Harrows. The other two companies named as fringe units were Airworks Ltd and Brooklands Aviation Co Ltd.

On paper it appears that a succession of different companies operated from Tollerton airfield during the war: the names of Rollason Aircraft Services, Tollerton Aircraft Services Ltd, Field Consolidated Aircraft Services Ltd, and the

Hunting Aviation Group all figure in the airfield's history. However, with the exception of Rollason Aircraft Services, they were all actually parts of the same organization. This has previously been fully described in Chapter 5. For the duration of the war the principal company working at Tollerton was Tollerton Air Services Ltd (TAS).

## The Handley Page Hampden

The aircraft that formed the mainstay of work at Tollerton in the early years of the war was the Handley Page Hampden. Designed during the first half of the 1930s, it first flew in June 1936 and became operational in August 1938. It was a new breed of (supposedly) fast twin-engine medium bomber. It had a crew of four, a maximum speed of 243 mph, a cruising speed of 155 mph and a range of 1,200 miles with a 4,000 lb bomb load. Its defensive armament consisted of either three or four .303 machine guns. It was nicknamed 'The Flying Suitcase' because conditions inside the fuselage were so cramped: indeed, with a fuselage width of only three feet it was virtually impossible to get from one crew position to another.

The aircraft's manufacturers, Handley Page, were so confident of its flying capabilities that they gave the pilot a fixed, forward firing gun and dubbed the aircraft a 'fighting bomber'. For its time it was both fast and manoeuvrable. Unfortunately for the Hampden, similar advances in performance were taking place in the air forces of other countries, notably Germany, where the new Messerschmitt 109 was one of the world's most formidable new breed of fighter aircraft.

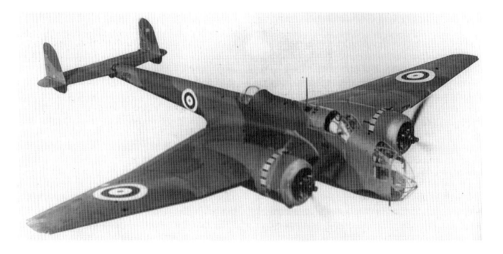

**Plate 46:   The Handley Page Hampden medium bomber.** The assembly of Hampden bombers formed the mainstay of TAS work at Tollerton during the early years of the war

When war broke out there were eight operational Hampden squadrons in the RAF. That number would increase as over 1,400 Hampdens were eventually built. As with too many other aircraft that the RAF was being equipped with, the operational career of the Hampden bomber was destined to be relatively short-lived. Within a few years of its introduction the all-round performance of the single and twin-engine fighter had improved to such an extent that aircraft such as the Hampden were totally outclassed when pitted against the vastly superior German Messerschmitt 109 and Messerschmitt 110 fighters. Without the protection of fighter aircraft the Hampden was simply too vulnerable to fly operationally during the hours of daylight.

It was not long before Hampdens were re-equipped and restricted to night flying operations, where they enjoyed some measure of success. Even so their operational life lasted only until September 1942 when they were all withdrawn from operational use to be replaced by larger and more effective four-engine bombers. However, for the early part of the war the Hampden was the aircraft that provided the employees at Tollerton with the bulk of their work.

The Hampden was another example of what, in theory, should have be an outstanding aircraft, but in reality was obsolescent by the time it became operational due to the advances being made generally in the performance of single seat, single-engine fighter aircraft. The story of the Hampden was an all too familiar tale that applied to too many of the aircraft introduced in the 1930s to equip the RAF. Along with the Hampden, aircraft such as the Fairey Battle (previously referred to in Chapter 7), the Whitley, Defiant, Skua, Blenheim, and Whirlwind all failed to live up to expectations and very rapidly found themselves withdrawn from operational use after relatively short-lived careers.

**Plate 47:    A Hampden tail plane being transported by lorry.** This photograph helps to give some impression of the relatively small size of the aircraft. Note the road haulage company name on the side of the lorry, Willowbrook. The company was based at Loughborough in Leicestershire. *J. Davis*

As has already been mentioned, one of the first contracts that Tollerton Air Services (TAS) secured was for the assembly and servicing of the Hampden. As the number of Hampdens in service grew so the amount of work undertaken at Tollerton also grew. Ultimately every damaged Hampden that required repairing by a civil repair unit was allocated to TAS at Tollerton. The years 1940 and 1941 thus saw the hangars at Tollerton visited by a steady stream of Hampdens for repair and modification. As the Hampden began to be replaced by larger four-engine heavy bombers the problem of what to do with the, by now, obsolete aircraft arose. One solution was to convert aircraft from bombers to torpedo bombers for Coastal Command, and some of these conversions were carried out at Tollerton.

However, the writing was on the wall for the ill-starred Hampden. From being a place of repair and modification, Tollerton then became a graveyard for Hampdens when, in 1942, they began to be withdrawn from operational duties and the obsolete aircraft were sent to Tollerton to be broken up and scrapped. Hundreds were flown into the airfield and systematically taken apart. Whatever usable parts could be salvaged were saved, the remainder were destroyed. The final nail in the Hampden's coffin occurred in the spring of 1944 when 230 of the surviving aircraft were sent to both Tollerton and Brush Coachworks to be scrapped.

As the Hampden was phased out, TAS found itself with less and less work to do. Temporary respite was found when a short-term contract was secured to carry out urgent modifications to the new four-engine Handley Page Halifax heavy bomber. A contract was also secured to do essential work on the Douglas Boston medium bomber, though this too was of a short-term duration.

## Lancasters at Tollerton

Prior to the outbreak of war the importance of the heavy bomber in aerial warfare had already been well established. With this in mind the Air Ministry had embarked upon a programme of re-equipping the RAF with a fleet of new heavy bombers which it was hoped would be capable of taking the bombing offensive deep into enemy territory. Technological advances in aero-engine design had resulted in engines that were becoming increasingly more powerful. This increased power made it possible to design aircraft that were larger and could carry a heavier bomb-load faster and further than had hitherto been possible. A new breed of four-engine, heavy bomber came into service with the RAF and these took over the duties that aircraft such as the Hampden, Blenheim and Whitley had previously performed, rendering the older aircraft obsolete. These new bombers were the Short Stirling, the Handley Page Halifax and the Avro Lancaster. Foremost amongst these three aircraft was the Avro Lancaster, an aircraft that set new standards in heavy bomber aircraft performance.

The Civilian Repair Organization designated four locations to undertake work on the new Lancaster bombers. Tollerton was one of those four locations and for the remainder of the war this would be the aircraft that formed the mainstay of all work undertaken by the civilian workers at the airfield. At Tollerton Lancasters were assembled, repaired, modified, and overhauled.

Along with the Supermarine Spitfire and the de Havilland Mosquito the Avro Lancaster has gone down in history as one of the truly outstanding aircraft of its generation, although its advent came about more by luck than judgement. Some aircraft, such as the Spitfire and Mosquito, came straight off the drawing board and were obviously exceptional aircraft from the moment they first took to the air. The Lancaster on the other hand was born out of the failure of another aircraft. That other aircraft was the Avro Manchester.

The Manchester was designated a 'heavy' bomber even though it only had two engines, namely Rolls-Royce Vultures. It was these engines that were to prove the Achilles heel of the new aircraft. Great things were expected from the prototype, which first flew on 25 July 1939, so much so that large numbers had already been ordered straight from the drawing board. However, after the aircraft's maiden flight the omens were not good. The power developed by the two Vulture engines was nowhere near as great as had been predicted. The aircraft also proved unstable in flight and difficult to fly. Even before this test flight though, an order for two hundred Manchesters had been placed with the manufacturers A.V. Roe, so desperate was the Air Ministry to replace the increasingly obsolescent Hampdens, Blenheims and Whitleys.

Modifications were made to the prototype and a second aircraft subsequently flew on 25 October 1939. Great secrecy surrounded these flights and no mention of the aircraft was made in the press. The first two Manchesters were sent to 207 Squadron at Waddington in November 1940 where they underwent intensive flight evaluation; but the Vulture engines continued to be remarkably unreliable. Since it was impossible to keep the aircraft airborne with only one

Plate 48:   The Avro Manchester. The unsuccessful aircraft from which the legendary Lancaster was developed. EM is the code for 207 Squadron.

engine, this unreliability did not endear the Manchesters to aircrew who were going to have to fly them over enemy territory where the consequences of losing an engine could be catastrophic.

However, further aircraft continued to be delivered and, following a visit from the King and Queen on 9 January 1941, 207 Squadron became operational and news of the Manchester was announced to the general public. Manchester numbers continued to increase and new squadrons were formed; but still the aircraft were bedevilled by engine unreliability. On 13 April 1941, following the discovery of a new fault traced to the engine bearings, all Bomber Command's Manchesters were grounded. Desperate situations call for desperate remedies and the manufacturers came up with two possible solutions. The first option was to replace the Vulture engines with two Bristol Centaurus engines. The second involved extending the wings of the aircraft and fitting four tried and tested Rolls-Royce Merlin engines instead. (It was the same Rolls-Royce Merlin that had powered the Spitfire and Hurricane in The Battle of Britain.) Fortunately it was the latter option that was adopted.

By the time that it was decided to replace the two Vulture engines with the four Merlins over two hundred Manchesters had already been delivered to the RAF. However, once the new engines were installed the transformation in performance and flying characteristics was stunning: a veritable transformation from carthorse to thoroughbred. The Manchester Mk III (as the four engine Manchester was named) first flew on 9 January 1941. The name Manchester was quickly discarded and the new aircraft re-christened 'Lancaster'. A legend was born.

The Lancaster proved to be vastly superior to all other contemporary RAF heavy bombers and would provide the mainstay of Bomber Command's strength for the remainder of the war. The table on page 141 provides some information relating to the aircraft.

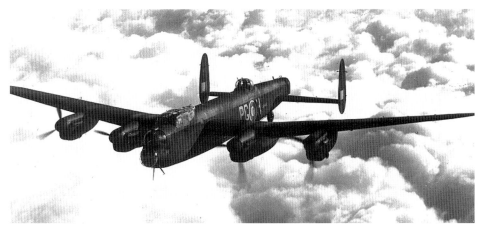

**Plate 49:    The Avro Lancaster.** Along with the Spitfire, Hurricane and Mosquito, were arguably the most successful and famous RAF aircraft of the war.

| | |
|---|---|
| Crew | 7 personnel comprising; Pilot, Navigator, Flight Engineer, Wireless Operator, Mid-Upper Gunner, Tail Gunner and Front Gunner/Bomb Aimer |
| Weights | Empty - 36,900lbs  Fully Loaded - 68,000lbs |
| Engines | Mark I & III had Four Rolls-Royce 1,460hp Merlin engines<br>Mark II had four 1,650hp Bristol Hercules radial engines |
| Performance | Maximum Speed - 287mph at 11,500ft<br>Cruising Speed - 210mph<br>Range with a 14,000lb bomb load was 1,660 miles<br>(The substitution of more petrol instead of bombs increased the range of the aircraft) |
| Bomb Load | Carried in the internal bomb bay - 14,000lbs<br>With modifications to the fuselage the Lancaster was capable of carrying a bomb load of 22,000lbs (the Barnes Wallis famous 'Grand Slam' bomb) |
| Armament | The Lancaster was provided with up to eight Browning .303 machine guns distributed in three power-operated turrets |
| Dimensions | Wing Span - 102ft 0in<br>Length - 69ft 4in<br>Height - 19ft 7in |
| Lancaster Feats | Tonnage of bombs actually dropped on enemy targets was 608,612 tons<br>The number of incendiary bombs dropped on enemy targets was 51,513,106<br>The average weight of bombs dropped per aircraft lost was 132 tons for the Lancaster<br>Similar figures for the Short Stirling were 41 tons and the Handley Page Halifax 51 tons |
| Lancaster Production | 7,377 Lancaster bombers were built |
| Lancaster Losses | 3,346 Lancasters were lost on operations |
| Victoria Crosses | Great Britain's highest award for bravery was awarded on no less than ten occasions to aircrew flying in Lancasters. Five of the awards were posthumous. |
| Over 100 'Ops' | 35 Lancasters completed 100 operational missions or more. The record number was completed by Lancaster III (ED 888) which completed 140 'Ops' |

**Table 7:    Avro Lancaster Facts and Figures**

**Plate 50** 'Wings Over Europe - Tollerton Issue'. The cover of a booklet of cartoons showing various scenes from Tollerton during the war.

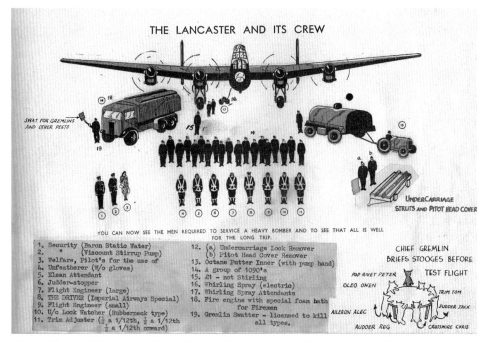

**Plate 51:** An illustration from 'Wings Over Europe - Tollerton Issue'. A comic view of the roles played by various employees of the TAS workforce.

The first squadron to be equipped with the new Lancaster bomber was 44 (Rhodesia) Squadron. On 24 December 1941 the squadron took delivery of their new aircraft. As the squadron had been flying the outdated Hampden the new Lancaster aircraft made a most welcome Christmas present. For the remainder of the war, the RAF would be supplied with a constant stream of the new aircraft as more and more of the heavy bombers took the air battle to targets all over enemy-occupied Europe.

Lancaster aircraft were involved in some of the most famous actions of the war. Perhaps the most famous of them all was 'The Dam Busters Raid' which took place on the night of 16/17 May 1943 when nineteen aircraft of 617 Squadron, led by Wing Commander Guy Gibson, attacked and breached the Mohne and Eder dams using Barnes Wallis' famous 'bouncing' bomb. For his outstanding bravery during the attack Guy Gibson was awarded the Victoria Cross though, sadly, eight of the nineteen aircraft that took part in the operation were lost, resulting in the deaths of fifty-three of the aircrew.

By the time the war in Europe ended there would be 57 squadrons flying Lancasters, giving the RAF a front-line strength of almost 1,400 aircraft. Without the significant contribution that Tollerton Aircraft Services Ltd and other companies like it made in modifying, assembling, and carrying out essential repair and maintenance work it would simply not have been possible to keep such a vast fleet of aircraft serviceable and available to play their vital role.

Before each Lancaster which had been worked on at Tollerton by TAS was ready to be returned to the RAF, it had to undergo a flight test to ensure that it was up to standard for operational duties. The chief test pilot at TAS was Walter Rogers, and he was usually the person who put each aircraft through its paces. The table on page 144 gives a sample of the aircraft that he test-flew at Tollerton. These aircraft represented just a small percentage of the total number of Lancaster aircraft that TAS worked on during the war years. We are indebted to Harry Holmes, author of *Avro Lancaster – The Definitive Record*, for providing the details.

Plate 52:   Walter Rogers, Chief Test Pilot for TAS during the war.
*Jan Krupa*

| Date | Number | Comments (Squadrons Flown With, dates Scrapped etc) |
|---|---|---|
| 28-04-44 | R 5618 | Lancaster I, 61 Squadron. Scrapped May '47 |
| 25-05-44 | JB 319 | Lancaster III, 103 Squadron. 5 LFS. Scrapped Oct '46 |
| 09-06-44 | W 4824 | Flew with 467 & 50 Squadrons. Lost on a day raid, 6 Aug 1944 having logged 619 flying hours |
| 17-06-44 | ED 727 | Lancaster III, 15 & 622 Squadrons. 5 LFS. Scrapped Nov '46 |
| 13-07-44 | DV 340 | Lancaster I converted to III. 460 & 9 Squadrons. SOC Apr '46 |
| 21-07-44 | W 4113 | 49 & 156 Squadrons. 5 LFS |
| 14-08-44 | W 4122 | 9 Squadron Scrapped Nov '46. 5 LFS |
| 15-08-44 | ND 521 | 207, 460 & 57 Squadrons. SOC Feb '46 |
| 01-09-44 | ND 843 | 44 Squadron 21-09-44 ME 781 460 Squadron. Crashed at Woolfox Lodge on 2/3 March 1945 |
| 14-10-44 | ND 934 | 35 Squadron. Sold for scrap May 1947 |
| 28-11-44 | ND 882 | 156 Squadron. Scrapped September 1947 |
| 05-12-44 | R 5855 | 49 Squadron. 5 LFS. Sold for scrap March 1949 |
| 30-12-44 | ME 754 | 166 & 100 Squadrons. SOC September 1947 |
| 17-01-45 | L 7539 | 44, 50 & 463 Squadrons. SOC December 1946 |
| 01-02-45 | PB 194 | 12 Squadron. Scrapped September 1947 |
| 10-02-45 | ME 862 | 90, 625 & 576 Squadrons. Scrapped 1947 |
| 19-02-45 | NN 701 | 57 & 429 Squadrons. Scrapped January 1947 |
| 24-02-45 | JA 872 | 57, 630 & 61 Squadrons. Scrapped January 1947 |
| 03-03-45 | LL 844 | 463 Squadron. Scrapped Jan '47 having flown 464 Flying Hours |
| 22-03-45 | PB 581 | 625 & 170 Squadrons. Scrapped December 1946 |
| 05-04-45 | ND 326 | 100 & 463 Squadrons. Sold for scrap in May 1947 |
| 24-04-45 | PB 458 | 83 Squadron. Scrapped May 1947 |
| 10-05-45 | LM 713 | 630, 9 & 189 Squadrons. Scrapped June 1947 |
| 18-05-45 | NN 749 | 576 Squadron. Crashed 5 Jan 1945. Scrapped September 1947 |
| 31-05-45 | HK 707 | Crashed on 19 January 1945. Scrapped October 1946 |
| 07-06-45 | R 5906 | 106, 15 & 622 Squadrons. Scrapped May 1947 |
| 03-07-45 | EE 108 | 156 Squadron. Scrapped 1947 |
| 24-07-45 | ED 888 | 103, 576 & 103 Squadrons. Completed 135 Ops. 941+ Flying Hours<br>Scrapped January 1947. One of only 35 Lancasters to complete 100+ Ops |
| 11-08-45 | PD 330 | 463 Squadron. Scrapped May 1947 |
| 24-08-45 | ED 425 | 97, 622 & 78 Squadrons. 5 LFS. Scrapped September 1947 |
| 03-09-45 | ED 801 | 106 & 207 Squadrons. Crashed March 1945. Sold for scrap Nov '47 |
| 14-06-45 | DV 383 | 207 Squadron. SOC November 1947 |
| 21-09-45 | JA 846 | 97 Squadron. 5 LFS. Scrapped September 1947 |
| 19-10-45 | ED 866 | 97 & 61 Squadrons. Converted to Flight-Re-fuelling Tanker. Crashed near Andover 22 November 1948 |
| 08-11-45 | ED 802 | 207 & 44 Squadrons. |
| 19-12-45 | ED 940 | 97 & 625 Squadrons. 5 LFS. |
| 19-12-45 | LM 420 | 619 & 213 Squadrons. 5 LFS. Sold for scrap May 1947 |
| 04-01-46 | JB 137 | 61 Squadron. 5 LFS. SOC October 1946 |

Notes:  SOC = Struck Off Charge (Disposed of)

LFS = Lancaster Finishing School (A Lancaster Training Unit)

**Table 8:**    **A sample of Lancaster aircraft tests flown by Captain Rogers**

## Recovery of Damaged Aircraft

Another vital job undertaken by TAS involved the recovery of crashed and damaged aircraft. Prior to the outbreak of the Second World War the recovery of crashed aircraft was primarily the responsibility of the technical staff of the RAF station nearest to the crash site. These specialist teams could call upon assistance, if they thought it necessary, from an Aircraft Maintenance Unit. Aircraft Maintenance Units were set up, as their name implies, to carry out any work that might be required on an aircraft that was beyond the capabilities of an RAF airfield.

Usually, if damage to an aircraft was not too substantial an RAF station would carry out whatever repairs were necessary. When this occurred RAF technical personnel would be responsible for carrying out the work. Often aircraft manufacturers would also have small working parties of their own employees lodged at an airfield to provide specialist technical back-up for the RAF units.

While this arrangement suited a peacetime situation, it would clearly be inadequate to deal with the huge increase of crashed and damaged aircraft that was predicted in a war. Therefore on 15 September 1939 the Air Ministry set up an organizational structure whereby specialized units would be responsible for

**Plate 53:** **Lancaster fuselages in the Main Hangar.** These aircraft are being assembled prior to delivery to 5 Lancaster Finishing School (5 LFS) based at Syerston.

the recovery of crashed aircraft and the repair on site of damage that was not of a major nature.

The aircraft manufacturers, in their turn, would establish central repair depots where the RAF could return any airframe that was deemed repairable. It was not long before this aspect of the organization became the responsibility of the Ministry of Aircraft Production (MAP), who designated the new body the Civilian Repair Organization (CRO).

Before September 1939 had ended five aircraft recovery teams had been dispatched to various locations on the east coast of England to create the new Salvage Centres. The Maintenance Units (MUs) employed personnel known as Categorizing Officers whose job it was to visit any incident and assess the situation. They categorised incidents as: repairable on site; repairable by the CRO; returnable to the Maintenance Unit for the recovery of spares; or complete write-off. Often a civilian representative of the aircraft manufacturer would accompany the Categorizing Officer and assist him in making his decision.

As a part of the CRO, Tollerton became involved in repairing crashed or damaged aircraft. A Categorizing Officer would assess a crashed or damaged aircraft and decide what action was necessary. If it were possible to load the aircraft onto a lorry and send it to Tollerton that would be arranged. It became a common sight in and around the villages of Tollerton and Gamston to see the articulated Bedford lorries known as 'Queen Marys' bringing in partly dismantled aircraft for repair at the airfield. If the aircraft needed to be dealt with *in situ* then a working party from the airfield would be organized. These working parties were known as 'outworkers' and so great did the demand for them become that it was not unknown, at times, for there to be almost as many people employed on work parties away from Tollerton as were working at the airfield.

Plate 54: **The 'Queen Mary' road transporter**. These Bedford articulated lorries were used to deliver aircraft parts to TAS at Tollerton and must have been a common sight on the roads in and around the village during the war years.

# The Air Transport Auxiliary

The Air Transport Auxiliary was responsible for flying into Tollerton any aircraft that was airworthy and required work to be undertaken on it. Once that work had been completed it was also the ATA that flew the aircraft to its next United Kingdom destination. The ATA was one of those organizations that worked well away from the public eye and their pilots never caught the limelight that fell on the 'Brylcreem Boys' of Fighter and Bomber Commands. Nevertheless, it did a vital job under trying and often hazardous circumstances. In some respects its contribution to the war was similar to that of the Merchant Navy: both services were overshadowed by their more glamourous and highly publicized military relations, the Royal Air Force and the Royal Navy. However, unlike the RAF and the Royal Navy, the ATA was exceptional in employing a significant contingent of women as pilots working on an equal footing alongside their male colleagues.

When war came in 1939 Great Britain was largely unprepared. New situations would inevitably arise which would require innovative solutions. Pre-war government planning had forecast that approximately 2,000 new aircraft would need to be produced each month to maintain the war effort. This would necessitate appropriate arrangements to ferry these aircraft from the factories where they were made to the maintenance units and squadrons that would require them for operational duties. However, when hostilities broke out no specific plans to do this were in place. Originally the RAF considered that it could do this job itself, but the impracticality of this soon became apparent: the RAF would need all its pilots for operational duties.

When war was declared it was obvious to the major civilian airline companies, Imperial Airways and British Airways, that some curtailment of their services

**Plate 55:** **A Lancaster at Tollerton with the bomb doors open.** Such sights were commonplace at Tollerton during 1944 and 1945. *Tom Myall Collection*

would take place and that this would create a surplus of pilots. The Air Ministry decided that these pilots would form the nucleus of a new organization which would provide a variety of services, including the transport of dispatches and mail; transport of medical supplies and medical personnel; and the provision of an ambulance service. (At this stage the RAF still had its own plans with regard to the ferrying of aircraft.) This new body was to be known as the Air Transport Auxiliary.

The original criteria for acceptance into the ATA were that a pilot needed to be male, between the ages of 28 and 50 years of age, and with a minimum of 250 hours flying experience. All pilots would be engaged on a civilian basis and the organization was to be run as a civilian operation. Originally 23 pilots signed contracts to work for the ATA, and they became the base from which the whole organization grew.

In the spring of 1939 the RAF had introduced a scheme whereby pilots from operational squadrons collected new aircraft for their own units from their places of manufacture. Aircraft needed for the new RAFVR units were to be collected by pilots from one of two RAF ferry pools that had been set up specifically for this purpose. One of these pools was based at Hucknall in Nottinghamshire; the other was at Filton, near Bristol. Each of the two pools comprised sixteen pilots and six Avro Anson transport aircraft. The Ansons performed the role of taxis that took the ATA pilots and aircrew to and from the ferrying points. Once the ferried aircraft reached its final destination the ATA pilot was picked up by the Anson and flown back to base. This was essential otherwise delivery pilots might find themselves stuck in the middle of nowhere with no available means of getting back to their bases.

By the beginning of 1940 it had become apparent that the RAF simply did not possess the resources required to conduct ferrying operations on the necessary scale. Another reliable source of pilots was required to perform this vital duty, and the ATA was a logical place to look. Thus the Air Transport Auxiliary was designated as a Civil Ferry Pool and No 41 Group RAF Maintenance Command took over responsibility for the overall running of the organization.

In the years immediately prior to the declaration of war the Government had set up two schemes for training civilians as the pilots who would be required in the event of war. These were the Royal Air Force Voluntary Reserve (RAFVR) and the Civil Air Guard (CAG). Both of these organizations have been dealt with previously in Chapter 5. Pilots in the RAFVR were destined to serve in the RAF but those pilots who had trained with the CAG could possibly be used in the ATA. A major problem, however, was that most of the ATA pilots had learnt to fly in small, single-engine aircraft like the de Havilland Tiger Moth. The aircraft they would be required to fly were larger, technologically more advanced, and usually much more powerful. To address this problem it was decided that suitable candidates should be sent to the RAF Central Flying School for further training and assessment. There they would learn to fly in the Harvard trainer and, if successful in that, go on to fly Battles, Blenheims, Hurricanes and Spitfires - or, for that matter, anything else that was available!

ATA pilots would be required to ferry whichever aircraft the operational squadrons required, encompassing a range of types and variants. The aircraft that a pilot could fly on ferry duties with the ATA were split into six categories and each pilot was classified according to the type of aircraft that he or she was qualified to fly. The categories can be seen in the following table:

| Category | Type | Aircraft |
|----------|------|----------|
| Class 1 | Light, Single Engine | Magister, Tiger Moth, Proctor, Hart, Gladiator and Swordfish |
| Class 2 | Advanced, Single Engine | Spitfire, Hurricane, Mustang, Lysander, Hellcat, Typhoon, Tempest, Corsair |
| Class 3 | Light, Twin Engine | Oxford, Dominie, Anson |
| Class 4 | Advanced, Twin Engine | Hudson, Wellington, Blenheim, Beaufighter, Mosquito, Dakota, Mitchell |
| Class 5 | Four Engine | Stirling, Halifax, Lancaster, Flying Fortress, Liberator |
| Class 6 | Sea-Planes | Catalina, Sunderland |

**Table 9:   Aircraft flown by ATA pilots by category**

All aircraft in classes 1, 2, and 3 could be flown solo. However in the remaining categories some assistance might be required according to the type of aircraft being flown. Thus, some aircraft would require any or all of the following: co-pilot, flight engineer, and pilot's assistant (usually an Air Training Corps member or a Sea Cadet). All the four-engine aircraft required at least a flight engineer to accompany the pilot to assist in the flying of the machine. However, there was no bar to women flying any of the aircraft provided that they had passed their training course on the respective type.

Mention is made in the following chapter of how amazed people were to see the sight of a heavy bomber being flown into Tollerton by a single pilot with no other aircrew. Such accounts of pretty young slips of girls bringing in mighty Halifaxes or Lancasters entirely on their own appear to have been widespread at the time, but they were simply not true in fact. It was physically impossible to perform from the pilot's seat all the flight duties necessary to take-off, fly, and land such aircraft safely. Nevertheless the tale had endearing qualities and certainly became an enduring myth.

As the war progressed so the ATA grew in size to meet the ever increasing demands placed upon it. By the end of 1943 it had made over 100,000 journeys ferrying aircraft for the RAF and the Royal Navy. The final figure for the whole of the war was in excess of 300,000 ferry journeys, a truly staggering amount. The highest number of deliveries in a single day occurred on 21 February 1945 when no less that 570 aircraft were moved. These remarkable figures were achieved with a workforce that never exceeded 700 pilots at any one time. Indeed, during the whole duration of the war only just over 1,300 pilots were employed by the ATA, of whom 166 were women.

To facilitate the smooth transportation of aircraft to the various operational airfields a series of ferry stations was established to provide a comprehensive network throughout the length and breadth of Great Britain. ATA headquarters was at White Waltham, between Reading and Maidenhead. The nearest ferry base to Tollerton was at Ratcliffe-on-the-Wreake, alongside the Fosse Way between Nottingham and Leicester. The Ratcliffe airfield was used throughout the war by the ATA, having been one of the first to be used by the ATA.

In most cases the ferry pilots had to do their own navigating. Navigating is a skilled art and most ATA pilots had not been trained as navigators. They had to learn their own way around the country, finding their way from airfield to airfield as best as they could, usually simply by visual means. This was all well and good when the weather was clear but it can be imagined what it must have been like on murky or, worst of all, foggy days. One of the biggest problems facing a ferry pilot was taking off in good weather only to have a sudden deterioration in conditions. However, the need to get on with the job and the urgency with which some aircraft deliveries were required meant that sometimes they were figuratively sailing decidedly close to the wind.

During the war over 150 aircrew with the ATA lost their lives ferrying aircraft, of whom 14 were women. Overall though, the accident rate was very low. This was a remarkable achievement, the more so when the range of aircraft flown, the conditions they were flown in, and the airfields that were used are taken into account. ATA pilots had to work very hard: they were required to work for thirteen days at a time followed by two rest days off. During the summer their working day could last from dawn to dusk, as they were expected to make as many deliveries as they could pull in during the hours of daylight. During the shorter daylight hours in winter they were expected to fly as long as the light and weather conditions permitted. Some of the pilots employed were even physically handicapped. There was an instance of a pilot having only one arm, his right arm having been amputated at the shoulder. This meant that there were certain aircraft that it was physically impossible for him to fly, but there were others he could ferry, and did.

At times adverse weather conditions would make all flying impossible. There is an amusing anecdote about Sir Arthur 'Bomber' Harris - a man well known for not suffering fools gladly - when he was Commander-in-Chief Bomber

Command. In January 1943 the winter weather had been atrocious: no flying had been possible for a fortnight and no aircraft had been delivered to the waiting operational squadrons. 'Bomber' Harris was less than impressed and made his displeasure known. An ATA emissary was dispatched to Harris to resolve the problem. Harris began by demanding how he was expected to get on with the war if the wretched ATA failed to deliver the aircraft that he needed. When asked by the emissary how many raids Bomber Command had carried out in the previous fortnight, the reply was, 'None, how do you expect us to carry out raids in this appalling weather?' The ATA officer pointed out that the weather was the same for ATA pilots. If Harris insisted, he said, then the ATA would try to deliver the aircraft, but it was likely that they would crash and Harris would not get his aircraft anyway. Faced with such logic, Harris apologised and invited the officer to dine with him that evening.

When victory was achieved in 1945 the need to ferry aircraft disappeared almost overnight. Before 1945 had run its course the ATA had been disbanded and its personnel released: within a few short months it was as if the ATA had never existed. Hardly a word of its demise was mentioned in the media of the day. When the Victory Parade was organized in London on 8 June 1945 to celebrate the winning of the war in Europe, twelve men and twelve women represented the ATA. However, rather than marching with the RAF representatives (which they had done earlier during the Battle of Britain celebrations) they were allocated places with the transport workers at the rear of the column. To those aircrew of the ATA who had given selfless service to the RAF throughout the war this seemed to be a snub, and unappreciative of their vital contribution to the war effort.

# Chapter 9

# The Way It Was

Throughout the war hundreds of people were employed at Tollerton airfield. They came from all walks of life and each brought their own particular skill into the work place. All however were united in a common aim, namely to ensure that Germany was defeated. The way that they personally could contribute in this vital struggle was to ensure that as many aircraft as possible were delivered to the RAF and the Royal Navy.

The following personal recollections are from a small cross-section of that workforce and offer a fascinating insight into what life was like at Tollerton during those hectic years from 1939 to 1945. One of those people who were at Tollerton in the very early days of the war was Harry James.

## One Man's Recollections

Harry James left school six weeks before the outbreak of war in 1939. He was determined to work with aeroplanes in some way or other. As luck would have it, Rollason Aircraft Services had just expanded their Croydon business to Tollerton and were recruiting workers, so Harry applied for a job and was fortunate enough to get one. When Harry began his employment with Rollasons at Tollerton, they were in the process of moving their Hampden repair facilities away from their premises in Croydon, along with some of the company's most experienced staff. The remaining vacancies at Tollerton were filled locally.

When Harry began working at Tollerton, Rollasons had a contract for converting Handley Page Harrow bombers into transport aircraft. The Harrow was a large lumbering twin-engine bomber, long obsolete. To convert it from a bomber to a transport aircraft required several modifications, one of which involved removing the bomber's three gun turrets and replacing them with streamlined fairings. The newly created aircraft was then used for transport duties and acquired the unofficial name of the Sparrow - hence the job became known as the Harrow/Sparrow conversion. This conversion work gave the new workforce the opportunity to hone their skills in readiness for the day when the Hampden production line would be up and running.

Such were the demands on Tollerton's workforce that it became necessary to work around the clock in order to meet the demands that work on the Hampdens was creating. Indeed, production pressures were so great that Harry remembers the workers being instructed to continue working even in the event of an air raid unless the bombs were actually falling on the hangars! As a precautionary measure teams of 'spotters' were set up to look out for enemy aircraft. Before he began work at Rollasons Harry had been on an Army Aircraft Recognition Course at RAF Hucknall, so it was logical that he should be given the job of training this team of 'spotters'. Once the team had been trained, volunteers were organized to provide a watch. To give the spotter the maximum field of view around the airfield a gun turret from a converted Harrow - basically a Perspex dome equipped with a seat which could be manually rotated in either direction - was placed at the top of the tower on the corner of the Main Hangar. Access to the turret was via a ninety-foot steel ladder. The spotter in the turret had a pair of binoculars, a telephone and a switch to operate alarm bells in the event of an air raid.

Within weeks the system was put to its first test. An alert sounded during the day but work continued. Harry decided that it would do no harm to climb up to the turret and see if he could lend a hand to the spotter on duty. Imagine his amazement when he found that the turret was empty: the spotter had taken fright and had beaten a hasty retreat. Fortunately the intruder aircraft encountered some strong anti-aircraft fire in the vicinity of Radcliffe-on-Trent and made for the coast and safety. Production had not been interrupted, so it may be said that the system had proved its worth.

Before being dispatched to the RAF, each aircraft was subjected to a test flight. As we saw in the last chapter, Captain Walter Rogers did this. On one of these test flights Harry was lucky enough to accompany him. It was only Harry's second flight in an aircraft. He sat behind Captain Rogers who performed a series of turns and banking manoeuvres. Suddenly there was a loud metallic

**Plate 56: The Handley Page Harrow.** The first contract that TAS secured at Tollerton was to convert the obsolete Harrow bomber into a transport aircraft, unofficially nicknamed 'The Sparrow', hence, the Harrow / Sparrow conversion.

bang. Neither Harry nor Captain Rogers had any idea of the cause, but since the aircraft continued to fly normally the flight continued - Harry breathing a sigh of relief that the order to bail out was not necessary. Another moment in the flight which Harry recollects vividly was when Captain Rogers checked the Hampden's stalling speed - the speed at which there is insufficient airflow over the wing surfaces to generate lift and the aircraft begins to fall towards the ground. Throttling the engines right back and applying full flaps achieved this. When the airspeed fell to 60 miles per hour the aircraft stalled and its nose dropped; Captain Rogers gently opened the throttles and recovered level flight. All of this was done within sight of the airfield and provided splendid excitement for Harry.

During his time at Tollerton Harry witnessed many memorable sights. Perhaps the saddest occurred at a time when a squadron of Wellingtons were briefly stationed at Tollerton. One Sunday lunchtime, whilst Harry was in the observation post on top of the tower, he saw a visiting Wellington take off to make the return trip to its home airfield. After half a circuit of the airfield the pilot, no doubt in high spirits, opened the throttles and did a low, fast run across the airfield, banked steeply and pulled the Wellington round in a very tight turn. The aircraft, already low, lost height, cartwheeled into the ground and burst into flames. There were no survivors.

A happier sight was the arrival of eight brand new Manchester bombers, which

**Plate 57:    A pill box inside the Main Hangar.** Why a pill box should be located inside the hangar is something of a mystery. To date we have no explanation as to why it was sited there since it appears to fulfil no practical purpose. *Nigel Morley*

155

flew into the airfield in close succession and taxied to their dispersal points before being taken away for modifications to be made on them. Another bit of excitement occurred for Harry during another of his 'spotting' spells. One day a fast sleek-looking twin-engine aircraft circled the airfield at low level and eventually came in to land. Even with binoculars and at close quarters, Harry was unable to identify the new arrival. It transpired that the machine was one of the prototypes of the de Havilland Mosquito bombers. The aircraft was being flown by none other than Geoffrey de Havilland himself, and was still on the secret list.

Perhaps Harry's most interesting sighting of all occurred in the spring of 1941. That day he saw a small fighter approaching the airfield from the direction of Nottingham. His instant impression was that it must be a Spitfire since it quite clearly wasn't a Hurricane; however through his binoculars he could see that it wasn't a Spitfire either, but a Messerschmitt 109. The plane banked to the right and Harry was relieved to see that it carried the familiar RAF roundels of red, white and blue on the aircraft. There is an interesting background to the story.

On 27 November 1940 Leutnant Wolfgang Teumer took off from Wissant (between Calais and Boulogne) in his Me 109 on a fighter-bomber mission to England. During the sortie RAF Spitfires attacked his aircraft, which was damaged to such an extent that he could not fly back to France. Teumer managed to fly to RAF Manton where, as the hydraulics on his aircraft were destroyed, he was forced to make a wheels-up landing. This manoeuvre was so skilfully executed that his Me 109 was only slightly damaged when it finally came to rest. The chance to evaluate the enemy's current equipment was not to be missed and soon the aircraft was repaired and was being test-flown at Farnborough, Boscombe Down and Hucknall, from where it was operating when Harry saw it. It was a common sight over the skies of Nottingham for several weeks. The aircraft survived the war and can now be seen in the Battle of Britain section of the Royal Air Force Museum at Hendon.

Harry recollects that reconstruction work on the Hampdens was not the most exciting work in the world of aviation, but it still had the odd moment that was a little out of the ordinary. One such occasion was when a standard Hampden arrived at Tollerton to be converted to a prototype Hampden Mk II. The standard Hampden was fitted with two Bristol Pegasus 885 hp engines, and these were replaced with two more powerful Wright Cyclone engines. This modification dramatically improved performance, but the writing was already on the wall for the aircraft. After undergoing the usual test flight, the aircraft was taken from Tollerton to undergo evaluation testing, but the results did not justify its going into production.

One role, however, that it was thought might suit the Hampden was that of torpedo bomber. The principal torpedo bomber flying with the RAF at that time was the antiquated-looking Fairy Swordfish biplane, for which no satisfactory replacement had yet been found. A project was set up at RAF Swinderby to look into the feasibility of converting the Hampden and Harry was one of a team sent from Tollerton to assist the work. The conversion was not a great success, however, and the project came to nothing.

As the bomber airfields in the East Midlands took delivery of increasing numbers of Stirling, Halifax and Lancaster bombers, it became a common sight to see streams of the aircraft in the evening skies around Nottingham preparing to attack targets in occupied Europe and Germany. The villages in South Notts reverberated with the roar of scores of Merlin and other engines, as the heavily laden aircraft struggled in wide circles to gain altitude. Harry recollects that a usual quip when faced with such a spectacle was, 'The boys are going out again tonight!' It was about this time that Harry left Tollerton to go and serve in the RAF. So ended a chapter of Harry's life, but one which holds many memories for him.

## Wartime Responsibilities and Everyday Trivia

Brian Hancock has written his own account of the time that he spent at Tollerton Air Services. The following reminiscences are taken from that account and from a taped interview.

Brian was a schoolboy in West Bridgford, Nottingham, during the 1930s. Around the mid thirties, Brian's father took him to an RAF display at Hucknall Aerodrome, and a lifelong love affair with the aeroplane was born. A couple of years later, Brian was at Tollerton being thrilled by the performers in the Sir Alan Cobham Air Show. The star attraction at that air show was a performer named Clem Sohn, billed as 'The American Bird Man' whose spectacular stunts are described in chapter 4.

Brian had no wish to emulate Clem Sohn; but the visits to the two air displays captured his imagination. From that time, Brian spent much of his pocket money on materials to make scale-model aeroplanes. In those pre-war days he never dreamt that within a few years Tollerton would play a significant role in his life. Brian's elder brother, George, began work at Tollerton around 1940 as a flying control fitter with Tollerton Aircraft Services Ltd. Early in 1942 Brian wrote to TAS seeking employment in the drawing office. Unfortunately there were no vacancies at the time, but he was offered the opportunity of starting a draughtsman's apprenticeship in six months' time. In the interim, TAS offered him temporary employment in the accounts department at 76 Musters Road, West Bridgford, which housed the company's secretariat, accounts, wages, cost offices, and stationery stores. Brian began work on a starting wage of fifteen shillings per week in what, to him, was a friendly working environment.

Some TAS workers were employed on 'working-out' parties (as described in Chapter 8) and it was one of Brian's duties to post their wages. These wage packets were made up (in cash) on Thursday mornings to ensure that they were received by the weekend; Brian cycled with them to the nearest Post Office where the envelopes were registered and posted. The following day, Friday, a van called at the Musters Road offices, collected the remainder of the wage packets, and delivered them to the airfield at Tollerton for distribution there. Security was never a problem: without motor transport would-be thieves had little chance of escaping from a crime-scene.

There were two tea breaks during working hours, one in the morning and one in the afternoon. Sometimes Brian would cycle to Major's Bread & Cake Shop for a one-penny currant bun or, as a treat, a two-penny cream cake. A five-minute cycle ride would see him home for lunch, though some days he would lunch at the Friary British Restaurant. This grand sounding establishment was actually the church hall behind the Friary Congregational Church on Musters Road, West Bridgford. The British Restaurants were a Government-backed scheme to provide workers with a good three-course lunch for 9d. They were open to anyone, though mainly favoured by office and industrial workers. And with food at these restaurants not 'on the ration' you could eke out your food ration.

When Brian's apprenticeship at Tollerton began during the autumn of 1942 he was transferred from Musters Road to the offices at Tollerton airfield. The Drawing Office at Tollerton was in offices attached to the Main Hangar just off the Gamston to Tollerton road. The Chief Draughtsman, Reg Hassall, proved to be a very good tutor (and indeed mentor). In general, the male workforce in the offices was composed of very young, or elderly, or disabled men, as younger,

**Plate 58:** A variety of aircraft parts stored in the Bridge Hangar, probably tail sections for Lancaster bombers. *Keith Hodgett*

fitter men had mostly been conscripted into the armed forces. Women of all ages were also employed in the offices at TAS - one such was Mrs Britt, a very attractive lady employed as a tracer. Another employee remembered by Brian was Eric Garlah-Watkins, son of an Irish mother and an Indian father, who was particularly noted for being well-mannered and always a gentleman.

Although a Barton's bus service ran daily from Huntingdon Street in Nottingham to Tollerton Brian's usual means of travelling to and from work was the bicycle. Strict petrol rationing meant it was virtually impossible to obtain petrol legally for a private car, so that a great many employees cycled from Tollerton, Plumtree, Keyworth, Cotgrave, Radcliffe-on-Trent, and further afield. The only exception occurred when the ground was covered with thick snow: then the only option might be to get off your bike and walk! Anyone without a bicycle who worked overtime would have to walk home at the end of the working day, as there were no late buses. A six-day week was the norm, with voluntary overtime on top of that, including Sundays, when required. Most people also found time to do voluntary jobs outside normal working hours, including such responsibilities as Air Raid Wardens, Auxiliary Firemen, Fire Watchers, Red Cross or St John's Ambulance Brigade workers. Many younger employees joined the army, navy, or air force cadets in readiness for when they were conscripted. Men of all ages from 17 years upwards joined the Local Defence Volunteers (LDV) - made famous as the Home Guard in the television series *Dad's Army*, and unkindly nicknamed the 'Look, Duck and Vanish' brigade by certain sections of the community! The general attitude amongst the

**Plate 59:    This group of men is believed to be the Tollerton Local Defence
          Volunteer Unit.** The unit comprised employees at TAS.
*Courtesy Melvis Phenix*

workforce was that what they were doing was important to the war effort and that personal considerations must take second place to the national good.

One of the first jobs that Brian was involved with at TAS concerned the Air Ministry contract for the overhaul of Hampden bombers. Brian particularly remembers one Hampden which came to Tollerton for repair. The aircraft in question was from 83 Squadron which had been involved in an attack on barges at the port of Antwerp on the night of 15/16 September 1940. During the attack it was hit by enemy fire and a shell appeared to explode in the aircraft's bomb compartment. A fire rapidly enveloped the compartment of one of the rear-gunners and the wireless operator, who was a Scot, Sergeant John Hannah. It fell to his lot to try to extinguish the flames. The rear-gunner had already bailed out of what he thought was a stricken aeroplane, and the pilot had his hands full attempting to keep control of the aircraft. Sgt Hannah could have bailed out, too, but he chose to stay and assist his pilot. The flames inside the aircraft had a firm hold and were melting the aluminium floor: indeed, after ten minutes the floor had disappeared and all that remained was a grid formed by the cross-members of the airframe. Through this grid a howling gale blew which fanned the flames even more and propelled great lumps of molten aluminium onto the rear bulkhead. Electrical wiring inside the fuselage was also destroyed in the inferno. Through all this, Sgt Hannah continued to fight the flames with

Plate 60:    A general view inside the Bellman Hangar, probably in 1944, showing engine nacelle covers, ailerons, undercarriage doors and wing sections for Lancaster bombers

whatever he could lay his hands on. He was lucky that his flying suit provided some measure of protection from the flames; even so, his parachute was badly burned, and if it ever came to bailing out his predicament would be parlous. To add to his difficulties live ammunition was exploding in all directions inside the fuselage. Notwithstanding all these dangers, Hannah continued to fight the fire. He eventually extinguished the flames and the aircraft was safely brought back to base at RAF Scampton. For his heroic actions John Hannah received the Victoria Cross, becoming at eighteen the youngest RAF recipient of the nation's highest award for bravery. So, from Scampton the Hampden was taken to Tollerton for repairs. This, perhaps, gives some insight into the type of work that might be undertaken at TAS.

As the Hampden was phased out of operational duties, a new contract was entered into with the Air Ministry for work on the new four-engine Lancaster. From late 1942 onwards an ever-increasing number of Lancasters began to arrive at Tollerton after sustaining damage whilst on operational duties. Despite extra staff being employed at the airfield and the addition of the facilities in the Bridge Hangar, Tollerton needed to work at full stretch to meet the demands placed upon it. This work fell into various categories including general maintenance, repairing battle damage, and implementing modifications that Avro introduced for improving the performance of the aircraft. Aircraft that were airworthy were flown into Tollerton; those that were not airworthy arrived in parts on the back of 'Queen Mary' transporters. On arrival, the aviation fuel was drained from the aircraft's tanks: aircraft were not allowed inside hangars with fuel on board. The aircraft would then be taken to the Bridge Hangar where, if necessary, the engines would be removed; then the aircraft might be towed to the Main Hangar for whatever work was necessary.

As the war progressed modifications were made to the Lancaster to improve its performance and make it a more effective weapon; these were a constant feature of work at Tollerton. One of Brian's earliest tasks in the Drawing Office was to compile a chart that kept track of these modifications. He did this in conjunction with Alec Brown, the Chief of Planning, and a well-known planning engineer by the name of Bill Shakespeare. The chart recorded such data as the reference number of the modification, the introducing source (Avro, Bomber Command, TAS, Maintenance Unit, etc.), a brief description of the modification, and, most importantly, the degree of urgency attached to the work.

Tollerton also repaired damaged aircraft, and Brian was involved in this side of things too. Major damage would necessitate replacement parts, but much of the minor damage (often caused by shell fragments, etc.) could be repaired *in situ,* and after a little tutelage from Mr Hassall, Brian was assigned to deal with such matters. Armed with a clipboard, pencil, rule, and measuring tape, he would make a detailed sketch of the damage and then return to his drawing board to devise a repair scheme. The plan had to be submitted to the

Aeronautical Inspection Directorate (AID), who were resident at Tollerton. AID was an independent body responsible for ensuring that all plans that were submitted could be justified on the grounds of cost and necessity. The AID representative at Tollerton Brian had to deal with was a Mr Noble who more often than not signed Brian's drawings as approved.

Sometimes Brian had to walk to the Bridge, Bellman or Club Hangars. (Cycling, which would have been much more convenient, was prohibited in any area where aircraft movements took place.) On warm days this walk could be a pleasant experience, but not so pleasant when the weather was inclement. If he was lucky he might get a lift from one of the transport vehicles that operated at the airfield. One vehicle that Brian particularly looked out for was a small utility truck used to distribute such things as wages, internal mail and spare parts around the site, which was often driven by Mrs Eskell, the attractive wife of the Commercial Manager.

Another vehicle that Brian recalls belonged to an important visiting official from the Ministry of Aircraft Production. Some of the TAS executives whisked this man away for the night, but completely overlooked his driver, who was left to face an uncomfortable night's sleep in the car. However, Brian offered him a bed for the night at his house, and Brian had the luxury of being driven home in

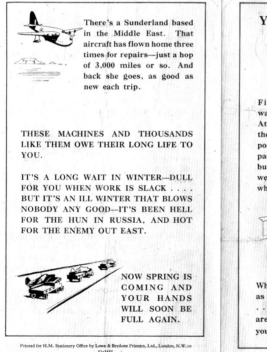

Plate 61:    The cover of a Government leaflet issued to TAS employees to increase output at the airfield. *Brian Hancock's collection*

the official car - a large American Buick convertible. The following day, the driver needed petrol. The nearest authorized fuel supplier was at RAF Hucknall. Rather than try to explain how to get there Brian went with the driver to show him the way. Despite thick fog, no signposts and the blackout, Brian found the way to Hucknall and back, and the Buick had a full tank of petrol.

Brian remembers what it was like to travel during the war on public transport. The buses that operated from Nottingham to Tollerton were double-deckers with a low ceiling designed to pass under low bridges. The Barton Bus Company operated four or five of these on the Tollerton run. On the rare occasions when Brian used the bus he caught it at Trent Bridge. During daylight hours this presented no problems. However, it was a different matter in the dark. To comply with blackout regulations all of the bus's windows, with the exception of those that the driver looked out of, were painted over with thick black or blue paint. This made them impossible to see out of. It wasn't such a problem on Brian's journey as the bus terminated at Tollerton but for other passengers it made life difficult trying to gauge where you were on your journey and making sure that you didn't miss your stop.

Every morning at Tollerton the workers had two separate ten-minute tea

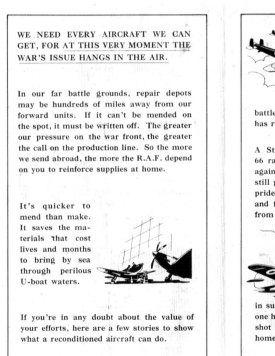

**Plate 62:** **Inside the Government leaflet shown opposite.** From the aircraft depicted the leaflet was probably published quite early in the war.
*Brian Hancock's collection*

breaks, five minutes apart, the start and finish of each signalled by a bell. The company nurse, resplendent in her uniform, was stationed outside the canteen door and as workers made their way into the canteen they were offered a spoonful of yeast extract, intended to make up for the vitamin deficiency that the shortage of fresh fruit could cause in the average diet. Inside the canteen, workers could buy a cup of tea and a bun for a few pence. Those wanting sweetened tea had to queue for their drink, which was poured into their mugs from a large brown enamelled teapot. The unsweetened tea queue poured out the hot liquid themselves, which was much quicker; so Brian decided to forego the luxury of sweetened tea. He soon became accustomed to the unsweetened drink and from that day onwards never had sugar in his tea again.

Brian remembers one incident that relates to the size of the tea mugs. The Progress Chasing Department were champions when it came to owning the largest mugs; but one of them had a mug that was so large it was the envy of his colleagues. So, in the mug-owner's absence, someone drilled a hole through the bottom of the mug and secured it to a shelf. When the time came for the tea break, the owner grabbed the handle and was stunned when all that came away from the shelf was the handle itself!

Another of the Progress Chasers' jokes could have had a serious outcome. Some of them were members of the Home Guard and they kept their uniforms in their offices. One day, while they were fooling around, a bayonet was thrust through one of the compressed cardboard partition walls that divided the offices. Sitting at her desk in the next office was Connie Gladwin, the department's clerk/typist, who only narrowly avoided being impaled. She never reported the incident to Sid Phelan, the Works Manager: had she done so then the perpetrator of the prank would certainly have been subject to severe disciplinary action. As it was, just to be on the safe side, Connie moved her seat to another part of the office.

On a lighter note, another prank that Brian vividly recollects involved Don Eskell, the Commercial Manager. At lunchtime one day Don sat alone at a table in the works canteen to eat his meal. When he finished, he got up and walked out. Immediately, a Progress Chaser sitting at a nearby table also got up and, passing the table where Don had been seated, gave a sly wink to his colleagues. When a canteen assistant arrived to clear away the dirty crockery, a scream rent the air. Before long everyone in the canteen was coming over to investigate the cause of the uproar. The girls covered their eyes and screamed; the men doubled up with laughter. There, in the middle of Don's plate, among the leftovers, sat what looked like a set of dentures. In fact the 'dentures' were half a set of pig's teeth that had been deftly dropped there by the departing Progress Chaser. The Canteen Manageress was livid and wanted to know who was responsible, but no one let on. It took some resourcefulness to get hold of half a set of pig's teeth at a time of acute shortages. Such occasional bits of silliness made a welcome break from the usual routine and helped to lift the spirits of the workers. Also, it was nowhere near as dangerous as fooling around with bayonets!

Another incident that Brian remembers relates to a test flight of a Lancaster bomber. Captain Rogers, the Test Pilot, had taken the Lancaster for its flight test but had aborted the flight immediately after take-off. Following a safe landing, he went over to the personnel responsible for preparing the aircraft and told them that there was something radically wrong with the tail unit. A visual check could not identify any problem but he was adamant that he would not fly the aircraft until a new tail unit had been fitted. The aircraft was taken to the Bridge Hangar and the new tail unit was soon fitted, along with the rear turret, flying controls and electrical systems. It was then necessary to ensure that all the flying controls, elevators, rudders, etc., worked satisfactorily. Settings of the flaps and the undercarriage mechanism were checked and then the fuel jettison valve was checked with startling results: to an accompaniment of a large whooshing noise, gallons and gallons of aviation fuel gushed onto the hangar floor. It was a golden rule that all fuel had to be removed from an aircraft before it is allowed into the hangars, but in the haste to get the job done this had been overlooked. The fuel from the aborted test flight was washed away; any which remained simply evaporated. However, as a safety precaution a no-smoking ban was enforced in the hangar for a week afterwards. It is interesting to note that, whilst it is now illegal to smoke in the workplace, then it was common practice!

While Brian's work did not bring him into contact with the Polish airmen at Tollerton, he did on one occasion persuade one of the Polish instructors there to take him on an unauthorized pleasure flight in one of the Harvard trainers that the Polish airmen were then using at Tollerton. Similar attempts to get a flight aboard one of the Lancasters were, however, fruitless. That was a disappointment, though Brian could console himself with the knowledge that he had actually flown in one of the famous aircraft before one had ever been seen at Tollerton. That memorable occasion occurred in May or June of 1942. Brian was a member of the Air Training Corps (ATC) visiting RAF Syerston. RAF Syerston was an operational Bomber Command airfield and the willing ATC lads were quickly put to work helping the station ground crew. As a reward for their efforts each of them was given a flight on one of the Lancasters' air-tests. Brian stood behind the pilot and flight engineer in the cockpit and had a spectacular view of the surrounding countryside as it flashed past beneath them. Sadly, the flight was over all too soon but it was nevertheless a memorable experience.

Later that same day, after the ATC lads had gone to bed, there was more excitement. Brian had just fallen asleep when an RAF officer woke all the ATC lads and told them to put their coats on over their pyjamas and go outside. Once outside they climbed aboard a Queen Mary articulated trailer which the officer drove around the airfield perimeter to the far end of the main runway. From this vantage point they watched the heavily laden Lancaster bombers of 61

Squadron take off on their operational sortie. The roar of Merlin engines filled the night air. The officer then told them that they were watching history in the making, but would say no more. Later, they learned that those Lancasters were heading for Cologne to take part in the first 1,000-bomber raid of the war. It was the night of 30/31 May 1942. Brian had been a witness to a significant milestone in the history of Bomber Command.

On many occasions when Brian was walking around the perimeter track at Tollerton he would see a Lancaster touch down and taxi round to a vacant dispersal point. The engines would stop and, a few minutes later, a pilot dressed in the dark blue uniform of the Air Transport Auxiliary (ATA) would climb out. The pilot could be a petite young blonde or a bearded old man and, Brian says, he never ceased to marvel that they had flown such a large, powerful machine and found their way to Tollerton single-handed. Sadly, however, as was explained in the section relating to the ATA on page 149, in spite of Brian's fond reminiscences, tales of huge Lancasters being flown by a lone pilot are, unfortunately, not founded on fact even though it was widely believed to be true.

By the time that the war drew to its conclusion around one thousand Lancaster bombers had been assembled and repaired at Tollerton. Brian was extremely proud to have been part of the team involved in this major contribution to Britain's war effort and looks back on his time spent at the airfield with pride.

## The Contribution of Women to the War Effort

Barbara Pearson was sixteen years of age when war broke out in 1939. At that time she was living on Shakespeare Street in Nottingham, and working as a shop assistant at Pearson Brothers, a large department store in the centre of the city. She was required to work six days a week, finishing at 9 p.m. on Saturdays, and for that was paid the princely sum of twelve shillings per week.

In 1941, at the age of eighteen, she and a friend decided to join the Land Army in order that they might make a more positive contribution to the war effort. Barbara's friend was accepted but Barbara, who had previously suffered severe bouts of bronchitis, was rejected as being unfit for the work. Undeterred, she went to the Labour Exchange, which suggested that she might like to apply for a job at Tollerton Airfield. It is interesting to note that even though Tollerton is only about four miles from Nottingham, Barbara had never heard of the place and consequently had no idea where it was!

She was successful in her application, and in 1941 commenced employment with Field Aircraft Services as an aircraft cleaner. The hours were 8 a.m. until 6 p.m. during the week, and 8 a.m. to midday on Saturdays. For this she was paid twelve shillings and sixpence a week. The working day began on Huntingdon Street in Nottingham at 7.30 a.m. when a Barton's bus would pick up the workers and take them to the airfield, picking up other workers along its route. Barbara remembers other girls who worked at the airfield travelling on the bus in their hair curlers, without make-up, and with packs of sandwiches for their lunch.

There were no security arrangements in place at the entrance to Main Hangar where Barbara worked - no security guards, no passes, no identification checks, nothing; you simply got off the bus and walked into the hangar. The first thing all the girls did was to disappear into the toilet, put on their boiler suits, take out their hair curlers, comb their hair, and put on their make-up. The transformation was astonishing: all of a sudden everyone looked glamorous. War was no excuse for letting personal standards drop, particularly with so many male workers to impress!

The aircraft cleaners normally worked in pairs, one male and one female. The partnership changed every day, so that there was no danger of anyone getting on too friendly terms with a member of the opposite sex. The woman's job was to clean inside the aircraft while the man did any repair jobs that he could manage without assistance. When they had finished these tasks, the fitters took over to complete whatever major repairs were necessary.

Barbara remembers that when she arrived at work each morning the aircraft were ready to be worked on in the Main Hangar and were moved out after she had gone home. She never saw planes arrive or leave; her impression was that they were brought in and flown out at night[1]. The workforce in the Main Hangar were all civilians and Barbara cannot recall seeing anyone wearing a military uniform all the time she was employed on the airfield.

The working parties were not issued with any protective clothing apart from a boiler suit, and, if the job was a particularly messy one, a pair of heavy rubber gloves. The first job on the damaged aircraft for the female cleaners was to sweep out any rubbish and broken glass or Perspex. It was a horrible job: there was often blood, urine, vomit and worse inside the aircraft. Once the dry rubbish had been cleared out it was a case of getting on hands and knees and scrubbing everything down with soap and water. The upholstery in the aircraft was cleaned with a special liquid that gave off highly noxious fumes. It was the same liquid that was used to fill fire extinguishers, and inhaling the fumes in such an enclosed space made you feel giddy. No protective masks were issued, so when the fumes became too strong you had to go outside for fresh air until you felt better. On those occasions when the cleaning liquid ran out, the nearest fire extinguisher was used instead, and this removed dirt and grease from both the aircraft and the hands and clothes.

The work was hard and there weren't many breaks. They ate their lunchtime sandwiches in the hangar if the weather was poor, or outside on the grass if it

---

[1] This is probably because after work had been completed in the Main Hangar aircraft were taken to Bridge Hangar for final checks before test-flying and eventual dispatch by the Air Transport Auxiliary. All ferrying duties by the ATA were done during daylight hours so there must have been a constant stream of aircraft flying into and out of Tollerton during the day. Aircraft brought in by road on the 'Queen Mary' transporters could have been delivered at night.

was pleasant. On particularly nice days the men might engage in a game of cricket. There was a canteen where you could get a hot meal but not many people used it. Barbara cannot remember any social activities outside normal working hours.

At the end of the working day, Barton's buses would be waiting outside the airfield to take the workers back to Nottingham. Barbara remembers one memorable journey home that occurred during a fog. On this particular day the fog was exceptionally thick and by 8 p.m. the bus had still not appeared. Barbara had no idea where Tollerton was in relation to her home in Nottingham but a male colleague offered to walk with her and show her the way. With the aid of a small torch (with tape across the lens to comply with the black-out regulations) they set off towards Nottingham. Barbara has no idea where they walked, and no recollection of crossing the River Trent. However, just after 10 p.m. she found herself arriving home where a very anxious mother was relieved to see her!

After eighteen months Barbara decided on another change of job and went to work at a garage in Nottingham that repaired and maintained army lorries. Thus ended her short association with Tollerton. The work that Barbara undertook at the airfield was often unpleasant, poorly paid, involved considerable travelling time and long working hours, was physically demanding, and for the most part was unappreciated. It was nevertheless another, albeit small, contribution to the war effort - a typical example of how everyone was expected to 'do their bit'. Such people as Barbara might not have been hailed as heroes, but 'they also served who cleaned the muck out of aeroplanes'!

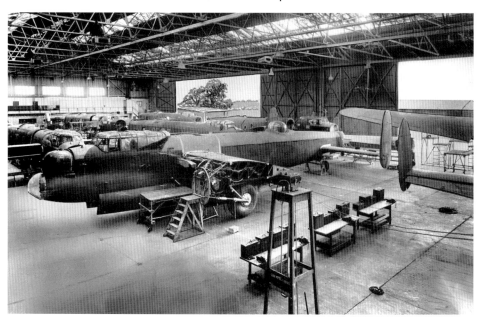

**Plate 63: Partially assembled Lancasters inside the Main Hangar.** *Keith Hodgett*

Bernice Squires and Betty Shelton began working at Tollerton in 1943 and continued there until the facility closed in 1945. Both had wanted to join the armed forces but their families had dissuaded them, probably because they were only seventeen years of age at the time. However they were both keen 'to do their bit' and, after applying to do war work, were recruited by the Labour Exchange to work at Tollerton.

Bernice lived in Burford Road, Forest Fields, and Betty in Gordon Road, Carlton. Their only means of getting to Tollerton lay with public transport and this involved catching a Nottingham Transport tram to Huntingdon Street. For this they used to buy a return ticket that cost 2d. From Huntingdon Street the special bus provided by Barton's Buses to take them to Tollerton cost them another 4d return. Working a six-day week, this involved spending three shillings a week to get to and from work - a substantial proportion of their weekly wage. They both left home at 7 a.m. to ensure that they arrived at Tollerton in time for the start of their shift at 8 o'clock.

Once at Tollerton they went directly to the Bridge Hangar where their duties lay. There was no security at the entrance to the site whatsoever: not only was there no one on guard-duty at the entrance there weren't even any actual gates to guard. They both simply walked from the bus drop-off point to their place of work. Their foreman, Mr Swingler, would check them in and allocate the girls their duties for the day. They were then expected to get on with their work. At various times he would wander round to keep an eye on things and check on their progress. The end of their working day was, on alternate days, either 6 or 7 p.m. They were both also required to work every other Saturday morning. For this they were paid £2.3s.11d. However wartime taxation was high and from this they were deducted 13s in income tax. After taking account of the 3s they paid for transport they were left with £1.7s.11d to live on. They were also expected to provide their own work clothes - using their own clothing coupons.

Their work was mainly on Douglas Dakota aircraft, though they worked on Avro Lancasters as well. Bernice did a variety of jobs, typically riveting or spraying panels or making Tufnel pieces (plastic-like pieces of material used to repair panels on aircraft). Betty worked as a riveter, replacing damaged sections of aircraft. The workforce in Bridge Hangar was divided into independent units. Neither Betty nor Bernice had any idea who else worked on the site or what their jobs were. Neither did they have contact with local people: at the end of their shift they simply caught the first bus back to Nottingham. The only variation to this routine occurred when Bernice worked Saturday mornings, when, on her way home, she would get off the bus at Trent Bridge, pop into The Trent Bridge Inn and treat herself to a drink.

Facilities for the workforce at the Bridge Hangar were poor. Unlike the Main Hangar there were no canteen facilities: you provided your own sandwiches and drinks and consumed them where you could. As far as Betty and Bernice could remember there wasn't even a first-aid post. Men and women worked alongside each other though the women were not expected to do any of the heavy manual tasks. Health and safety regulations were rudimentary. When Bernice was spraying panels with oil or paint, for example, the chemicals could cause giddiness and nausea; to counter this she was given pieces of dried yeast, which she was to place in her mouth where, supposedly, it would cure the effects of the chemicals. Bernice used to eat hers!

When the aircraft that Betty and Bernice worked on were ready for service they were filled with aviation fuel. Often the drivers of the petrol-bowsers that were used to fuel the aircraft were Polish servicemen stationed on the military side of the airfield. It was one of these Polish servicemen that Betty met, fell in love with, and married.

The example of Betty and Bernice is typical of the minor, but vital, role that ordinary civilian workers at Tollerton contributed to the war effort.

*

When war broke out in 1939 Edith Lyons lived at Aspley, Nottingham, and was still at school. Her parents favoured teaching as her future career; but for Edith

Plate 64:   'The Führer takes over command.' A leaflet found inside one of the aircraft at TAS Tollerton. Bomber Command devoted a considerable amount of time and effort in dropping these propaganda leaflets on German towns and cities early in the war, risking the lives of many aircrew in the process. The Germans engaged in similar activities early in the war. The British found them very useful as firelighters and toilet tissue. One suspects that the Germans put theirs to a similar use! *Brian Hancock's collection*

the prospect of a life in teaching seemed dull and boring, and at eighteen she decided to pursue a different direction. A visit to the local Labour Exchange revealed that there were vacancies on the airfield at Tollerton. The job sounded interesting and so she applied for an interview, which led to a post with Tollerton Air Services.

So it was that in August 1941 Edith made her first journey from Aspley to begin work at Tollerton airfield. Edith's first job, in a ground-floor office attached to the front of the Main hangar, involved keeping records of the various components used on the Hampden bombers that TAS were then repairing. Edith particularly remembers a girl in the office named Mary Simpson: she had a chemist friend in West Bridgford who was adept at making cosmetics to his own formulae - a real boon when such things as lipstick and face powder were becoming hard to obtain. Another of Edith's duties entailed walking to the other hangars each day to see how work on the Hampdens was progressing. Should more parts be required, then Edith would get that organized.

By the time Edith began work at TAS in November 1941 the airfield was a hive of activity. Repair work on the Hampden bombers had ensured that the workforce at TAS had burgeoned. By the autumn of 1941 the concrete runways had been laid down and there was a massive expansion of the on-site facilities for the military side of the airfield, although the number of military personnel on site was still relatively small.

Dieser Brief wurde bei einem deutschen Soldaten in Russland gefunden. Die Schreiberin hat bereits am 7. September gewusst, was ihr Mann in Russland brauchen werde. Aber Hitler, der „alles von vornherein einkalkuliert hat", kam erst 3½ Monate später darauf. Am 21. Dezember erfuhr das deutsche Volk, dass es seine Woll- und Pelzsachen abgeben müsse, um Hitlers Versäumnis gutzumachen.

## DAS VERDANKT IHR EUREM FÜHRER!

Plate 65: **'So you are indebted to your Führer'.** The leaflet mocks Hitler's failure to supply the German Army with adequate warm clothing to combat the severe winter weather in the Soviet Union. *Nigel Morley*

In 1942 TAS opened a new Parts Department on Daleside Road, Colwick, Nottingham. Edith was sent there for about a month to help set up the records section. When she returned to Tollerton it was not to work in the offices attached to the Main Hangar but to the Club Hangar instead. At that time the Club Hangar was being used to repair and assemble instrument panels for the Hampden bombers. Edith was still engaged in record-keeping but the team she worked with now was very much smaller. Her new supervisor was Eric Garlah-Watkins, whom Edith, like Brian Hancock mentioned earlier, found to be exceptionally polite and a perfect gentleman. He was a pleasure to work with, as was Edith's other colleague, a middle-aged lady called Pat Bushnell who lived locally at Tollerton. Pat and Edith were responsible for ensuring that every pack of instruments allocated to a Hampden contained all the essential 37 or 38 separate items. Each of the instruments in the panel was checked in the Club Hangar before it was fitted. Any that proved to be defective would be repaired in the hangar workshops if that were possible. If it was impossible to mend an instrument, an expert from Brush at Loughborough might be sent for to try to sort out the problem. Pat and Edith were lucky in that they enjoyed a large degree of autonomy in their work. They were detailed tasks to undertake and then left to do the work in the best way that they saw fit.

Edith remembers seeing Queen Mary articulated lorries bringing in by road those Hampdens which could not be flown into the airfield. One lorry driver in particular, whose journeys to pick up damaged aircraft took him as far afield as Leuchars in Scotland and down to Devon and Cornwall, was a most obliging character: if anyone needed to travel to where he was going, he was more than happy to give him or her a lift - a real bonus given that wartime public transport could be slow and overcrowded.

Edith remembers with pleasure the social side of life at TAS. Invitations to attend socials, dances and parties were frequent and usually came in the form of a visitor to the office asking if any of the girls fancied going to such-and-such a do. Socials were always being organized locally, often on the airfield but also in Tollerton, Plumtree, Keyworth or further afield. At these events there never seemed to be a shortage of drink, but food was usually in limited supply. Edith particularly remembers the Christmas parties held at The Griffin at Plumtree. All those going piled into several cars and headed for the pub; once the festivities were over they were taken home in the same cars. Where the petrol came from was never questioned; but given that petrol was stringently rationed it is a fair guess that gallons of aviation fuel must have found their way into the tanks of some of the cars! Also the attitude to drink-driving was very different then.

One Saturday, Stan Ashmore, one of the lads at TAS and a Bristol University graduate, asked Edith if she fancied popping into 'the TBI' on their way home from work. She accepted without having any idea what the TBI was! It turned out to be The Trent Bridge Inn, a pub near Trent Bridge cricket ground in West

Bridgford. The date was August 6th, and it was the first time that Edith, just 18 years old, had ever been in a public house. She was surprised to see six or seven other TAS employees from the offices there as well: it was evidently a popular dropping-in place after a hard week at work!

Edith's working day was usually from 9 a.m. to 5.30 p.m., but she could always work overtime. Then she might begin at eight and work until whatever time was required. She recalls with particular pleasure working on a Sunday. On Sundays the office canteen was closed, so the works canteen had to be used instead. There, for a penny or so a slice, you could get toast with pork or beef dripping - a real treat!

It was expected that all TAS employees would volunteer either as a firewatcher or a first-aider. Edith elected to be involved in first aid. At that time TAS had a full-time nurse on site. Edith remembers that one of the benefits available was that you could go and see the nurse each day and have a spoonful of yeast to eat in the belief that it had beneficial health properties. Edith also vividly recollects visiting the Bellman Hangar and being stunned by the overpowering smell of the aircraft dope that was being applied to the canvas fabric skin of aircraft. Before the advent of stressed metal skins on aircraft it was common practice for the outer surfaces of an aircraft to be covered in fabric material which helped to keep the weight of the aircraft down, an important factor in the days when engines were not very powerful. However, this material covering needed to be weatherproof and a plasticised lacquer known as dope was painted or sprayed onto the covering to tauten, stretch and weatherproof the material. This dope was highly inflammable and gave off very heavy fumes whilst it was drying out. Those employees who were engaged in applying the dope were entitled to an extra ration of milk in the belief that it ameliorated the adverse effects of the chemical. One suspects that some of the

**Plate 66:** **A Lancaster bomber in front of the Bridge Hangar.** *The Hunting Group*

workers must have been 'as high as a kite' from the effects of the fumes in the hangar.

Amongst the incidents that Edith remembers was the accident in which Leading Aircraftman Forrester was killed while driving a tractor when the propeller of a taxiing aircraft struck him. That occurred on 26 August 1942 and word of the incident seems to have spread rapidly around the workforce. Bad news has a habit of travelling fast.

In 1944 a new section was being opened in the Bridge Hangar. The Office Manager, Mr Ashnall, initially asked Edith to set it up and then take charge of it. Subsequently, however, he changed his mind and gave the job to her friend Pat Bushnell. This was the only occasion in Edith's time at Tollerton that gave rise to unpleasantness. Edith was not pleased, assuming that her relative inexperience and a lack of years had counted against her, and she decided to leave TAS to seek employment elsewhere. She later discovered via Mr Ashnall's secretary, Mrs Harrison, that he had given the job to Pat Bushnell because he thought it would be unfair to put Edith, at such a tender age, in an office where she would be the only female.

During those wartime years it was not possible to leave your job simply because you wanted to: permission had to be sought from The Ministry of Employment. A 'man from the ministry' was duly sent to see Edith and, on being told that she wanted to join the 'Wrens' (the Women's Royal Naval Service) or something like that, permission was granted to leave TAS.

However, a little over a week later, in May 1944, Edith was involved in a serious car accident while travelling from Grantham. She sustained a broken pelvis and as a result was off work for over a year. By the time she was fit to return, the war in Europe had ended and with it the contract that TAS had with the CRO. Most of the workforce at TAS had been disbanded and Edith's job no longer existed: consequently her association with Tollerton airfield came to an end.

*

A common comment made by people interviewed for this book who worked at Tollerton - and Edith is no exception - was how little they each knew about what others employed at the airfield did. There was little or no fraternizing with people from other departments; you did your own job and left others to get on with theirs. Maintaining security never seems to have posed problems. There may not have been guards on the entrance gates, nor regular patrols around the airfield; but the self-imposed security amongst the workforce itself seems to have been tight. After all, there was a war on, and slogans such as 'Careless Talk Costs Lives', 'Keep Mum, She's Not So Dumb', and 'Walls Have Ears' could be seen on propaganda posters everywhere.

All of the people previously mentioned in this chapter were very conscious of the heavy responsibilities that the war placed on them. At times, particularly early in the war when Great Britain and her Empire stood alone against the might of Nazi Germany, the task in front of them must have seemed Herculean indeed. However, in keeping with the rest of the population they rose magnificently to the challenge. When Winston Churchill pleaded to the USA 'to give us the tools and we'll finish the job' he could equally have said to the employees at TAS, 'here are the tools, now do the job'.

For their part the workforce at Tollerton did sterling work during the years 1939 to 1945. It has proved impossible to obtain any definitive figures for TAS production but it is believed that contracts involving approximately 1,700 aircraft and 2,000 components were completed for the Ministry of Aircraft Production. That must surely be considered a valuable and significant contribution to the war effort.

# PART III: POST-WAR – 1945 to 2007

## Chapter 10

# Adjusting to Peacetime

For most of the first twelve years after the war (1945 to 1957), Tollerton Airfield was largely given over to the same two organizations that used it during the war: the Royal Air Force and Field Aircraft Services. They are dealt with in this chapter. In addition there was some commercial flying, while the pre-war Nottingham Flying Club made a brief reappearance. These are considered in chapters 11 and 14 respectively.

## The Royal Air Force

The end of the war did not signal the immediate end of military involvement with Tollerton airfield. Wartime training of Polish pilots based at RAF Newton continued for a few months after the end of the war but finished early in 1946. Tollerton's relationship with Newton during this period was that of a satellite or relief landing ground under the command of the Commanding Officer of RAF Newton. In 1946 the airfield was turned over to civilian use, only to be returned to military use in 1949, when Tollerton became a relief landing ground for No 22 Flying Training Squadron at RAF Syerston, under the command of that station's commander, engaged in the initial training of pilots for the Fleet Air Arm. This continued until 1956, when Syerston's relief landing ground requirements were transferred to RAF Wymeswold.

Throughout the period 1945 to 1957 Field Aircraft Services (alternatively known during the war as Tollerton Aircraft Services), a civilian business which worked on aircraft brought from all over the country and some from abroad, continued its wartime occupation of nearly all the buildings on the airfield which had been erected before and during the war, including three of the four hangars. The fourth, the Club Hangar, which had been used by the Nottingham Flying Club (which was moribund after 1949), was still used by nominal or former Club members, by private aircraft owners, and by T.Shipside, who serviced their planes. When the RAF returned in 1949 it hangared its planes at Syerston and had little need to use other Tollerton buildings. Civilians and military occupied different parts of the airfield, worked amicably as neighbours but had very little to do with each other. There was, however, some sharing of facilities, such as the provision by Fields of fire and crash services for all RAF flying, with the RAF providing the necessary vehicles. Nevertheless, there appears to have been some confusion regarding the rights and responsibilities of the military and civilian tenants of the airfield.

This led to a meeting of representatives of the RAF, Air Ministry and Civil Aviation Authority in January 1952, at which the RAF spelled out its requirements, which were:

1. Unrestricted use of the airfield whenever required - normally on weekdays, but excepting three periods of two weeks each year when No. 22 Flying Training Squadron stood down;
2. The RAF to control all flying during periods when the airfield was being used as a relief landing ground;
3. Authority to limit flying as may be considered desirable in the interests of safety, to be vested on the Officer Commanding RAF Syerston;
4. Facilities for housing an Air Traffic Control caravan and tractor and for providing a rest room for ground crew. (It was assumed that aircrew would not normally get out of their aircraft at Tollerton but just use it for landing and take-off practice.)

One implication of these requirements was that civilian flying would be severely restricted, which was no doubt a reason why Nottingham Flying Club suspended its activity (as we shall see in Chapter 14). Even test flights by Fields of aircraft they had converted had to fit in with RAF schedules, as did recreational flying by private aircraft owners. On the other hand, if these flights took place while the RAF was also present, they could take advantage of RAF Air Traffic Control cover.

**Plate 67: Fire and Emergency vehicles outside the Bellman Hangar** *Arthur Cronk*

All RAF flying instructors, ground crew and pupils were housed at Syerston, some of whom flew to Tollerton when Syerston became congested. The instructors and ground crew were all RAF personnel; the pupils naval midshipmen - presumably destined to fly off Royal Navy aircraft carriers as well as shore bases. The aircraft used for instruction were initially Tiger Moths and Prentices. Perhaps to prepare pupils for more difficult landing and take-off on carrier decks, they were required to use grass rather than the concrete runways. Terence Lucas, who was a radio mechanic (one of the RAF ground crew) in the early 1950s, has given an account of what went on:

We used the grass airfield at Tollerton for (1) use by the first year student pilots for circuits and bumps [repeatedly circling the airfield, landing and immediately taking off again] and (2) when they progressed further the pilots were, as part of their training in the cross-country element of the course, invited to touch down at Tollerton. … I think we fired more red flares at Tollerton than anywhere else, when we saw that they had not yet got their wheels down. [This must relate to aircraft other than the Tiger Moths and Prentices on which training began, because both of these had fixed undercarriages.]

Tollerton was used quite frequently for circuit and bump 'rides' by most of the Instructors and pupil pilots alike - I estimate we had as many as six to eight touch-downs per hour some days whilst the following day that could be halved. We were there on average five weekdays per week but not usually at weekends. There were exceptions of course: I can remember one period in the early winter of 1951 when, due to fog on site, we lost around 1000 hours of flying, so we flew non-stop for eight days and nights to catch up with the flying schedule. One must remember that our initial training schedule was inter-linked with those that were to follow when our pilots passed out and went on to Scotland to convert to jets, so it was very important to keep within the overall programme. All this was against a background of the Korean bust-up and our involvement there [referring to the Korean War, 1950 to 1953, with China and the USSR backing the North and the USA and UK backing the South].

Fog was always a problem in the winter as the field was near the Trent and this caused trouble at the drop of a hat, it could close us down in a matter of minutes, not a good thing when many of those aloft were pupil pilots! We often wondered why the RAF chose to put a training school in such a vulnerable position. [In fact, Tollerton had a marginal advantage over Syerston - and Newton, which was also used by No. 22 Flying Training School - in respect of fog, in that it was further from the Trent than either].

One further point: just before the pilots went off to further training in Scotland the C.O. got someone to mark off the length of a carrier deck space on the Syerston runway and then got the lads to land on it as though they were trying to hook on to an arrester wire. He even had a go himself just to show them that it could be done with safety … he was a man who led from the front. [We do not know if he did the same at Tollerton].

# Field Aircraft Services

During the war, as we saw in Chapter 8, the most important work done at Tollerton was the assembly, repair, maintenance and modification of aircraft – particularly the patching up of damaged bombers returning from missions over Germany. The prime organisation involved in this work was Field Consolidated Aircraft Services, which also went under the name of Tollerton Aircraft Services. When the war ended Fields changed almost overnight from construction to destruction: the dismantling and break-up of bombers for scrap. This had happened before, in 1942, when Hampdens were scrapped and replaced by Lancasters (see page 138). Now it was the turn of Lancasters. A substantial workforce was still required, but one former employee (Cyril King) estimates that it nevertheless fell from about 750 in May 1945 (VE Day was 8 May) to around 150 by December of that year.[1]

For about a year, Tollerton specialised in the break-up of Lancasters. These workhorses of Bomber Command during the latter part of the war flew in or were brought in by Queen Mary lorry (see Plate 54, page 146) to be dismantled. For much of that year they covered the perimeter track nose to tail, waiting their turn to be taken apart in one of the hangars. Little was recycled: there was limited demand for the alloy of which their bodies were made (known as duralumin) and unless the engines were as good as new they were too expensive in labour costs to recondition or cannibalise for further use[2]. Even minor items like first aid kits and navigators' tabletops were destined for the scrap heap unless they were purloined by workers - if they had not already been removed by RAF personnel flying the aircraft in.

Within the year several hundred Lancasters had been thus dismantled, until work came to an end. Fields did not, however, abandon Tollerton. It changed its name by dropping 'Consolidated', becoming simply Field Aircraft Services; and it looked for alternative work.

After the war there was a surfeit of military and a shortage of civilian aircraft; so the company turned to adapting some of the military aircraft - particularly troop carriers and air freighters that were more amenable to adaptation - to civilian use. In addition it continued to repair and overhaul planes to maintain their airworthiness. Its work was very largely concerned with

---

[1] It has not been possible to pinpoint exactly when the change-over from repair to break-up occurred – whether it was VE Day, VJ Day (14 August 1945), sometime between those dates, or even later than VJ Day. A table on page 144 showing test flights of repaired or modified Lancasters undertaken by Fields' test pilot Walter Rogers from April 1944 dates the last such flight as 4 January 1946, implying that constructive work on the planes continued at least until the latter date. Also, in the table's 'Comments' column, no Lancasters are shown as having been scrapped before 1946. If the table refers only to flights by Rogers from Tollerton, the change-over did not occur before January 1946. But neither constructive work nor break-ups by Fields took place exclusively at Tollerton.

[2] New Duralumin was used in pre-fabricated housing, for which there was a great demand in post-war years, but it was of no use 'second-hand'.

machines brought in from elsewhere, however; Tollerton's own small number of planes, mostly light and privately owned, were maintained 'in-house' by T. Shipside using the Club Hangar.

Initially orders were slow to come in and involved small planes like the Percival Proctor - the Percival Company was, like Fields, part of the Hunting Group. When Derrick Brooks joined Fields in 1946 the total workforce was down to perhaps twenty. He has described it as 'small, cliquey and good'. At that stage, all the work took place in the Main Hangar; the Bridge Hangar was used only as a store and the Bellman was not used at all[3]. The canteen, which had operated while Fields was employing hundreds, closed, and there were no organized social activities on site.

One particular order recalled by Derrick came from a Mrs Morrow-Tait, a newly qualified pilot whose heart was set on making a round-the-world flight. It involved increasing the range of a Proctor by replacing the back seats with extra fuel tanks taken from a Rapide. When the conversion was complete she christened the plane 'Thursday's Child'. The name implied it had 'far to go', but sadly it did not go far enough: it crashed in Alaska.

After this slow start, work began to expand. Conversions were supplemented by overhaul, repair and servicing, which included cleaning and maintenance work on Dakotas which carried coal during the Berlin Airlift of 1948/9 (dealt with further on page 196). Many of the conversions were for export; the very first Dakota (much larger than a Proctor) went to India. In 1949 a big order came from BEA for converting a batch of twenty military Dakotas for civilian use, into what were called 'Pionairs'; thereafter contracts mostly involved larger planes, though these were small by today's standards.

An article in *Flight* (21 April 1949) describes in some detail the work involved in both overhaul and conversion, with particular reference to Dakotas.

An inventory is made of the equipment received with the aircraft. ... The aircraft is then stripped: wings, cowlings and fairings are taken off, control surfaces [flaps, tailplane, etc.] removed and undercarriage and tail wheel dismantled. Fuel and oil tanks and coolers are removed, together with the hydraulic tank and reservoir, de-icer tanks and autopilot servo unit. All radio sets and similar equipment is taken out, together with all instruments, seats, flooring throughout the fuselage. ... Inspection is carried out and a report prepared calling for all replacements and repairs necessary to comply with ARB [Air Registration Board] requirements. ... In general an aircraft will be given to a gang of men, although specialised trades, such as instruments, radio and electrical are catered for by trade gangs ... [who] deal with all aircraft needing attention.

---

[3] The term 'Bellman' refers to a type of hangar. Both the Bridge and Bellman Hangars were of this type and were similar, but one was called the Bridge Hangar to distinguish it from the other; it was located near a small bridge across the Grantham Canal.

At the time the article was written Fields at Tollerton employed about 150 personnel, who had 'over the last two years' converted about 20 ex-Service Dakotas and overhauled a further six for renewal of their Certificate of Airworthiness (C-of-A), a requirement of the Air Registration Board. Each conversion took about six to eight weeks and an overhaul about four weeks. The aircraft were then rigorously flight tested, involving 'not less than three flights covering in all a period of five hours'.

Dakotas were not the only machines Fields worked on. To quote from the same article, which was based on a visit from a team of *Flight* staff, 'at the time of our visit, four ex-BEA Vikings were undergoing modification and C-of-A renewal. ... A good deal of work is also concerned with C-of-As for the smaller aircraft types, ranging from Rapides down to Proctors.'

**Plate 68:    A Douglas Dakota or C47 at Tollerton.**  *Arthur Cronk*

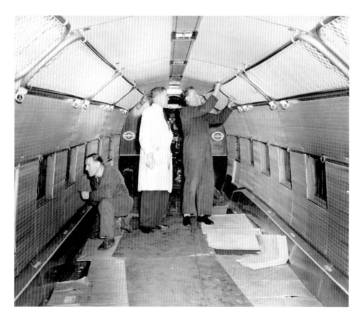

**Plate 69: Refurbishing a Dakota's Interior to become a Pionair**
Seating would be among the last items installed. The fuselage could take eight or nine rows of double seats on either side of a central aisle – about a tenth the capacity of a modern Boeing 747 Jumbo Jet.
*Arthur Cronk*

182

Orders and therefore employment increased rapidly during the following year, with the workforce reaching 500 by 1950. One of those workers was Jeff Redshaw, who started work with Fields as an apprentice aircraft fitter in 1949 on the conversion of Dakotas. Before undertaking precision work he was introduced to more basic operations, as he recalls:

My job as an apprentice was to empty the fuel from each aircraft as it arrived; it could not be taken into the hangar with any fuel in the tanks. ... The plane was left some distance from the hangar and I approached it armed with a bucket and a very high pair of stepladders. I would set up the steps under the wing, climb precariously to the very top and was just able to reach the fuel tap. With a bucket in one hand I would endeavour to release the fuel from the tap while getting my arm away before it cascaded. Of course I never did. When the bucket was as heavy as I could manage to keep steady I would turn off the tap, once again getting aviation fuel down my sleeve, and climb down the steps.

In 1953, Fields won a contract to refurbish a hundred Dakotas for the United States Air Force - in fact to update them for further military use. When these were completed an order for the refurbishment of another hundred was received and for the next few years, Fields carried out this work under American Air Force supervision.

Many of the aircraft to be refurbished or converted were able to fly in - Dakotas for the US contract were flown in from, and returned to, RAF Silloth in Cumbria. Those that were not airworthy were brought in by road, as during the war: the fuselage and wings lying alongside each other on 60 feet-long trailers (almost the length of a cricket pitch) called 'Queen Marys'; other components arriving separately in smaller vehicles. After work was complete, every aircraft had to be test-flown before leaving Tollerton. The test pilot was Freddie Cronk, a former RAF pilot who had been chief pilot and co-founder of Trent Valley Aviation and had also revived the social arm of the Nottingham Flying Club under the new name of the Eagle Flying Club (see page 247).

Rex Morris, who worked for Fields from 1953 and was, with Len Henson, the last Fields employee to leave Tollerton in the 1960s, has given a detailed account of its activities from the mid-fifties until the firm moved to Wymeswold, including the use to which each of the buildings was then being put, as shown in Figure 9 on page 184.

A glance at that map shows that there were then many more buildings on the site than are there today, mostly erected during the war and the majority at that time still in use. With the exception of the Club Hangar and Clubhouse, all those in use were now occupied by Fields, which was also using a building not on the map - the Bridge Hangar, on the northern periphery of the 1950s airfield. The site of the Bridge Hangar is now occupied by a group of mobile homes called Tollerton Park, just beyond the present airfield boundary.

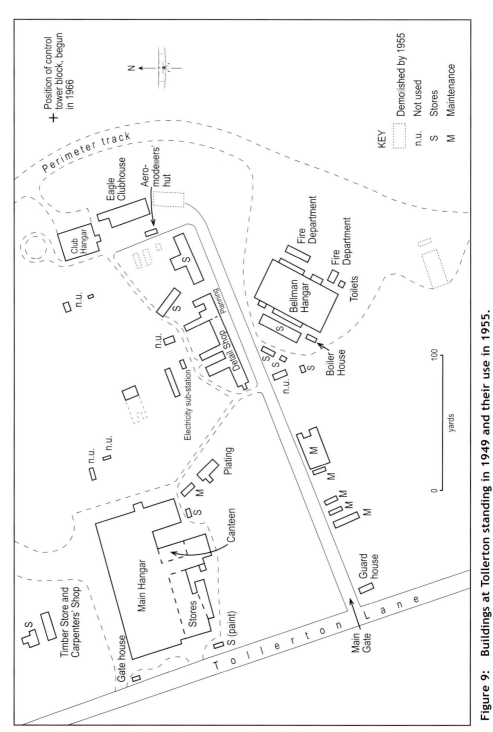

**Figure 9: Buildings at Tollerton standing in 1949 and their use in 1955.** *Dr Anne Tarver & Rex Morris*
The Bridge Hangar is off the map near the airfield's northern boundary.

From occupying only one hangar in the late forties, within a few years Fields was using three, as it had during the war: the Bridge, where the American contract to refurbish Dakotas for the USAF was carried out; the Main, where most of the conversion work on main frames for British and overseas civilian airlines took place; and the Bellman, where parts such as ailerons and wing flaps were serviced or made for both Fields and for other aircraft manufacturing and maintenance companies working elsewhere. Another job carried out in the Bellman was the cleaning of fuel tanks, which tended to corrode where small residues collected; they had to be cut open, thoroughly cleaned out and re-welded. Engines and instruments were not serviced at Tollerton; they were dealt with by Fields' other two bases at Croydon and Bovingdon respectively.

Each hangar had its own storerooms but other, smaller buildings were also used for more specialist stores. The fourth hangar on site, the Club Hangar, continued to hold and service Tollerton's own resident aircraft. Unlike the others, it was built well before the war, was owned by Shipsides and operated quite independently of Fields.

The Main Hangar was bigger than the others and could house several large aircraft being worked on simultaneously. A great variety of contracts were carried out under its roof, including conversion or refurbishment of Dakotas, Vikings, Viscounts, Ambassadors, Prentices, Princes, Rapides, Marathons, DC 4s and Lincolns. Some were for fleets like BEA, others for individuals. Two of the Vikings were converted for use in the Queen's Flight. In addition, a Tollerton

**Plate 70:** **Inside the Main Hangar c.1950.** Aircraft being serviced: two Dakotas (monoplanes), a Rapide (large biplane) and Tiger Moth.

team went to Burnaston (Derby) to adapt a Dakota for use by Field Marshal Montgomery ('Monty'), Deputy Supreme Commander of NATO forces in Europe between 1951 and 1958. Among overseas contracts undertaken were conversions of two Viscounts for the President of Brazil (including luxury interior furnishing, much of which was sub-contracted to a Derbyshire firm, Reeve and Kenning of Pilsley), of three Lincoln bombers into meat carriers for Argentina to export carcasses across the Andes to Peru (only one was completed and that was never paid for or sent), and special orders from countries all round the world.

Fields also took part in on-site recovery operations almost anywhere in the world, usually on behalf of Lloyds, the premier aviation insurers. If a plane crash-landed and could not take off again to reach a repair workshop, a Fields team might be called out, either to render the plane airworthy to be flown back for a thorough overhaul at Tollerton; or if that was not feasible but the aircraft was worth saving, to be dismantled and brought back in parts. On one occasion in 1956, a team of nine (eight of whom were from Tollerton) called out on one such mission to Eastern Syria to recover a crashed Convair 340 of Saudi Arabian Airlines, found itself in difficulties not of its making. While they were in the middle of their work the Suez crisis erupted: Britain and France, with Israeli collusion, invaded Egypt to try to regain control of the Suez Canal, recently nationalized by the Egyptian government. This aroused the wrath of Arab

**Plate 71:  The Fields' Team after retrieving the Convair from Syria, 1956.** A young Gordon Williams is holding the team leader's headdress. *Gordon Williams*

states, of which Syria was one. Britons in the country were in danger of being interned or worse, and to avoid that possibility the Fields team hastily bought some Arab head dresses from local tribesmen, drove in disguise through the night across the Syrian Desert to Aleppo, from where they were escorted to Damascus and Beirut, where they boarded a plane to England. In the words of one member of the party, Gordon Williams, 'when the warring factions calmed down some months later, the party returned to Syria, completed the temporary repairs and the aircraft was flown to Tollerton where it underwent major repairs prior to return to service'.

Some idea of the growth and variety of work carried out by Fields at Tollerton, and the range of customer contracts won is given by this extract from the December 1952 edition of *Tally Ho*, the house newsletter of the Hunting group.

During the past year ... some 42 aircraft passed through [Tollerton's] hands [compared with a similar number over two years reported in the 1949 *Flight* article quoted earlier]. This included eight ... Pionair conversions for BEA and two Pionair convertible freighter aircraft, which are now undergoing operational trials. ... 1952 also saw the last two Liberators on their way to France and also the last of the ... Proctors for the RAF. ... Prentice aircraft are passing steadily through the works. ... 19 aircraft are for modification as Radio Trainers ... [and] last but not least, three outside working parties are touring RAF Training Command to embody modifications on some 360 Prentice aircraft in service. ... There is also a steady flow of Prentice and Proctor components passing through the Component and Detail manufacturing shops. Perhaps the most interesting contract of the year was for eight C47B [Dakota] conversions to de-luxe passenger standards for East African Airways Corporation. ... The Production and Machine shops are being kept busy with various contracts for de Havillands, Vickers-Armstrongs, Armstrong Whitworth and Hawkers. ... The most outstanding achievement of the year has been ... the repair on-site of the remains of the Viking in Beirut.

With the exception of a small number of American Air Force officers overseeing work on their aircraft in the Bridge Hangar, the workforce was entirely civilian. The majority commuted in from Nottingham by double-decker bus or bicycle. Normally they worked a single shift - manual workers clocking on at 8 a.m., 'staff' at 8.30 – though some, known as 'ghosters', worked nights and at week-ends. A canteen in the Main Hangar, with segregated area for staff, served cooked meals. When there was pressure to fulfil an order, overtime or whole additional shifts were worked. Men, who comprised the majority of the workforce, were engaged in most of the manual and heavy work - as fitters, machinists, truck and tractor drivers - and also in more office-bound positions as managers, supervisors and draughtsmen; women worked on stock control, in the canteen and fabric shop, and as typists and secretaries. There were a small number of overseas workers: Keith Hodgett recalls in particular the Poles and Lithuanians, some of whom had trained as pilots or aircraft fitters at Tollerton during the war and who had a reputation for conscientiousness and high quality workmanship.

Fields' employees and others using the airfield saw little of each other. The clubhouse, operated in the 1940s by Nottingham Flying Club and in the 1950s by Eagle Flying Club, was open to all but used mainly by flyers and their friends. There was little contact between those earning their living on the ground for Fields in the Main, Bellman and Bridge Hangars, and those flying their own light aircraft, whether for leisure or business, out of the Club Hangar. The same separation occurred while Tollerton was being used as a relief landing ground for RAF Syerston. Segregation was not deliberate; there was simply little occasion for mixing.

There were some clubs for Fields' employees however: an aero-modelling club, housed in a small hut near the Eagle clubhouse; a cricket club with its pitch on the airfield margin near the Bellman Hangar; rifle and archery clubs, using The Butts (see Figure 9). These were organized by the workers for the workers. There were also more informal recreations. Caroline Smith, who worked as a comptometer operator in 1949 and 1950, recalls: 'There was a table tennis table in the hangar. A lot of us used to play every lunchtime.' And: 'The girls in the office were sometimes allowed up for test flights ... [even though] there were no proper seats.' This would be with Fields' test pilots, not pilots of the Nottingham Flying Club. Some used to attend Saturday night dances at the Burnside Hall in nearby Plumtree. Works outings were organized periodically. Caroline recalls a weekend in Paris:

> We hired a converted Dakota. The return fare was £5 and our test pilot ... flew us from Tollerton to Le Bourget. We had to stop at Lympne both ways for customs. We had to find [our own] accommodation in Paris. ... It was a fantastic two days for a 16 year-old.

More formally, management held an annual dance at a venue on Sherwood Street, Nottingham, for all employees and their partners, which was also attended by one or more directors and senior managers from Fields' headquarters in Croydon.

Towards the end of Fields' stay at Tollerton social facilities improved and activities expanded. The December 1956 issue of *Tally Ho* refers to the complete renovation of the canteen, including resurfacing 'the old cold concrete' floor, making it more suitable for dances and other such occasions; organizing a series of pre-Christmas whist drives and a Christmas party for employees' children - the first ever to be held at Tollerton (the following issue of *Tally Ho* reported an attendance of 200 children, with special buses bringing them in from Keyworth, Ruddington and Clifton); a planned social evening and choral concert; the annual Sports Club dance; and a visit by 60 employees to the Farnborough Air Display the previous September.

By the mid-fifties, the volume of work undertaken by Fields was stretching the capacity of Tollerton's three available hangars. Also, as aircraft increased in size they needed longer runways. RAF Wymeswold was a bigger airfield, with more and larger hangars and longer runways. (When the Civil Aviation Authority was looking for a site for the planned East Midlands Airport at about this time, Wymeswold was preferred to Castle Donington, but it was still being used by the RAF and was therefore unavailable.) The RAF, which had been using Tollerton as a satellite of Syerston since 1949, had left the previous year, a possible signal that the Air Ministry would soon derequisition Tollerton. In fact, according to minutes of the City Council's General Purposes Committee, derequisitioning of that part of the airfield belonging to Nottingham City followed in two stages: 192 acres in September 1958 and the remaining 38 acres in May 1960. Meanwhile, Fields had been receiving a growing number of contracts from the RAF for which a site on one of its stations was considered an advantage. For all these reasons - runways, hangars and RAF links - in 1957 Fields decided to move from Tollerton to Wymeswold. Most of the removal took place in 1958, but some work continued at Tollerton into the 1960s. The Bridge and Bellman Hangars, together with some of the smaller buildings, were shut down first and all work

**Plate 72:    Inside the Main Hangar c.1960.** Work on whole aircraft (as shown in Plate 70) has been replaced by making aircraft components

on whole aircraft, which had been concentrated in the Main Hangar, moved to Wymeswold. Some 'detail work' (making of components) continued for a few years, transferred to the Main Hangar as shown in Plate 72. The Plating Shop, alongside the Main Hangar, was the last to close in 1963, covering metal components from Rolls-Royce, the Nottingham Royal Ordnance Factory and elsewhere with a protective coat of non-corrosive metal. Rex Morris and Len Henson were the last two Fields workers to leave Tollerton. The company stayed at Wymeswold until 1970, when it moved again, this time to East Midlands Airport.

# Chapter 11

# Post-war Commercial Flying – 1946 to 1951

When Tollerton airfield was transferred from RAF to civilian use in 1946, the question which immediately arose, but which remained unanswered for the rest of the decade, was whether Tollerton would be developed into a major civil airport.

In that same year, the Labour government published a white paper indicating its intention to nationalise all airports used by regular passenger services. Private and municipal airfields were to be restricted to club, taxi and charter flying. As Tollerton had operated scheduled services before the war (see chapter 3), initial indications were that it would resume scheduled flights and therefore be nationalised. In 1946 a letter from the Civil Aviation Authority to the City's Deputy Town Clerk expressed the view that Tollerton was 'one of the most suitable aerodromes in the region' to operate scheduled flights on grounds of size, approaches, weather and the fact that it had hard runways.

The local Chamber of Commerce thought so too. In a letter to Lord Amherst of BEA (reported in the *Nottingham Journal* of 1 October 1946) it said that it wished

to put forward the claim of Nottingham to be included in the network of air services, with an airport at say Tollerton or Hucknall with frequent services to Glasgow, Bristol and Liverpool with connections for Ireland, and definitely a regular service to connect with the London airports for continental and overseas routes.

However, over the next few years it became clear that civil aviation was changing: aircraft were increasing in size, jets were replacing propellers, and commercial airports would need to become bigger and fewer. Not every town or city the size of Nottingham could sustain an airport running scheduled flights as had seemed feasible before the war. Tollerton was too small for the requirements of large, jet-propelled aircraft. East Midlands Airport, serving the three cities and counties of Nottingham, Derby and Leicester, would be the eventual solution in this region but it was not opened until 1965. In the 1940s, the future was still unclear, and Tollerton was left in limbo: would it or would it not be nationalised? Should the airfield operators invest in maintenance facilities and other improvements if the airfield was shortly to be taken over by the state? In July 1947 Hansard listed the airports to be nationalised and the list included Tollerton. However, in 1950 the government let it be known Tollerton would not become a national airport.

\*

Meanwhile, following the departure of the RAF, Tollerton was returned to Nottingham Airport Ltd, with Field Aircraft Services still present, now converting to civilian use rather than repairing or dismantling military aircraft, and operating on a much reduced scale with far fewer workers. But the leaseholder, Shipside, was still keen to attract other commercial users to cover rent and airfield maintenance costs.

This was a time when small airlines were springing up all over the country. There were few regulations of the kind now required by the Civil Aviation Authority; aircraft were cheap to buy at the end of the war, with an over-supply of decommissioned military aircraft on the market; and there were many former RAF men available to fly them. Four such airlines came onto the scene at Tollerton between 1946 and 1948: Hunting Air Travel Ltd, Blue Line Airways, British Nederland Air Services, and Trent Valley Aviation.

However, they faced one major difficulty: Nottingham was relatively well connected by rail and road to other major business centres and holiday resorts, and from its midland location distances to most were not large enough to give more expensive air travel a significant advantage in saved journey time for all but a few businessmen. Only overseas destinations gave air that advantage. Hence the Channel Islands and Isle of Man were more viable destinations, but these offered only limited and largely seasonal demand. The four airlines were soon struggling and either moved away, joining up with other airlines, or went into liquidation. None stayed at Tollerton more than three years.

There were, however, a few individuals who continued to use Tollerton as a base for either recreational or business flying. Referring to the latter, an up-beat piece in the *Nottingham Journal* of 25 September 1950 states that:

in all, two textile firms, one engineering firm, three firms of motor engineers and a photographic firm base aircraft at Tollerton, and in addition the charter company [Trent Valley Aviation, already bought up by Eagle Airways and about to move away from Tollerton] is often called upon to fly businessmen to their destinations. ... Hendon [now the RAF Museum] is the most popular London aerodrome for these businessmen as it connects with the Underground and they can be in the City in 20 minutes or so.

The tone of this article implied that Tollerton had a promising future as a base for local business people - a promise that at best was only partly fulfilled, as chapters 12 and 13 will show. The airfield never really took off as a significant commercial airport and, once the RAF had left, most flying activity came to be associated with flying schools, flying clubs and a limited air-taxi service. In addition the airfield was used by a handful of private owners using it as a base for business or recreational flying; and as a drop-off and pick-up point for VIPs or special missions like air ambulance cases or rushing donor organs for transplant to a specialist hospital like Harefield or Papworth.

One of the private business users of Tollerton in the 1940s and 1950s was H. Tempest, the photographic firm referred to in the *Nottingham Journal* article quoted above. The firm was one of the biggest of its kind in the country, specializing in school photographs for which it had nation-wide contracts. Mr Tempest kept two planes at Tollerton and was also a member of the Nottingham Flying Club. One of his former employees, George Alford, recalls accompanying Mr Tempest on business trips to Luton, Coventry, Cardiff and Hendon, and also on pleasure trips to Shoreham (Sussex) and Lands End – Tempest worked a rota system whereby his workers were offered places to fill the plane when he had to fly on business. He evidently took very seriously the welfare of his employees: a picture in the *Nottingham Journal* of 26 July 1956 shows four girls who, the caption reads, 'had been let down over their holiday travel booking[4] to Jersey. When their boss, Horace Tempest, heard about the sad business he decided to fly them there himself – in his own aircraft ... [from] Tollerton'. In fact, one of the girls, June Stevens, has added to the story fifty years later: his plane would only take two passengers, so he asked another employee, a Pole called Alec Gertner who was also a pilot, to take the other two in his second plane. A week later both pilots flew to Jersey to bring the four girls home. On their return, all four girls were made honorary members of the Eagle Flying Club.

One unusual mission recorded in the *Evening Post* (17 September 1947) was that of a Miles Gemini which was touring the country to gather support for the Mildmay Pathfinder project prior to its flying out to several central African countries to provide a service for missionaries. Before moving on, the crew attended a well-supported meeting of the Missionary Aviation Fellowship held in Friar Lane, Nottingham.

All these and many other aircraft using the airport earned it landing fees and usually payment for the hangarage, refuelling and maintenance facilities provided, thereby enabling Tollerton to survive as an airport, unlike many comparable small airfields.

## Early Post-war Air Services

As we have noted, in the years following the war four small independent companies trying to establish themselves in the embryonic civil aviation market used Tollerton airfield. On 13 April 1946, for example, before Tollerton Airfield had been formally transferred to civilian use, the *Nottingham Journal* reported that **Hunting Air Travel Ltd** was planning to run an air taxi service from Tollerton, initially with a single Percival Proctor. The potential market was thought to be primarily business people needing to fly to the continent. The following month the same journal had a picture of the said Proctor at Tollerton, preparing for take-off to pick up passengers at Walsall bound for Guernsey. Nothing more has been found of this venture, so it must be assumed to have been dropped shortly afterwards.

---

[4] The booking was to fly from another airport; there was no commercial flying from Tollerton between 1951 and 1963.

Hunting was an umbrella group embracing companies engaged in, among other things, commercial flying, aerial surveys and aircraft maintenance. One of these companies was Field Aircraft Services, which had been repairing and servicing aircraft at Tollerton since 1939 (see chapter 10), so perhaps it is unsurprising that Hunting Air Travel should try it out as a base for chartered flights. However, it soon dropped Tollerton and concentrated its activity first on Luton, then moving successively to Gatwick, Croydon and Bovingdon, all nearer London, where the market was more promising. Fields continued servicing aircraft at Tollerton for another eleven years.

Again in 1946, passenger and freighter charter flights operated by **Blue Line** began from Tollerton with two Percival Proctors – passengers in summer and freight (requiring reorganization of the planes' interiors) in winter. The company was briefly a pioneer in a business we now take for granted: holidays by air. The following year it joined forces with the Air Transport Association of Guernsey (ATA) in running regular passenger services between Nottingham and the Channel Isles, using Avro Ansons. In 1948 ATA ceased operations and Blue Line continued on its own with five newly leased Ansons. Its owners also opened a travel agency in Nottingham, working from an office on Long Row. One must remember, however, that Ansons could only carry about a dozen passengers apiece, so the scale of operations was modest by today's standards. 1948 also saw the airline and travel agency merged into a single company, still called Blue Line Airways.

During the winter of 1948, the company obtained charter work flying freight to Europe from Croydon, Blackbushe and Bovingdon, all near London where the potential for such work was more promising than at Tollerton. It continued its passenger services to the Channel Isles in the summer of 1949, by which time it had also acquired a Douglas Dakota, which made the occasional flight from Tollerton to the Isle of Man. But the company was no longer profitable, and on 15 August of that year it went into voluntary liquidation. 20 of its clients were left stranded in Jersey and over 200 who had booked holidays with Blue Line for later that season lost both their money and their holidays.

At a meeting of creditors held at the Black Boy hotel on 17 November 1949 and reported in the next day's *Nottingham Journal*, the Official Receiver, Mr A.J. Rogers, declared that the company had gross liabilities of £42,405 and total estimated assets of £1,668 'though the position is very complicated and ... the liquidator might succeed in realizing much more than £1,668'. Creditors' claims totalling over £24,000 could not be met, and although the amounts lost by individuals, averaging some £120, appeared to him small (worth over £2,000 in today's money), Mr Rogers observed that they were grave to the creditors concerned. He went on: 'I found my heart rather heavy when they kept coming in to claim their money. It is a very sad thing for them.' He implied that this was a disaster waiting to happen to the clients of small under-capitalised businesses. It was the kind of situation which led government, in the interests of consumer protection, to put pressure on the multiplicity of post-war airlines to amalgamate into larger concerns. Not that it put an end to such unfortunate occasions, as the 1956 experience already cited of four H. Tempest employees illustrates – though this had a happy ending thanks to the generosity of their boss.

Most of Blue Line's fleet was sold to a larger concern, Eagle Aviation, which subsequently became part of an even larger concern, Britannia Airways.

Another airline called **British Nederland** operated from Tollerton for one year only, from 1947 to 1948. It ran charter flights in two Miles Aerovans, mostly carrying both freight and passengers to and from Holland, and was associated with a similar airline called Aero Holland operating from The Hague. Much of the freight from Holland was market garden produce. In 1948 it moved to Bovingdon (Hertfordshire). Only three of its aircraft flew out of Tollerton, but at its maximum the fleet numbered seven.

The fourth of these short-lived post-war companies operating out of Tollerton was **Trent Valley Aviation**. In terms of the number of aircraft owned this was the smallest of the four with, at maximum, only four planes - a Dakota, two Dragon Rapides and a Miles Gemini. But while Blue Line flew mainly to the Channel Isles and British Nederland to Holland, Trent Valley had a greater

**Plate 73:** **Trent Valley Aviation crew.** From left: A.Bamfield (navigator), J.Brooks (engineer), J.McCarthy (radio op), B.Brind (air hostess), F.J.Cronk (captain), G.Ford (first officer). *Arthur Cronk*

variety of destinations, which included Scandinavia, Switzerland, the Channel Isles, Berlin, the Middle East, the Dutch East Indies (shortly to become Indonesia) and Australia. Its base remained exclusively at Tollerton, though like a taxi service, it picked up its clients from their nearest airport.

Most of its flights carried passengers, the more newsworthy of whom included a football team from London to Brussels and London boy scouts to a jamboree in Stavanger (Norway). Some carried a mixture of freight and passengers - for example, oil drilling equipment and personnel to the Middle East; others took freight in one direction and passengers on the return – on one occasion, ships' spares to Australia and a ship's crew from Bombay to England on the way back. Apparently Trent Valley Aviation was ready to undertake almost anything. Among its more unusual cargoes were a flock of pigeons; a pack of 56 foxhounds from Birmingham to Italy; and a cargo of empty milk churns to Ireland - to get round a dock strike at Liverpool.

The most colourful episode, and one of the earliest in Trent Valley's brief life, was its contribution to the Berlin Airlift.[5] From 4 August until 10 November 1948, one of its aircraft – the Dakota, named Maid Marian, shown in Plate 74 – flew 186 sorties (three or four return trips each day, with short breaks after every seven days) between bases in West Germany (first Fassburg, then Lubeck, and finally Hamburg) and West Berlin, carrying in all 665 tons of coal. During this operation, all aircraft had to be serviced after every 72 sorties, which in the case of the Trent Valley Dakota meant returns to Tollerton. By November the military air forces of the occupying powers were able to manage the airlift without civilian help, so Maid Marian, no doubt after a thorough clean-out, returned to normal charter services.

Throughout the summer of 1950 Trent Valley ran a regular, scheduled passenger service, in association with British European Airways (BEA), from Tollerton to Jersey and the Isle of Man. Announcing the forthcoming service, the *Nottingham Journal* of 13 January 1950 stated that flights would begin on Saturday 6 May: 'At first, these two services will operate each Saturday.' Perhaps in view of the predicament of creditors after the collapse of Blue Line

---

[5] After the war, Germany was divided into four zones, under the control of the four occupying powers: the British, American, French and Russian zones. Berlin was similarly divided, but the whole city was located within the Russian zone. In 1948, the four became two: three of the zones combined to form the Federal Republic of West Germany, while the Russian zone became the Democratic Republic of East Germany. A similar amalgamation occurred in Berlin, where the two zones became known as West and East Berlin respectively. The four occupying powers continued to have a strong presence throughout.

As a result of a dispute between Russia and the Western occupying powers, the Russians blockaded the road and rail corridors linking West Germany and West Berlin on 24 June 1948. From then until the blockade was lifted over a year later (on 6 October 1949) all supplies of food, fuel and other necessities for the 3 million people of West Berlin were ferried in by a continuous relay of aircraft of the American, British and French Air Forces, supplemented in the early stages by a small number of civilian aircraft, one of which was provided by Trent Valley Aviation.

Airways the previous year, booking agents for the service were to operate a voucher system whereby payments for bookings were not transferred to the airline until after the trip was completed. The service was maintained until the autumn, but the take-up was insufficient for it to be renewed the following summer.

One of the problems of small airlines like Trent Valley Aviation was that much of its business was seasonal and to a limited number of holiday destinations, chiefly islands, which could not be reached by train; winter trips to the Mediterranean Costas and beyond had not yet been developed. When even summer services were not flying full, Tollerton lost its last scheduled service and the last of its small independent airlines. In September 1950 Trent Valley was bought by Eagle Aviation (which had also bought Blue Line Airways' aircraft but not the company), though it retained the name Trent Valley Aviation for its Tollerton charter services for another year. Thereafter, Eagle Aviation continued to operate under its own name, but no evidence has been found of its continuing to fly out of Tollerton.

The name did stay on however as the Eagle Flying Club. For, with the demise of Trent Valley, its chief pilot, Freddie Cronk, took over the clubhouse at Tollerton, formerly run by the now moribund Nottingham Flying Club, and renamed it the Eagle Flying Club. But it was a flying club in name only; in fact it was a social club, occupying the old clubhouse as a restaurant and bar, with no direct involvement in flying though many of its members were no doubt users

MESSRS JONES & PIKE
*Staff Outing to Blackpool • June 12th. 1949*

**Plate 74: Staff Outing to Blackpool with Trent Valley Aviation.** *Arthur Cronk*

of the airfield. The club carried on under the name Eagle into the mid-sixties (see chapter 14).

The name Trent Valley Aviation also resurfaced. It was, however, a different firm, with a different base - East Midlands Airport - and only operated during 1968 and 1969, when it provided pleasure flights at air displays in the Midlands. But there is no record of its ever visiting Tollerton.

# Chapter 12

# Truman Aviation I – 1963 to 1980

For twelve years following the departure of Trent Valley/Eagle Aviation in 1951, no commercial flying took place from Tollerton other than test flights by Field Aircraft Services of former military aircraft it was converting for civilian use, and of aircraft overhauled to renew their Certificate of Airworthiness. Towards the end of the 1950s, the Air Ministry indicated its intention to derequisition Tollerton, which it finally did in 1960. By then the RAF had already left in 1956 and most of Fields in 1957, while the 30-year lease taken by Nottingham Airport Ltd in 1934 was nearing its end, a lease its shareholders were not anxious to renew. The only positive development during this period was the start of the Sherwood Flying Club in 1956. Its Council did consider applying for a new lease but members drew back from such a costly undertaking. It therefore looked as though the airfield would close. A minute of Nottingham City Council General Purposes Committee dated 29 May 1958 states:

> It is understood that the corporation was not proposing to continue [Tollerton] … as an airfield and that it would revert to agricultural land. Resolved:
>    i.   the Corporation do not wish to purchase any buildings or installations …
>    ii.  the Corporation will expect land to be restored to its original condition or compensation paid
>    iii. on derequisition the land will be regarded as available for such purposes as the Corporation decides, subject to planning approval.

A subsequent minute on 14 July 1958 states that 'the present users [of the airfield] - Nottingham Airport Ltd and Sherwood Flying Club - have been given notice to quit', though it went on to record that the Corporation would allow them to continue using the airport rent-free until it decided what to do. Thereafter inertia seems to have afflicted the Corporation for several years, allowing Derek Truman to appear on the scene in the early sixties and effectively save the airport. He believed it could survive profitably by a combination of non-aeronautical activities and what was called 'general aviation' - private and club flying, together with air-taxis, using small propeller-driven machines.

By the early sixties the future of commercial aviation was clearer than it had been in the forties: most would involve large jets flying out of a few major regional airports rather than small propeller-driven machines from a multiplicity of small municipal aerodromes. Truman understood that airfields like Tollerton would only be suitable for general aviation, and though he may have viewed its future over-optimistically, he thought the airfield's commercial viability would be more secure if part were given over to other activities.

# The Start of Truman Aviation

C. H. Truman & Co. therefore applied to Nottingham Corporation to take out a lease on the airfield; terms were agreed and Truman Aviation came into being. The airfield continued to be known as Nottingham Airport Ltd, as it had been for most of the then 33 years since it was formally opened (though originally it was called Nottingham Aerodrome or Nottingham Air Port). Truman proved to be sufficiently correct in his calculations for the airport still to be active 44 years later, but, as we shall see, not all his vision materialized and he had to adapt, particularly with the non-aeronautical activities he had in mind. Much later, the airport also changed its name to Nottingham Tollerton Airport, to distinguish it from East Midlands Airport when the latter was for a short time renamed Nottingham East Midlands Airport. However, EMA has now formally dropped 'Nottingham' from its name while Tollerton has become Nottingham City Airport plc.

Truman Aviation Ltd has been the principal leaseholder at Tollerton Airfield from December 1963 until today (2007). During that time, the company has been led by two Managing Directors: Derek Truman from 1963 to 1980, and Derek Leatherland, who has retained the Truman name of the company, from 1980 onwards. This chapter covers only the first of these periods.

After the departure from Tollerton of the bulk of Field Aircraft Services in 1957, the airfield remained largely untenanted for six years, during which Sherwood Flying Club was the main occupant. It was allowed to stay as 'tenant on sufferance' (effectively a rent-free squatter) in recognition of its having maintained the airfield in reasonable condition before Truman's arrival. There were, however, other occupants: the remnants of Fields, who took several years to transfer everything to Wymeswold; T. Shipside Ltd and the social club called Eagle Flying Club based in the old Nottingham Flying Club clubhouse in which Shipside retained an interest; and two companies that occasionally used the airfield grass for grazing and hay-cutting. Consideration was given to developing the site for housing, but it was greenbelt land and there was already sufficient development going on elsewhere to satisfy medium-term projected needs around Nottingham - the 1960s saw the rapid expansion of a number of nearby villages like Keyworth, Cotgrave, Ruddington and Tollerton itself.

Then on 10 September 1962 the General Purposes Committee of Nottingham Corporation considered a request from C.H. Truman & Co, dealers in luxury cars (Rolls-Royce and Bentley), to obtain a lease 'to develop a flying centre for the sale and hire of private and executive aircraft in conjunction with entertainment facilities such as restaurant, motel, etc.'. A year later, on 9 September 1963, the terms of a 75-year lease were provisionally agreed. The existing tenancies mentioned above were to continue, and Truman was asked to deal with Sherwood Flying Club 'as sympathetically as possible'. After the agreement was ratified, Truman Aviation was born on Christmas Day 1963, with

Derek Truman as its Managing Director. Sherwood's 'tenancy on sufferance' was allowed to continue for a number of years and although it now pays Truman Aviation for use of the airfield and its facilities, no formal contract has ever been drawn up between the two.

It will be observed that there were two dimensions in Truman's original vision: flying and entertainment. The latter was extremely ambitious, as this extract from the *Guardian Journal* of 10 June 1964 makes clear:

> Plans for developing Tollerton Airfield as a £650,000 fly-in leisure centre, thought to be the first in the world, were announced yesterday. ... The 65-acre scheme will also include a 122-bedroom motel. Golfing facilities ... an automatic driving range with provision for 150 tees - which will be floodlit for night-time opening - a nine-hole par three golf course, a miniature golf course and a practice pitching area. An indoor arena will offer ten-pin bowling, archery and artificial ski slopes for beginners and comparatively advanced skiers.

While the flying took off, with both the sale and operation of private aircraft, entertainment did not. The pre-war Nottingham Flying Club clubhouse, already renamed the Eagle Flying Club in the 1950s, now changed its name again to the

**Plate 75**
**Derek Truman**
*Valerie Truman*

Tollerton Flying Club, still a social rather than a flying club; otherwise, none of the items mentioned in the above quotation ever materialized. In 1966, planning permission was sought for a drive-in cinema; it was refused. Thereafter, Truman scaled down his social plans to do no more than arrange lounge and relaxation facilities, primarily for those who flew with the company or visited the airfield.

Over the first few years of Truman's tenancy, the most important developments were the start of a Piper agency, the launch of an air taxi service and improvement of the infrastructure, particularly by servicing and improving the runways, and by erecting a control tower.

## The Piper and Beagle Agencies

Piper is an American firm specializing in the manufacture of light aircraft, which, in the mid-sixties, was looking to make inroads into the British general aviation market after import restrictions on foreign aircraft had been lifted. Derek Truman sensed that the market for light aircraft was expanding and that Piper products offered as good value for money as most of its rivals. In the former respect he was only partly right - the market has expanded, but not at the rate he had hoped. In the latter he was vindicated: Pipers became increasingly popular among amateur flyers throughout most of Truman's tenancy. The dealership was conducted with energy and considerable success,

Plate 76: A Truman advertisement for Piper.

using advertisements like that in plate 76 and going out to meet likely customers. The first two aircraft he bought for Truman Aviation were Pipers: a Cherokee 180 and a twin-engined Comanche, the latter used for both demonstration flights and for charter work. In May 1972 he took the Lord Mayor and Sheriff of Nottingham on a trip over the city, though this was largely for publicity rather than in the hope that the Council would be a customer. Truman became the leading British dealer in the Midlands and North. By 1973, he had sold more than a hundred new and second-hand Pipers, and in March 1980 he celebrated sales of over £1 million during the previous twelve months.

Truman Aviation was also appointed agent to sell Beagle Pups in 1968. Beagle was a British firm based at Rearsby near Leicester and Pups were single-engined two or three-seater aircraft. Truman held the agency for a few years and the Pups sold well until Beagle went into liquidation in the early seventies. This occurred after the firm had developed a new model for military training, the Bulldog, which did not sell immediately. The Liquidator sold the rights to manufacture, using the plane's design plans, to Scottish Aviation, who subsequently sold large numbers, first to the Swedish Air Force and then to the RAF. A Bulldog has found its way back to Tollerton today, owned by Brian Wells, Sherwood Flying Club member and joint director of Nottingham City Airport plc, the recently formed company which has bought the airfield.

Truman delegated the agency side of the business to a Sales Manager, first John Hogg (for both Piper and Beagle) and later Damien Mannix (Piper only).

**Plate 77:** **Brian Wells's Bulldog.** *Brian Wells*

They maintained an office in Nottingham where catalogues were available and specifications and prices could be discussed. When a potential buyer thought he knew the model he wanted (either new or second hand), arrangements were made to demonstrate its handling qualities and capabilities either at Tollerton or wherever was most convenient to the buyer. Agency sales were the company's main source of revenue throughout most of Derek Truman's time at Tollerton (1963 to 1980).

## Air Taxis

Early in 1964 Truman announced that he proposed to start an air taxi service, primarily for business people, but for anyone who could afford the convenience that air travel offered. Roads were becoming progressively more congested and rail services were being cut following publication of the Beeching report in 1963. It was widely believed that British business people would follow their American counterparts by taking to the air, appreciating that time saved travelling to meetings by air would outweigh the additional cost; and that while the large commercial airlines only flew between a limited number of airfields, often situated a long way from central areas of cities, with tedious check-in procedures, light aircraft from small airfields like Tollerton, generally closer to city-centres, could take their passengers with a minimum of fuss to many more destinations. There are, and were then, over 200 airfields in Britain accessible to light aircraft, and hundreds more on the continent. On the other hand, many were, and still are, not equipped with the navigational aids allowing planes to land in bad weather; nor were they all manned at night. Business people need a reliable, all-hours service, which not all small airfields provide.

Before Truman's taxi service could be launched it ran into a difficulty: the lease agreement with Nottingham City forbade use of the airfield for charter business. However, after further negotiation with the Town Clerk, it was agreed that Truman could run air taxi or ferry services provided the aircraft carried no more than six people, including the pilot, or an equivalent in cargo. A pilot with a Commercial Pilot's Licence (more demanding than a Private Pilot's Licence) was appointed – Peter Thomas.

The taxi service slowly built up and Truman was optimistic for its future. Here he is talking to a reporter from the *Newark Advertiser* in January 1972:

> The original reluctance of business houses to use air taxi services is rapidly disappearing as they find that the slightly extra cost is easily compensated by the tremendously increased flexibility of a personal air service, which also has the advantage of departing from the doorstep in their area.

In January 1969 the Air Taxi Operators Association, with members in London, Birmingham, Manchester and Glasgow, moved its headquarters from London to

Tollerton. In May 1973 Tollerton hosted a day conference on the business potential of air-taxis, under the slogan 'TIME FLIES; WHY DON'T YOU?' It was sponsored by the CBI and addressed by the Under-Secretary of State for Air Transport among others. This was the year of Britain's entry into the Common Market, promising closer ties with, and therefore more frequent business trips to other members of what then was called the European Economic Community.

Meanwhile private aircraft ownership was also slowly increasing: by 1975 some three-quarters of the 35 planes based at Tollerton were privately owned, mostly by local businessmen or by share-ownership syndicates. Many were Pipers bought from Derek Truman. Their owners, if on business, enjoyed a clear cost advantage over taxi users: they did not need to hire a pilot, and if they could also afford recreational flying, overheads could be spread between business and pleasure. Some potential taxi users therefore preferred to fly their own aircraft.

For this and other reasons, the taxi side of Truman Aviation did not expand as had been expected. Whether through innate conservatism or hard-headed calculation, not enough business people bought the time-versus-cost argument. Even light aircraft cannot deliver door-to-door as cars can; England is not like America where distances between cities and business centres are much greater. Furthermore, as the motorway network expanded, intercity travel was becoming faster, with roads not seizing up as frequently as expected. Tollerton's airport manager, Eric Johnson, summed up the somewhat disappointing position in an interview for the *Newark Advertiser* in April 1978:

> I think the use of light aircraft, though still expanding, is not increasing at the rate envisaged when we first started here fifteen years ago. The main reason is the general economic depression. Another big reason is that there are so few people in the business world who appreciate the value of aircraft as a business tool.

Well before that was said, only a year after making the optimistic forecast cited earlier, Truman had sold the air taxi side of his business to the Mosley Group of Loughborough (primarily coach bodywork builders), who continued to run a service from Tollerton for a few years, though with no more success than Truman. This business left Tollerton after Mosley's death in the late 1980s.

## Infrastructure

After the RAF finally left Tollerton in 1956 they took their flying-control caravan with them. Thereafter until 1966 Tollerton had no control tower, although the Sherwood Flying Club operated a ground/air radio service on their club flying days (weekends and Thursdays). Otherwise, those flying in or out relied solely on their own eyes with no external guidance, observing simple rules of courtesy and safety: if the coast was clear they could land or take off; if one wished to take off when another was about to land, the plane in the air had priority; if two wished to land at the same time, the one nearer ground-level had priority. Flying only took place when visibility was adequate. After the Cotgrave colliery headstock towers were built in the early sixties, a rule of thumb was that if they were visible from take-off point (about two miles away), it was safe to fly.

However, as airspace was becoming more crowded and aircraft more sophisticated, and as safety standards became more rigorous, Truman responded with the 1966 control tower still in use. It gives an all-round view at sufficient height to see to the end of runways on clear days, and has no doubt enhanced safety, particularly for aircraft with radio navigation equipment, which can be warned of any lurking danger. Nevertheless the tower is not strictly a control tower, though it looks like one: those who staff it are not fully qualified air traffic control operators and legally can only advise. It is still ultimately the pilot's responsibility either to take or ignore that advice. The

Plate 78:
The Control Tower shortly after its erection in 1967.
*Derek Leatherland*

Plate 79:
The Control Tower block in 2006.
The Club Hangar is in the background.
*Rod Gill*

tower was placed some 50 metres away from the existing buildings, and at first was a simple tower, with an office at ground floor level with the control room immediately above. Additional offices were added soon afterwards, and a 'pilots' lounge' installed in a caravan nearby. Further extensions to the control tower block were made during the 1980s.

However, the control tower's position has one disadvantage: it is too near the north-west to south-east runway for safety. The runway has therefore been out of use as a runway ever since. Plans are now afoot to re-site the tower, together with all the offices and social facilities, into a single complex set far enough away to allow the runway back into service. In the meantime it can be used for taxiing and parking planes (as seen in plate 80).

According to the lease, maintenance of runways, along with hedges and ditches, was Truman's responsibility. One of the first improvements Truman made was to install electric lights (involving also the laying of buried cables) along both sides of the main east-west runway as replacement for paraffin-lit flares to assist night flying. In addition, 'glimmers' (battery-powered lamps) were introduced, chiefly to assist night-time taxiing. The flares had been labour-intensive, taking about three man-hours to take out, light, and later extinguish and bring in again at the end of one evening's flying. But despite the advantage of electric illumination, it has not been extended to the other runway; all night flying uses the east-west runway.

Runway maintenance involved periodic resurfacing, which was an expensive procedure (over £5,000 every five to ten years at 1968 prices). In 1967 Truman

**Plate 80:    A Piper Tomahawk on the disused runway.** The runway close to the control tower is used for taxiing and parking aircraft. *Rod Gill*

Aviation applied to the landowner (the City Council) for financial assistance, which the Council eventually approved in principle in 1970, but only if ground rent was increased. After negotiation, a variation in the terms of the original lease was agreed, leading to reduced ground rent, the lease running for only a further nine years - until 1979 instead of 2038 - but with Truman paying in full for runway maintenance. However, it was a heavy financial burden, and some of the surfaces were allowed to become pock-marked with holes in the tarmac, revealing underlying concrete laid down in the 1940s (see plate 88 on page 222).

The cost of runway maintenance would occasion another revision of the lease in 1978 (only a year before the then current lease was due to expire). The City Council proposed a doubling of the rent to take account of rapid inflation in the late seventies; Truman Aviation claimed it could not afford the increase, particularly in view of the prospect of a by now £20,000 bill for runway renewal it was about to undertake (there had been high inflation in the 1970s). Negotiations led to a compromise and a second new 15-year lease; this would be revised again during the Leatherland era.

**Plate 81:** **The Tollerton Runways in the 1990s.** The numbers on the runways indicate the first two digits of their magnetic bearing from the point of view of an approaching aircraft. So, 27 means a bearing of approximately 270 or magnetic west. *Derrick Brooks*

## Company and other Aircraft Visitors

Like other airfields, Tollerton was and is used frequently by visitors from elsewhere. Richard Randall, a long-time local aviation enthusiast, has compiled a list of companies using Tollerton in the 1960s to bring in and carry out either business executives or goods or both. It includes Charles Forte (hotels), Rolls-Royce and Hawker Siddeley (aircraft engines), McAlpine (motorway and other construction), Tube Investments (bicycles), Vernons (Football Pools), The Central Electricity Board and Skegness Air Taxi Services. This last, based at Ingoldmells, operated a weekly ferry service carrying Saturday editions of the Evening Post and sports results in two fully loaded Austers from Nottingham to Skegness, for holiday makers and for those who had retired from Nottingham to live in 'Nottingham-by-the-Sea'.

A distinguished individual visitor was Prime Minister Sir Alec Douglas Hume during the 1964 general election campaign, while Lord Robens called frequently during his spell as Head of the National Coal Board. In addition, jockeys making for Nottingham and Southwell racecourses were then, and continue to be, frequent users of the Airport.

## Air Pageants

A feature of pre-war Tollerton was the frequent air pageants or flying displays, as already described in chapter 4. They were revived briefly after the war, but with the demise of the Nottingham Flying Club, were discontinued. In 1967 Derek Truman was ready to resume them, and from that year until his retirement in 1980 they occurred every summer, though usually with external sponsorship by businesses like John Player & Sons and the *Nottingham Evening Post*. Much of the organization was also conducted in collaboration with outside bodies like the RAF and Royal Aeronautical Club.

The 1967 pageant was held on Saturday 19 August, and contained many elements of displays which would be featured in future years, with most provided by the RAF: fly-pasts by wartime veterans like the Spitfire, Mosquito and Lancaster; formation flying, this year by the RAF Red Pelicans, later by the RAF Red Arrows; aerobatics by RAF planes - on this occasion a Gnat and a Hunter; and a drop by the RAF Falcons parachute team. Civilians were involved in two outstanding events however: the final of the King's Cup Air Race, the first of three of this national event to be held at Tollerton (the other two would be in 1968 and 1970); and the first helicopter race ever to be staged in the United Kingdom.

The final of the King's Cup Air Race, an annual event first held in 1922, visits airfields throughout the country. It is open to aircraft of any type provided they are British-registered or are flown by a British pilot. The course in 1967 involved four laps of a quadrilateral between points near Tollerton, Kinoulton, Cropwell

Butler, Radcliffe-on-Trent, and back to Tollerton - about 50 miles in all, flown at low level. (The course was devised to avoid the villages themselves, to minimize noise nuisance.) The race at Tollerton had been preceded by eliminating heats held at Plymouth, Middleton and Tollerton itself, to reduce the number of entrants in the final to about twenty.

The helicopter race course was shorter - three laps of a six-mile circuit - with

## SATURDAY 1st JULY

| | |
|---|---|
| From   10.00 a.m. | Formula 1 Air Race Practice |
| 13.15   15.30 | **FINISH OF INTERNATIONAL AIR RALLY** |
| 15.30 – 19.00 | Formula 1 Air Race Practice |
| | Display Practice |
| | **AIR DISPLAY** including |
| | Ray Hanna (Spitfire), RN Sea Fury |
| | The Blue Chips RAF Chipmunk Team |

## SUNDAY 2nd JULY

| | |
|---|---|
| Commencing 14.00 | The Macaws RAF Jet Provost Aerobatic Team |
| | Formula 1 Air Race Heat |
| | Sherwood Flying Club Demonstration |
| | RAF Varsity Formation |
| | RAF Meteor |
| | RAF Vampire |
| | Truman Aviation Ltd. Piper Display |
| | Falco F8L Aerobatics |
| | The Blue Chips RAF Chipmunk Team |
| | RN Sea Fury |
| | Zlin Aerobatics |
| | Stampe Duo Aerobatics |
| | Interval   – Vintage Car High Speed Trials |
| | **JOHN HOWITT TROPHY FORMULA 1 AIR RACE** |
| | RAF Lancaster |
| | RAF Hurricane |
| | Ray Hanna (Spitfire) |
| | The Red Arrows RAF Formation Aerobatic Team |
| | The Falcons RAF Free-fall Parachute Display Team |

Plate 82:   Order of Events at the 1972 Pageant. *1972 Pageant Programme*

competitors in view from the airfield all the time. Trophies were presented to the winners by television celebrity Hughie Green (a former pilot with the Canadian Air Force) and Sheila Scott, famous for her record-breaking round-the-world solo flights.

Subsequent pageants followed much the same pattern as the 1967 event, though the helicopter race was not repeated and the King's Cup race did not revisit Tollerton after 1970. They all had similar programmes: a combination of fly-pasts, races and aerobatics, together with parachute drops and stunts like flour bombing. There were, however, variations, some of which will be mentioned.

In 1968 the Red Arrows made their first appearance at Tollerton with an impressive display of formation flying, leaving smoke trails of red, white and blue as they thundered overhead. In 1970 the first Formula-One race was introduced to Britain from America at Tollerton: ten laps by very small and manoeuvrable single-seater aircraft capable of making tight turns, over a three-mile circuit entirely within visual range of spectators at the airfield. That year's King's Cup race was also markedly different from others, being flown over a much larger circuit between Tollerton, Lowestoft, Goole and back to Tollerton, so that spectators could only see the start and finish. Both the Formula-One and King's Cup races were open to competitors from all over the country and beyond.

A page from the 1972 programme (plate 82) illustrates what was on offer. The pageant was spread over two days, with the RAF still making a significant input. On this occasion and in the following year, a local businessman, Pat Howitt, managing director of the local printers J Howitt & Son, sponsored the Formula-One event as well as an International Air Rally, with trophies and generous prize money. The International Rally was open to any aircraft weighing less than 12,500 lbs, from any airfield within five hours flying time of Tollerton, which they had to leave at 8 a.m., arriving at individually pre-set times after 1 p.m. at Tollerton. Points were awarded for distance flown, number of intermediate airfields on which they touched down, customs clearance (for overseas competitors) and for number of passengers carried. Points were deducted for arriving before or after the pre-set time.

Meanwhile, in addition to what was taking place overhead, there were ground events and displays, including those involving vintage cars and motorcycles.

The following year saw two pageants: the first on 1 July, the International Air Rally, and the second on 28 September, Nottingham Air Day. The programme for the former was similar to that of the previous year, but not identical. It included balloon bursting and streamer cutting, demonstrations by a Fleet Air Arm helicopter team and the Goodyear Airship, together with the first of many appearances at Tollerton of the Rothman aerobatic team of five new biplanes, said to be 'the finest aerobatic aeroplanes in the world'. BBC Television was there for a 45-minute colour film to be broadcast the following month, and at the end of the pageant Group Captain Douglas Bader, the wartime fighter ace, presented the trophies.

Nottingham Air Day saw the first of many visits by another aerobatic team, the Barnstormers. Tragically, this was preceded by a mid-air collision between a Tiger Moth of the Barnstormers' team with two men on board, and a single-

**Plate 83: Rothman's Aerobatic Team at Tollerton, 1973.** *1973 Pageant Programme*

seater visiting plane unconnected with the event. Both were preparing to land, collided, and crashed to the ground, killing both pilots and the Moth's passenger. Remarkably, the rest of the Barnstormer team carried on with their display later that day.

The repertoire of the Barnstormers included 'wing walking' - a Tiger Moth flew over the airfield with the intrepid 'walker' standing on the upper wing above the cockpit. This was introduced in 1975 with a woman as walker, and repeated the following year with a man. There is no record of further repeats - perhaps it was tempting fate too far. Yet this daredevil event was tame compared with pre-war wing-walking. Then, as described on page 79, the walker climbed out of the cockpit while the aircraft was flying and moved about with very little support. The Barnstormers' walker was not really a walker at all

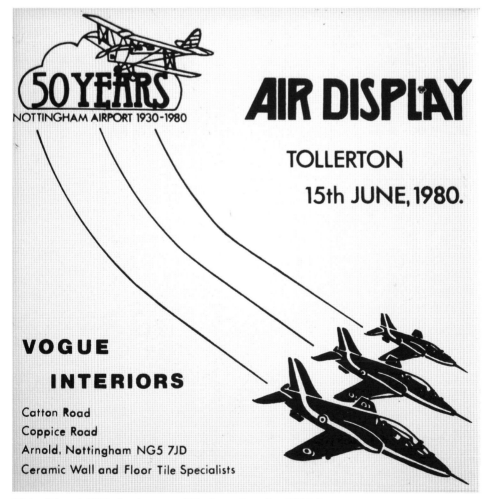

**Plate 84:    A 50th Anniversary Tile issued at the 1980 Pageant.** Tollerton Airport was officially opened in 1930. *Nigel Morley*

- he or she stood still, strongly supported by struts. Nevertheless, still hair-raising stuff!

It must have become increasingly difficult for organizers of these pageants to think of something new to draw and entertain the crowds. On the one hand, what once seemed spectacular becomes commonplace when seen frequently, whether in the flesh or on television; on the other hand, increasingly stringent health and safety regulations limit, no doubt quite properly, what is allowed.

The rest of Truman's reign saw pageants follow a by now familiar pattern. However, his swansong in 1980 coincided with the 50th anniversary of the official opening of Tollerton aerodrome, and was an opportunity to select planes and events to illustrate its history.

Many of the old favourites were there: The Falcon parachute team, Rothman's aerobatics and The Red Arrows; the fly-past of Spitfire, Hurricane and Lancaster. But also in the air were the Puss Moth, billed as the fastest entrant in the 1931 King's Cup race, a Blackburn B2 pre-war trainer, a wartime American Flying Fortress and a German Messerschmitt 108, a post-war trainer (Vickers Varsity), two early jet fighters (the Meteor and Vampire), and the modern Jaguar ('spearhead of Britain's aerial defence'), Nimrod (submarine hunter-killer) and Sea Harrier (Royal Navy vertical take-off and landing aircraft), together with civilian light aircraft.

Why did Truman stage these pageants? They rarely yielded a financial profit,

**Plate 85:    An early Jet Fighter - the Vampire.** *1980 Pageant Programme*

and although much of the organization was outsourced to other bodies, they must have involved a good deal of work and worry. Sometimes the weather was disappointing on the day: events had to be cut (parachutists, for instance, would not be released in cloud when they could not see their landing ground or be seen by spectators) and fewer people came to watch. In 1974 when the weather was bad, attendance was only 3,000; in 1978, under blazing sun, over 10,000. A more frequent complaint, also made about similar events in the 1930s, was that many spectators would watch from vantage points beyond the airfield's perimeter to avoid paying entry and car-parking charges, clogging up the surrounding roads. One observer who remembers the enthusiasm of crowds who came to pre-war pageants in their thousands by bus, bike or on foot, has commented that the largely car-borne spectators of the 1970s were generally fewer and less excited by what they saw. Perhaps the novelty of flying had diminished by the 1970s, and there were more counter-attractions.

No doubt there was a 'feel-good' factor for the organisers in bringing together aviators, watching them show off their skills, and meeting them socially. The main spin-off from these air shows, however, was publicity: the promotion of air-mindedness, inducing more people to use the airfield by joining a flying club or school, or even buying a plane (preferably a Piper) which would then require the use of Tollerton's hangar, maintenance and refuelling facilities.

## Pilot Training

Until 1974 Truman Aviation provided no flying lessons; it was left to the clubs, chiefly the Sherwood Flying Club, and briefly the Player Flying Club as well (see chapter 14). However, in that year a flying instructor, Frank Spencer, came to Tollerton from East Midlands Airport, together with two of his protégées, both women. Together they established the Spencer Flying School, with Spencer as chief instructor and the two women as assistant instructors. Two aircraft and a small piece of land on which to place an office-caravan were leased from Truman. After the caravan was blown over in a gale, it was replaced by a portacabin.

Unlike the clubs, the Spencer School charged for tuition as well as for fuel, maintenance and other overheads, but it was open seven days a week whereas the clubs had only limited opening hours on Thursdays and at weekends. One of Spencer's leased planes was a four-seater, which could be used for touring, presumably for pilots who had advanced beyond initial training. It could also be used for business trips. The other was a two-seater trainer. Curiously, both were Cessnas; one might have thought that a Piper agent would have provided it with Pipers. There is said to have been some tension between Truman and Spencer over this issue.

One of Spencer's early students was Derek Leatherland. He already held his

Private Pilot's Licence, but now trained as an instructor and, on qualifying, joined the School as a flying instructor. However, after Spencer's death in the late 1970s the School declined. An attempt was made to revive it under a new name - the Nottingham Flying School - which lasted into the Leatherland era.

Tollerton has also provided training in piloting helicopters since 1974. Helicopters briefly linked Nottingham to Leicester and Birmingham in 1956, when a firm, Midland Helicopters, started an experimental scheduled service, with three flights a day linking the three cities. Tollerton was only marginally involved, in providing fuel; Nottingham flights took off and landed at Trent Lane. The experiment failed however: there were insufficient customers, with the Suez crisis and consequent fuel rationing finally killing it off. Tollerton also saw the country's first helicopter race in the 1967 pageant, as already mentioned.

But it was not until 1974 that helicopters established a permanent presence on the airfield, with the arrival of William Howes of Spondon, who started a helicopter school and taxi service. If fixed wing aircraft are expensive to buy and fly, helicopters are considerably more so. Nevertheless there has been a continuous demand ever since, mainly from business, for both helicopter instruction and taxis, and also for private hire by those who have learnt to fly them. Today the service goes under the name of Central Helicopters.

**Plate 86:** A Central Helicopters' Robinson 22 in the Truman Hangar. *Rod Gill*

# Keeping the Planes Flying

Aircraft need maintenance and regular check-ups - equivalent to MOTs, but more rigorous, with inspections after every 50 flying hours, again annually, and a thorough overhaul every three years to retain the necessary Certificate of Airworthiness (C of A). For nearly half Tollerton's post-war history, this service was provided by Harold Hall & Co of Leicester and Nottingham.

Hall's connection with Tollerton goes back to the 1940s, when he was employed by Field Aircraft Services as a fitter. By the late 1940s he was a qualified licensed aircraft engineer and in the late fifties renewed his association with Tollerton by servicing planes belonging to the newly formed Sherwood Flying Club in his workshop at Leicester Airport. Then in the early 1960s, with the departure of Shipside (who had until then provided most of the maintenance at Tollerton) and with the arrival of Truman Aviation, Hall & Co was invited to become the resident maintenance firm, a position it already held at Leicester. Hall bought the Club Hangar as a workshop in which up to four aircraft could be serviced at the same time. He also recruited engineers - for most of his time at Tollerton he employed four. His own role was administrative and supervisory, both here and at Leicester. He also made frequent trips to collect spare parts from manufacturers or their agents, who included CSE of Oxford for Pipers and either Rogers of Bedford or Northair in Yorkshire for Cessnas.

Truman's early confidence in Hall and his keen eye for publicity are illustrated by the following anecdote. Shortly after Truman came to Tollerton he asked Hall to bring a Piper Cherokee to his car showroom on Huntingdon Street in Nottingham. The aircraft was dismantled; the parts stacked on a lorry and brought to the showroom where it was re-assembled. After a week or two the process was reversed and the aircraft again re-assembled and prepared for flight at Tollerton.

Hall stayed at Tollerton until 1991, right through the Derek Truman era and well into the Leatherland era, when he retired. Throughout that time he provided the full range of services required by fixed-wing aircraft, including those like the Tiger Moth and Auster aircraft, whose canvas covering needed periodic replacement, but excluding helicopters. In support of Truman's Piper agency, Hall became a certificated Piper maintenance engineer. He also serviced some aircraft that flew in from elsewhere - he estimates this constituted up to 20% of his work at Tollerton.

After Hall's retirement, the firm was bought by Skyline Helicopters, which included maintenance of helicopters as well as fixed-wing aircraft, but it remained only two years before leaving Tollerton. Subsequently Truman Aviation established its own maintenance unit.

# Neighbours and Nuisance

One of the arguments routinely put forward against airports and their expansion is the issue of noise. Such complaints have not infrequently cropped up in connection with Tollerton airfield. To minimize noise and nuisance to neighbours, users of the airfield are periodically reminded to try to avoid flying low over residential areas, and to climb and descend as steeply as is safe. Nevertheless, nearby residents complain from time to time with letters in the press about noise from low-flying aircraft, particularly after pageants. They are normally countered by replies from other members of the public. Recent replies have pointed out that the airfield has been there since 1929, probably long before the complainants, who should have been aware of the noise hazard when they chose to live nearby. Earlier replies reminded people of the role Tollerton played in training pilots who helped to save Britain from invasion during the war - we might need such men again. More recently in 2006, when the airfield was up for sale and there was the possibility of it becoming the site for 3,000 houses or of an industrial estate, a majority of local press letters were in favour of the airfield staying. News that the site had been bought by Nottingham City Airport plc, who had undertaken to continue and develop it further as an airfield, was greeted with relief by many though not all correspondents. Airfields do not make comfortable neighbours, but many people travel by air, and there could be worse neighbours than a lightly-used base for light aircraft.

In the late seventies the boot was on the other foot: the airfield was faced with a development which, it was felt by those who flew, would threaten the safety of the public and airfield users alike. Instead of being complained about, users of the airfield became the complainers. A Roma caravan site was to be placed on its doorstep. (At that time the term 'gipsy' was generally used.) The government had decreed that every county should provide such a site; Nottinghamshire County Council chose land on the northern boundary of Tollerton airfield, where the Bridge Hangar had once stood, some 150 yards from the end of one of the runways.

Truman Aviation and the Sherwood Flying Club both pointed out the dangers of children or dogs straying onto the airfield, and of smoke from bonfires obscuring pilots' vision. Tollerton and Holme Pierrepont Parish Councils and Rushcliffe Borough Council also registered their objections, but were overruled by the County. The issue was then referred to the Secretary of State for the Environment, who supported the County. Derek Truman challenged either the government or the County Council to offer him indemnity against the possibility of a Roma child being killed by straying into the path of an aircraft taking off or landing. No such indemnity was offered and the plan was put into effect. Roma moved in but were ejected after only a short stay because of vandalism. Eventually a group of twelve mobile homes was erected on the site and occupied by people with more conventional life-styles. It is now called Tollerton Park. There have been no further complaints from either Truman or Sherwood.

# Chapter 13

# Truman Aviation II - 1980 to 2007

In 1980, Derek Truman retired and sold his company, Truman Aviation Ltd, to Arrowband Equipment Ltd of Nottingham, whose subsidiary was Leatherland Business Equipment Ltd of Castle Boulevard. The sale included the lease of the airfield, which had been renewed two years earlier. The new Managing Director was to be Derek Leatherland, a keen aviator who had been an instructor in the Spencer Flying School and owned his own Tiger Moth. His brother Ray, together with Barry Thomas, became co-directors. One of their first decisions was to retain the company name of Truman Aviation. Twenty-seven years later, Derek Leatherland is still Managing Director.

In January 1984 a new lease was agreed between Truman Aviation and Nottingham City, to run for thirty years from 25 March 1983. Under the agreement Nottingham leased to Truman 230 acres of land together with 'all the buildings, structures and erections standing and being upon the said piece of land, and the fixtures and fittings therein'. The terms were similar to those of previous lease agreements, which included clauses stipulating that: (i) the land was to be used as a private airfield only; (ii) it should not be used for scheduled or charter air services, except for air-taxi or ferry services employing not more than six aircraft, each with a seating capacity of not more than 19, including the pilot (this was considerably larger than the ceiling capacity of six imposed in the original 1963 lease – there are few 19-seater taxis!); (iii) Truman would be responsible for all site and building maintenance; (iv) sub-letting should be subject to the City's approval and, with the exception of unbuilt-on land (which

**Plate 87:  Ray and Derek Leatherland.** *Derek Leatherland*

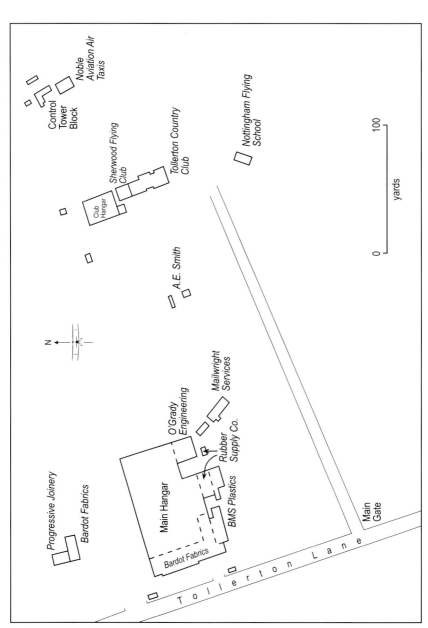

**Figure 10: Map of Tollerton Airfield's Buildings in 1981 and their uses.** The Bellman Hangar and most of the smaller buildings shown in Figure 9 have gone, as has the Bridge Hangar outside the map area. The Main and Club Hangars and the clubhouse are still standing. The Control Tower Block and the clubhouse are still standing. The Control Tower, not on Figure 9, is shown surrounded by a number of caravans and portacabins. *Dr Anne Tarver & Rushcliffe Borough Council*

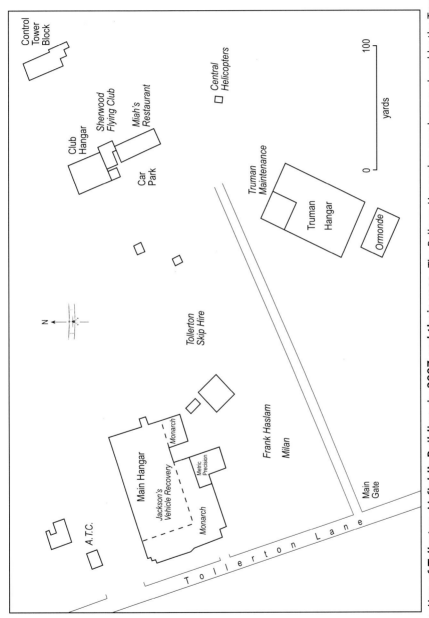

**Figure 11: Map of Tollerton Airfield's Buildings in 2007 and their uses.** The Bellman Hangar has now been replaced by the Truman Hangar. Alongside is a much smaller hangar occupied by Ormonde Aircraft Ltd. The Control Tower is now part of a single block, containing offices, briefing rooms and a lounge. *Dr Anne Tarver*

could be used for agriculture) and the Main Hangar block, should be confined to aviation-related activity; and (v) Truman should pay all rates, taxes and the cost of insurance cover.

The new regime brought both continuity and change. Those elements which continued much as before will be dealt with first. Most basic was maintenance of the flying infrastructure, which carried on much as before though there were some significant developments.

## Infrastructure

Soon after Leatherland took over Truman Aviation the 'pilots' lounge' caravan installed in the 1960s was replaced. In its place three adjoining interconnected Portacabins were provided beside the control tower block, primarily to house the flying school, but open to all flyers using the airfield. In 1990 these were replaced in turn by two prefabricated structures bought from Rushcliffe Borough Council, then about to move its offices into its present premises on Pavilion Road, West Bridgford. These were joined on to the control tower block, more than doubling its floor space and providing offices, a lounge and briefing room.

Maintenance of the runways was a continuing financial burden. Inflation had raised the cost of resurfacing to £100,000 by the late 1980s when it was scheduled to take place. Coincidentally, cracks began to appear on the two operational runways. A survey revealed that parts had sunk by two feet, which was put down to subsidence caused by mining from Cotgrave colliery. Happily for Truman Aviation the National Coal Board acknowledged responsibility, repaired and resurfaced the parts it had damaged, thereby saving Truman a considerable expense.

Two new hangars were erected in the 1980s: the first was a second-hand

**Plate 88:   A runway prior to resurfacing in early 1980s.** Much of the top layer
of tarmac had worn away exposing the original concrete surface. *Derek Leatherland*

double hangar brought in from RAF Desford in Leicestershire and erected on the site of the old Bellman Hangar removed in the late 1950s; the second was a much smaller one beside it. The former, after standing as a skeleton of girders for several years, was eventually clad and roofed, to replace the Main Hangar beside Tollerton Lane for hangaring aircraft. Part was partitioned off for maintenance work previously carried out in the old Club Hangar. The small hangar was erected for specialist work described in chapter 15.

## Other Airfield Users

Sherwood Flying Club continued under the 'squatting' arrangements it had enjoyed since it was first established, occupying the same club rooms and using the hangar, fuelling and maintenance facilities provided on site. Private owners of aircraft continued using Tollerton as their base - the number of 'resident' aircraft has remained fairly stable at about 35 fixed-wing (over half privately owned) and four helicopters (one privately owned).

Helicopters have also continued to operate, run by a succession of private companies. The most recent is Central Helicopters, which provides both its own flying school and a heli-taxi service. Central Helicopters currently has three machines (two two-seater Robinson 22s and one four-seater Robinson 44) and some 40 students on the books, though only about 25 are classed as 'active'. Most activity is at weekends, and once qualified, former students can hire the helicopters as members of an unofficial club. Truman provides hangarage and fuel, but maintenance is carried out by East Midland Helicopters at Costock, beside the A60 Nottingham to Loughborough road. Because of the different skills involved (and different expenses - helicopters cost at least twice as much to buy and fly as light fixed wing aircraft) there are few associated with both Central Helicopters and the Truman Flying School or Sherwood Flying Club.

Occasional use of the airfield has continued by a select few visiting Nottingham and its environs from elsewhere: jockeys, pop stars, politicians and others with either busy schedules or comfortable bank balances or both. The Army Air Corps, and to a lesser extent Naval and RAF aircraft refuel at Tollerton from time to time. Perhaps the most notable visitors have been the red or maroon aircraft of the Queen's Flight, usually helicopters conveying members of the royal family on their way to attend nearby events or institutions. Tollerton is often preferred to East Midlands Airport because there are fewer formalities at the smaller airfield, and no queues awaiting landing or take-off clearance during the intervals between arrivals and departures of commercial airliners – intervals that become shorter as East Midlands becomes busier. Commercial flights generally have priority over private flights.

Non-aviation activities have continued in the Main Hangar block and clubhouse, and are dealt with in chapters 14 and 15. The rest of this chapter will focus on the changes that have occurred since 1980.

## Major Changes

Derek Leatherland took over the Piper franchise, which Derek Truman had held since 1963. The year prior to transfer, 1979, saw sales topping a million pounds for the first time, so future prospects must have looked promising. But the market in light aircraft had peaked and rapidly declined thereafter - it appears to have become saturated. Leatherland bought two Pipers when he took over the lease; he sold one and kept the other (which is still in use) but never sold another, despite persevering with the agency for a few years. A 1983 advertisement offered free flying lessons to any Piper purchaser. No-one took the bait and the franchise was then dropped. With it the company lost what had, only a few years ago, been its most profitable enterprise. Subsequently, Piper's main agency in Britain at Oxford, sole provider of spare parts for Pipers, also finished.

Leatherland therefore looked for alternative revenue sources, and eventually, but not immediately, took over two activities previously conducted on the airfield by others. Both were new starts for Truman Aviation: the Truman Flying School and the Truman Maintenance Unit. The Nottingham Flying School had replaced the Spencer Flying School towards the end of the Truman era; it was in turn replaced by the Truman Flying School soon after the beginning of the Leatherland era, with one significant difference: while both the Spencer and Nottingham schools were run independently of Truman Aviation, from 1983 onwards the Truman Flying School would be run directly by Derek Leatherland.

The Truman Flying School has gradually grown and in 2007 there are four full-time flying instructors (paid, unlike their counterparts in Sherwood Flying Club) and a membership of 250, of whom 40 are student pilots. The rest are able to use Truman's planes once they are qualified, and enjoy facilities in the control tower block, rather like members of an unofficial club. Unlike Sherwood club members, however, they have no share in the ownership of the planes they use and have no constitutional right to influence the School's policy and practice - they are customers, not shareholders. Like Sherwood Flying Club, the Truman School advertises trial lessons and gift vouchers to recruit new members: a voucher gives its recipient a flight with an instructor and the opportunity to take over the controls while in the air. Hundreds are dispensed, particularly before Christmas but also to mark birthdays, wedding anniversaries and the like.

One further short-lived flying school appeared on the airfield, based in a small building adjoining the Club hangar and calling itself The Pilot Assist College. Peter Clark of Sherwood Flying Club recalls:

We [Sherwood Flying Club] were approached by a Roger Easton in June 2002 to consider a joint undertaking with this organization to train *ab initio* students (up to Private Pilot's Licence standards) who wished then to proceed to become commercial pilots. We were not keen since, because they were obviously commercial and we are not, the tie up would be awkward and upset our relationship with Truman Aviation.

We were very pleased not to have got involved since the outfit went bust less than 18 months later, leaving a number of students high and dry.

Aircraft maintenance, carried on by Harold Hall for thirty years and then by Skyline Helicopters for a further two, was taken over in 1993, to be run directly by Truman Aviation. Part of the large new Truman Hangar was partitioned off to become Truman Aviation's maintenance unit, which has since that date provided a full range of services for all fixed-wing aircraft resident at Tollerton (see plate 89). The rest of the Truman Hangar is used to hangar aircraft, as is the old Club Hangar, which Hall had used for maintenance.

A new enterprise introduced by Leatherland is advertised on the Internet as 'Aerial photography and site surveys'. People may wish to see what their property looks like from the air, while companies or local authorities may wish to monitor progress in site development. An example of the latter is the landscaping of disused collieries, such as those at Pleasley and Shirebrook, near Mansfield. Truman Aviation conducted monthly photographic surveys over these areas for four years and continues to do so every quarter.

Less frequent and regular aerial photography from Tollerton is carried out by businesses other than Truman Aviation. One such is the British Geological Survey, based in nearby Keyworth. After serious floods a BGS plane is dispatched to a convenient airfield, from where it carries out a photographic survey of

**Plate 89:    Inside the Truman Hangar.** A Socota TB10 being serviced in the Maintenance area of the Truman Hangar. *Rod Gill*

affected areas to produce a flood map which will help predict future floods and ameliorate their impact. The *Nottingham Evening Post* of 30 June 2007 reported such a flight after one of the most severe floods in living memory:

> The BGS plane's flight path took it from Tollerton Airport over towards Derbyshire, over Worksop into Humberside and then back past West Burton and Cottam power stations, the A1, Newark, Radcliffe-on-Trent and back to Tollerton. ... Dr Howard [Principal Geologist at BGS] said: 'From the plane, I was able to see where this modern flood matched long gone rivers and channels shown on our geological maps. Every time man builds on the floodplain, it modifies the next flood. ... So every time there's a major flood we try to get a plane up and see what is different'.

Apart from the two new hangars and the control tower block extension already mentioned, the other building developments since 1980 have been: (i) rebuilding the Country Club restaurant (formerly Nottingham Flying Club's clubhouse) after it had been destroyed by fire in 1982; (ii) enlargement of Sherwood Flying Club's premises; and (iii) the erection to the north of the Main Hangar of a small building which now houses the South Nottinghamshire Air Training Corps Squadron. These are all considered in chapter 14.

## Pageants

Annual pageants, which were a feature of Truman's tenure, continued for a dozen years under Leatherland, though organization was no longer shared with outside bodies. Familiar names and events still appeared on the programme: The Red Arrows in formation flying, The Barnstormers in aerobatics and the Falcons in free-fall and parachute drops. Time-honoured fly-pasts by wartime veteran aircraft, notably the Spitfire, Hurricane, Lancaster and Flying Fortress, also continued.

The 1981 pageant was held in June. In August of that year another notable event took place at Tollerton, spread over three days: the fourth International Precision Championships, the first to be held in Britain (it had previously been held in Canada, Austria and Sweden). Competitors were required, among other things, to fly a series of navigational tests without electronic aids, equipped only with map, compass and photographs of a destination revealed an hour before the flight; and to land with both wheels on a one-foot target. Unfortunately ground officials placed themselves dangerously near a runway for some of the tests, causing alarm among airport staff. Organisers of the event were not invited to return.

A highlight of the 1985 pageant was a visit from Concorde. Derek Leatherland learnt that, on 27 June, it was due to fly from Heathrow to East Midlands, to bring passengers to the official opening of Britannia Park, near Ilkeston. As this was also the day of the Tollerton pageant, Derek enquired into the possibility of the plane being diverted to fly low over Tollerton – the runways were too short for it to land and take off again. He received a positive reply: not only would it come but it would do so free of charge. Unfortunately the sky was overcast on the day, but nevertheless at the expected time Concorde suddenly appeared out of the clouds with its undercarriage down and flew very low overhead. David Kidger of Bassingfield, whose back garden faces the airfield, was ready with a camera to record the visit - see plate 90.

The 1990 pageant marked the airfield's sixtieth anniversary with a special programme, but attendance was disappointing, in part because a growing number of spectators were avoiding payment of entrance and parking fees by taking up positions with their cars along surrounding roads. The 1993 pageant made a loss of £8,000, after which the directors called a halt. There have been no pageants since. Instead, annual 'Fly-ins' have been arranged, in which flyers of light aircraft are invited to come from all over the country to Tollerton on a Sunday in summer to meet fellow flyers socially and to view their aircraft - an aviators' jamboree. Several dozen normally take part though numbers vary with the weather and other factors, such as extra publicity when the journal *Today's Pilot* adopted Tollerton as 'its' airfield in 2005 and 2006.

**Plate 90:   Concorde flying over Tollerton, 1985.** *David Kidger*

# Chapter 14

# Clubs and the Clubhouse

Flying clubs differ from the Air Training Corps in that they are for adults and are owned by their members, which the ATC isn't; and offer pilot training to their members, which the ATC doesn't. The clubs should also be distinguished from flying *schools,* which are not owned or run by members; the latter are commercial ventures whose primary function is to offer pilot training in return for payment. They are considered in chapters 12 and 13.

Nottingham Flying Club was started in the 1930s as a successor to the Nottingham Aero Club. It suspended activity during the war, revived soon after the end of hostilities (its first post-war minuted meeting is dated 6 June 1946), became moribund in the fifties, and wound up in 1963. The Sherwood Flying Club started in 1956 and is still active today. The Player Flying Club operated at Tollerton between 1967 and 1970 for the benefit of Player's directors and employees.

The Eagle and Tollerton Flying Clubs were flying clubs in name only: membership did not involve learning to fly or the ability to do so. They ran the clubhouse with bar facilities, were licensed to sell alcohol to club members only, and provided flyers (or anyone else) who joined somewhere on site to enjoy a tipple. They and their successors will be considered towards the end of this chapter, together with a more aviation-oriented club which has neither 'flying' nor 'club' in its name: the Air Training Corps.

## Nottingham Flying Club

Most of what we know about the post-war Nottingham Flying Club is derived from a minute book, a few press reports, a correspondence file and some bank statements. We have found few today with memories of its activities.

In 1946 Tollerton was transferred by the Air Ministry from military to civilian use, after which activities of the Club were resumed. Its revival was led by pre-war members G. Simpkins and T.W. Shipside, the latter being director of Nottingham Airport Ltd, which had regained use of the aerodrome and clubhouse, but not of the numerous buildings erected during the war.

The Club got off to a promising start. By mid-August 1946, with membership already touching 130, the *Nottingham Journal* reported an inspection tour by members of the Association of British Aero Clubs. At its close their chairman said:

> We are extremely impressed by what is being done here. So far as I am aware the flying rates that the Nottingham club are charging are the lowest anywhere. In my opinion, the club is one of the most efficient in England.

Within a year membership had risen to 200, though only about half were flying members; the other half were 'social', and included spouses and partners of the flyers. The flying members were mostly but not exclusively men. The Club differed from its successor, the Sherwood Flying Club, in that it ran a clubhouse and employed staff to provide lunches, teas and bar facilities. Lunch was 2/6d (ground staff 1/6d) and tea 1/3d (ground staff 9d). This aspect of the Club's activities is dealt with towards the end of the chapter, headed 'The Clubhouse'.

On 21 September 1946, the Nottingham Flying Club held an Air Pageant. Two days later the *Nottingham Journal* enthused that a crowd of 10,000 had watched

> an air display that was full of interest with many of the very latest military and civil aircraft including jet-propelled machines. ... In this respect alone it was the most important display held at Tollerton, and probably the finest air show ever staged in the Midlands. ... Chief interest of course centred on the jets - represented by a de Havilland Vampire, a Gloster Meteor ... and the Avro Lancastrian[6], which is powered by two Nene jet units and two Merlins [with propellers]. ... [The Lancastrian] took off with all four engines working. Then both Merlins were silenced and the Lancastrian flew low over the crowd on the two jets only, having worked up a speed that must have amazed those who had not seen this aircraft in flight before. ... Proceeds of the display will be divided between the RAF Benevolent Fund and the funds of the Nottingham Flying Club.

These proceeds amounted to the apparently modest sum of £67.19s.2d, though with an inflation factor of 20:1 (probably an underestimate) this would be worth nearly £1,400 in today's money. There was a down side however: three years later the club minute book refers to an unspecified accident, which had incurred legal costs. Two club members were involved, who would be required to foot the bill, but other members were invited to support them with donations. No record has been found of members' response.

Further pageants were held in the following three years, in which one of the events was a three-leg navigation competition sponsored by the *Nottingham Journal*. At the annual dinner and dance in January 1949 a club member, Ben Dowson, was presented with a replica of the trophy for achieving a hat trick: he had won the event in each of the last three years. At that same dinner/dance another way in which the *Journal* supported the club was alluded to by its chairman, Mr Shipside: scholarships enabling two young people to learn to fly each year, foreshadowing the flying scholarships awarded jointly by the Nottinghamshire County Council and Sherwood Flying Club in the 1960s and

---

[6] The Lancastrian at this event, with its two jet engines, was a one-off experimental modification of the standard Lancastrian, which was powered by four Merlin engines and was a civilian version of the Lancaster bomber. Both the Merlin and the Nene engines were made by Rolls-Royce.

1970s (see page 240). One of the old scholarship winners was John Stafford, now in his eighties, who recalls that some sixty years ago he was awarded 21 hours of flying lessons at Tollerton as the prize for a short story he had written on an aviation theme. Although he did not gain a pilot's licence he subsequently took up gliding as a life-long recreation 'until a few years ago when increasing fees and decreasing pension income made it impossible to continue'.

The last Nottingham Flying Club pageant was held in 1949 and was pronounced a 'distinct success' at the following AGM in spite of unfavourable weather, which curtailed attendance. A donation was made from the proceeds to the RAF Benevolent Fund, after which the event showed 'only a small deficit'. In retrospect, this boded ill for the future of the Club: it was already running into financial difficulties and appears to have been generous beyond its means. Moreover, annual subscriptions had been *reduced*, and reduced substantially, in 1947 - from five guineas to three for individuals, and six guineas to four for couples; there is no mention of a subsequent increase. One member, H.Tempest, the photographer mentioned in chapter 11, made a donation to the Club of £100 and was voted to be made a life-member in May 1949, but his example does not appear to have been followed by others.

However, in November 1949 a committee meeting discussed the Club's financial difficulties and decided on some cut-backs in expenditure: catering in the clubhouse was to be closed during the winter except at weekends, and flying instruction should also be restricted to weekends. This meeting turned out to be the last (at least, the last to be minuted) until 1960. Either the return of the RAF referred to in chapter 10, or the Club's parlous financial position seemed to put a stop to all its activities.

**Plate 91:** **The Avro Lancastrian with two jet and two propeller engines.** *Tom Myall*

These economies illustrate how the Nottingham Flying Club differed from its successor, the Sherwood Flying Club: it depended more heavily upon paid staff. In 1947 the Nottingham club appointed a flying instructor (H.C. Rogers) on a salary of £375 a year plus 2/6 per hour flying time; all Sherwood's flying instructors are club-members and are unpaid, apart from the costs of insurance premiums, periodic medicals and licence renewal tests. And while Nottingham Flying Club ran a licensed clubhouse serving alcohol and meals involving paid bar-tenders and catering staff, Sherwood members wanting these facilities have to go to an independently run enterprise next door - currently a Bangladeshi restaurant, only open in the evenings and Sunday lunch-time; if they want a cup of tea in their own clubhouse, they make it themselves. Only some of the time-keeping - the booking and logging in and out of all flights by club members - is paid, and even that was once done exclusively by volunteer members; some still is.

Returning briefly to pageants, those of the early post-war years, which attempted to carry on what had been part of Nottingham Flying Club's annual pre-war programme, were organized entirely by the Club. In contrast, pageants held in the 1960s and 1970s were hosted by Truman Aviation, organized by outside bodies, and the only contribution of Sherwood Flying Club was the participation of members in individual events or as stewards.

Other than pageants, the minute book of the Nottingham Flying Club refers to the following activities: teaching people to fly - the 1947 AGM reported 16 'A' licences (the rough equivalent of today's Private Pilot's Licence) had been obtained during the past year; flying competitions - there is no indication what they involved, but in 1947 the Shipstone Cup was won by T.K. Shipside; and social events like a dinner at Christmas. In short, the Club was responsible for everything that happened on the airfield other than aircraft repair and conversion, the domain of Field Aircraft Services.

By 1949 the Club had two aircraft - an Autocrat and a J.4 (both Austers) - and some members owned their own aircraft. They were housed in the Club Hangar (Tollerton's original hangar), situated next to the clubhouse, which was owned by T.W. Shipside. Presumably there was some recreational and, perhaps, business flying undertaken by Club members, either as individuals or in groups. One former member, E. Cox, recalls how, in the severe winter of 1947, an Autocrat was fitted with skis and made several take-offs and landings on the snow.

Although the Club was in financial difficulties by the late forties, it had a potential asset. An appropriately named Mrs Wing had bequeathed £1000 'to be used for the benefit of flying' to the Nottingham Aero Club before its name-change in the early thirties. The origin of this bequest is more fully described on pages 67 and 75. It had by now accrued a further £200-plus in interest. Apparently the Club could not touch the money until lawyers were satisfied that the Nottingham Flying Club was the legitimate heir to the Nottingham Aero Club, and that took many years - and legal fees. Until 1956 in fact!

There is a large gap in the minute book from November 1949 to March 1960, so we know little of the Club's activities in the 1950s. The gap is probably explained by the fact that Tollerton airfield (but none of the buildings) was again taken over for use by the RAF in 1949, and became a satellite of RAF Syerston until 1956, when it was transferred to civilian use for a second and (so far) final time. As during the war, the Flying Club apparently ceased to function as a club. However, the total ban on civil flying which had pertained throughout the war no longer applied and individuals who had been members of the Club continued to fly and enjoy use of the Club Hangar. It is perhaps to these individuals that an unsigned letter of 1956 refers when it states that the Club proposed to use the Wing legacy to buy a second aircraft 'as it appears they have 60 members and only one aircraft'. There are no records of Club membership fees being paid into its account, and no minutes of Club meetings, and the plane was never bought. Indeed, during the fifties bank statements indicate virtually no transactions until loans were made to the Sherwood Flying Club (see below), which, together with the gap in the minute book already referred to, suggests the Nottingham Flying Club was moribund throughout the 1950s.

Instead, the Wing fund seems to have been used to advance loans to the Sherwood Flying Club, formed in 1956 and incorporated in 1957 - first of £400 in 1957, to be paid back in monthly instalments of £5; and then of £1000, to be repaid at £20 a month. Finally, in November 1963, Nottingham Flying Club was dissolved and effectively absorbed by Sherwood Flying Club. A minute of a meeting of the directors of the Sherwood Flying Club on 16 November 1963 reads:

> It was unanimously resolved that the Sherwood Flying Club agree to take over the Nottingham Flying Club with all its assets and members and under the terms as detailed in their letter signed by Mr. K. Smith dated 11th November, 1963.

That letter uses the word 'absorbed' and states:

> Assets consist of £1,227.12s.6d … and one silver cup. There are no liabilities. … The total membership, including myself, is four, of whom two are already members of the Sherwood Flying Club.

The assets evidently did not include an aircraft, which makes one wonder what happened to the two it possessed in 1949, mentioned above. It seems likely that Nottingham Flying Club had been little more than a bank account for at least the six years since Sherwood Flying Club began operating alongside, and probably since 1949.

## Sherwood Flying Club - the Early Years

The origin of the Sherwood Flying Club has been described by the widow and daughter of one of its founder members, Michael (Mike) Gani, a South African who had settled in Nottingham after World War II as an estate agent. Mike placed a notice in a Nottingham paper in 1955 or 1956, inviting anyone with flying experience interested in teaching others to fly to get in touch. The encouraging response from local businessmen and ex-service pilots led to an approach being made to the Air Registration Board (predecessor of the Civil Aviation Authority) for permission to establish a flying club at Tollerton Airfield. This was granted and a committee was formed of those willing to make an advance payment towards the purchase of an aircraft, a Tiger Moth. The Sherwood Flying Club was born.

Whether or not Mike Gani's notice started the ball rolling or was written on behalf of a like-minded group who were already nurturing the idea of a flying club is not clear. An article in the *Evening Post* on 17 October 1955 refers to air-minded men who 'are hoping to give the city [of Nottingham] an aero club again and bring it into line with Leicester and Derby'. One of the men mentioned in the article was Paul Cash, who would, with Mike Gani, become a leading member of the Sherwood Flying Club. Clearly there was a gestation period of informal discussion and planning before the Club was born in 1956.

Membership then increased rapidly so that fees made it possible to return the advances within 18 months to those who had made them. Growing numbers and funds led to the purchase of a second plane, a Taylorcraft Model plus D. But it also led to a consideration of limiting the liability of the committee should the Club run into financial difficulties.

The result was the formation on 8 July 1957 of a limited liability company, now named The Sherwood Flying Club Ltd. There were seven founder members, listed as 'subscribers' in the Articles of Association and presumed to be the original committee making the advance payments. They included both Mike Gani and Paul Cash and comprised the nucleus of the limited company, the membership of which subsequently elected a governing Council, including Harry Adcock as Chairman, Charles Taylor as Vice-chairman, Mike Gani as Secretary and Frank Kirk as Chief Flying Instructor[7]. The Club now had a formal constitution and was also on a sounder financial footing.

On the other hand, loans from the Nottingham Flying Club already mentioned suggest that finances were still somewhat precarious. This did not inhibit the Club's ambitions, however: the Articles of Association state that 'The number of members with which the Association proposes to be registered is 500'. It is doubtful if that number was ever reached: membership climbed to well over 200 in the early 1970s; it now stands at about 175. The recent downturn largely reflects a nationwide declining interest in recreational flying: the award of Private Pilot's Licences (PPLs), has fallen nationally by 40 per cent in the past ten years, which is steeper than Sherwood's fall.

---

[7] Frank Kirk succeeded Paul Cash, who had been the Club's first Chief Flying Instructor but left the area to take up a post in South Wales at about the time the Club was incorporated. So Frank was the Incorporated Club's first CFI.

Sadly, two of Sherwood's founder officers died comparatively young: Mike Gani in 1964 and Frank Kirk in 1972. Mike was self-effacing, working diligently and efficiently behind the scenes, and few remember his relatively brief tenure today. The few who do, such as Richard Randall who was introduced to Mike as a twelve year-old boy in 1963, and Wilf Dale who knew him from 1957, speak very warmly of his friendliness, particularly towards youngsters like Richard. Frank was a professional pilot, first in the Fleet Air Arm and then with Rolls-Royce. As Sherwood's Chief Flying Instructor he had a higher profile in the Club than Mike and his period of office lasted longer. Today he is perhaps the most revered of the Club's founding fathers. In 1963 he succeeded Mike as Secretary while continuing as CFI and held both positions until shortly before his death. Although he flew for a living, over half the total of 16,000 flying hours he amassed during his career were devoted to the Club, mostly training pupil pilots voluntarily and unpaid.

It has not been possible to obtain access to minute books of The Sherwood Flying Club Council, and few of those we have interviewed were involved with the Club in its first few years. Apart from Wilf Dale and Richard Randall already mentioned, Mrs Gani and her daughter are other exceptions: they recall accompanying Mr Gani to Tollerton on frequent weekends. While he flew, his

**Plate 92:  Five Founder Members of The Sherwood Flying Club Ltd.** Left to right: Cyril Marson, Harry Adcock (Chairman of Council), Frank Kirk (Chief Flying Instructor), Bob Ockleford, Hector Taylor. *Wilf Dale*

wife met with other wives in the clubhouse, while their children played outside in some of the wartime bunkers away from the flying area - nearly all the pilots were men, though there was at least one woman.

Although the Club was growing in numbers it retained something of a family atmosphere. Teenagers like Richard Randall, too young to start pilot training, were encouraged to get involved in some of the ancillary jobs associated with flying, like manning fuel pumps or cleaning aircraft, for which they were often rewarded with free flights. Sometimes members' wives and children were given 'rides' - on one occasion Mr Gani took his wife up and looped the loop twice! She was unruffled. Then as now, Thursday was also a flying day when the club was open and those who could take time off work to fly did so, normally leaving the rest of the family at home or at school.

Documentary sources lent by Will Dale relating to the early days include two issues of a *Newsletter* dated September 1957 (Number 2) and March-May 1958 (Number 6), and a photocopy of a 1958 description of the Club, source unknown. From the description, we learn that the Club in 1958 had 140 members of whom 40 were 'fully licensed [pilots]'; that in the two years of the Club's existence 14 members had been trained *ab initio* to gain their Private Pilot's Licence while 'a good number of ex-pilots have renewed their licences which had lapsed because of the lack of [accessible] flying facilities'; that 'there are cross-country flights to all parts of the United Kingdom' and that 'one of the most popular trips is to places like Skegness to take tea with a fellow pilot.' From the *Newsletters* we infer that it began as a monthly or bi-monthly issue but became quarterly (it seems to have lapsed altogether for some years until revived in 1966); that the Club had held its second annual dinner/dance in March 1958; that many members attended the Air Display at Hucknall on May 1958 – 'our club aircraft were busy

**Plate 93:**
**Mike Gani.** Founder Member and first Secretary of the Club. *Bunney Hayes*

flying members to Hucknall well before the start of the show while a good number went by car with their families'; that from its formation in June 1956 to March-May 1958 (23 months), the Club had accumulated a total of 1308 hours 40 minutes flying hours (about 57 hours per month), which had grown in the last three months from 59 hours in March to 91 hours in May 1958 as both Club membership and hours of daylight had increased. With a flying membership of 40, the figures imply an average of between 1.5 and 2.25 hours per month per member. To put them into context: every licensed pilot, who has to renew his Private Pilot's Licence every two years, has to put in at least twelve flying hours during the second year, while the present Chief Flying Instructor, Peter Clark, estimates that these averages were somewhat higher than they are today – probably because fuel and other costs were lower then than now, and many members used to go on weekend tours to the Continent which they rarely do today.

Operating happily as a club within a club in the early 1960s, and illustrating the point just made, was the Southwell Air Touring Club. This consisted largely of Sherwood Flying Club members, mostly from the Mansfield and Sutton area. They owned their own aircraft – a Miles Messenger – which members could use to take family and friends on continental trips (hence the word 'touring' in the title) or to attend aviation rallies in the UK.

There were also special occasions at Tollerton when competitions were held, though not on the scale of later pageants. They were mainly for the benefit of members (flying), their families and friends (watching), rather than being open to the general public. We have few details of what took place, but Mr Gani's logbook refers to his taking part in the Masefield Trophy competition. There were meetings at which competitive flying between Sherwood members, or between Sherwood and other clubs took place.

One member, Jack Marriott, was a particularly keen racer who also took part in several King's Cup events in other parts of the country. In addition he was, in the early 1960s, UK distributor for the Italian aircraft manufacturer Falco and owned one of its planes, together with a variety of others which Richard Randall recalls as being uncommon: Mooneys, a Tipsy Nipper and several Piper models not usually seen in England at the time.

## Sherwood Flying Club - From the Mid-sixties

The period from 1966 to 1978 is well documented in the Sherwood Flying Club's twice-yearly *Newsletter*, which after a few issues was named *Straight and Level*. Unfortunately, regular production ceased in 1978, though occasional newsletters have been produced since, a few in the 1990s under the name *Sierra Fox Charlie*, the Club's initials in air-speak. There are also many long-time members with remarkable memories to compensate. Much of what follows, particularly outside the dates covered by the newsletters, comes from interviews with them.

The Sherwood Flying Club's birth coincided with the departure of Field Aircraft Services and the end of the lease held by Nottingham Airport Ltd, so that for the seven years until Truman Aviation appeared on the scene, Sherwood was virtually running the airfield. Perhaps for that reason, the owner, Nottingham Corporation, allowed the Club to stay and use the facilities rent-free. When Truman Aviation took over the running of the airfield in 1963 these rent-free 'squatters' rights' continued for a few years and there is still no formal sub-letting agreement between the Club and Truman Aviation. However, Sherwood does now pay to use the airfield and hangars; it also pays for aircraft maintenance and buys most of its fuel from Truman.

By the issue of the first revived *Newsletter* in 1966, Sherwood already had three aircraft and was looking forward to the delivery of a fourth. One may assume that the loans from Nottingham Flying Club referred to earlier went towards the purchase of two, and the transfer of that Club's assets in 1963 was spent on the third, but with light aircraft then costing anything upward of £3000 a piece, members' subscriptions, together with flying and instruction fees must have provided the bulk.

The Club was flourishing between the mid-sixties and mid-seventies. These were its halcyon days. According to *The Newsletter*, membership stood at 250 in 1966, reached 285 in 1970, and over 300 in 1973, with waiting lists when there were insufficient 'instructional hours' (available instructors and planes) to train those who wanted to learn to fly. However, the Club Secretary and Treasurer from 1972 to 2006, Derrick Brooks, disputes these figures: he

Plate 94: A Piper Warrior belonging to the Sherwood Flying Club over the National Water Sports Centre at Holme Pierrepont. *Peter Clark*

contends that they include those on the waiting list; full membership never exceeded 250, and averaged below 200 in the early 1970s. This implies substantial waiting lists. Also, many members only stayed for a short time, so the queue for membership moved fairly quickly.

Between July 1970 and March 1973, there was an intake of 177 and a loss of 149 - a net gain of 28, but also a substantial wastage. Part of this was due to student pilots leaving once they had obtained their Private Pilot's Licence or achieved their first solo flight - they never intended to stay longer. Some left the area and perhaps joined other flying clubs. But in other cases, suggested reasons include the increased cost of flying, the growing popularity of alternative leisure pursuits from golf to local history, and the knock-on effects of growing gender equality. These last included complaints by wives that husbands were spending too much time and money on their hobby to the neglect of the family (only 15 members were women pilots in 1973); and more women going out to work so that there was more for their husbands to do in the home. These trends became more apparent later on, but were already beginning to make an impact, not only on Club membership, but also on the amount of time members devoted to Club activities.

Meanwhile a good deal was going on. In 1967 the King's Cup Air Race came to Tollerton for the first time, as part of an annual weekend pageant held normally in the summer. Although this was a Truman rather than a Sherwood event, several Club members took part, and in 1972 it fielded an aerobatic display team.

Navigational tours were organized by Club members in the spring over several years, involving a group flying together to other airports in the United Kingdom or abroad - one year to Brittany, another to south-west England, another to Ireland - again, usually over a weekend. And in the autumn, flying competitions were held, in which Club members displayed their prowess in skills such as forced landing, spot landing (touching down on a particular spot), aerobatics and navigation.

A particularly noteworthy trip was undertaken by three of the youngest members of the Club in July 1968: Gary Ferriman, Richard Randall and Robert Taylor. Gary (18) and Robert (17) were fairly newly qualified pilots; Richard (17)

**Plate 95:**
**Sherwood's Private**
**Pilot's Licence Badge.**
The Civilian Equivalent of
RAF Wings

was still learning. They hired the Club's four-seater Cherokee 140 for a fortnight for £108, and after rigorous briefing from Frank Kirk (Chief Flying Instructor) and Gordon Ferriman (Gary's father and a future CFI) they flew to Cannes via Stansted, Paris, Lyons and Marseilles, returning via Dijon and Stansted – a total of nearly 1700 miles in 18 hours flying. The rest of the time was spent sightseeing and relaxing beside the Mediterranean. The trip is said to have been further than anyone else has taken a Club plane, before or since.

In June 1976 a special event took place: a highly successful two-day visit to Sherwood by members of a German flying club from a city twinned with Nottingham and boasting the oldest flying club in the world, the 'Karlsruhe Flugsportsverein 1910'. This was followed by a group of Sherwood members visiting Karlsruhe, and subsequent reciprocal visits by individual members of the two Clubs who became good friends.

These were all, in varying degree, communal flying activities - socializing in the air. Today they no longer happen: there is the occasional communal day-trip to Le Touquet and back, but flying has generally become more individualistic, with socializing confined to the clubroom and the annual dinner in town. Christmas parties for members' children which featured regularly on the Club calendar are also a thing of the past, as are 'Ladies Only' evenings, the latter reflecting a desire by today's women to be members in their own right.

There are of course today, as in the past, many members who have devoted a great deal of time, skill and effort to the Club. Perhaps most notable are Derrick Brooks, the Secretary/Treasurer for nearly 35 years already mentioned, loyally assisted throughout by his wife Gill; the CFIs (successively Paul Cash, Frank Kirk, Gordon Ferriman, Len Stapleton and Peter Clark); and the numerous Assistant Flying Instructors, some of whom travel over 60 miles between home and Tollerton to give their service. They are all unremunerated and have no expense accounts, while lucrative jobs exist in flying schools which some could be doing instead. But such people require time as well as dedication, and the Club has to depend heavily on the retired for its instructors. Fortunately there is no age limit on flying, only more frequent fitness tests (the current CFI is in his mid-seventies). It is the willingness of members to work without payment that has enabled the Club to build up its healthy bank balance from precarious beginnings.

Another part of Sherwood's programme in the 1960s was the Junior Wings scheme, supported by the Nottinghamshire County Council, an echo of a scheme in the 1940s involving collaboration between the Nottingham Flying Club and the *Nottingham Journal*. The new scheme's title arose from the Wing bequest made to the Nottingham Aero Club referred to earlier. It was agreed by the Sherwood Club Council (its elected ruling body) that interest on the £1000 bequest should be devoted to flying instruction, and after discussions with the County Youth Service the scheme was launched in 1966. It offered flying scholarships to members of youth clubs in the county, entitling successful applicants to ten hours instruction at a nominal rate of 10/- per hour (the normal fee at that time was about £6 an hour, to cover fuel and overheads). Initially the cost of the scheme was borne entirely by the Club, but when funds from the Wing legacy ran out Nottinghamshire County Council stepped in: the cost of flying the aircraft would be borne by the County, and the Club would continue to provide free tutoring. It proved to be a qualified success: after six years, the January 1973 issue of *Straight and Level* reported that 24 had benefited from the scheme; of these, seven were still flying with the Club, others were satisfied to have achieved flying solo and taken it no further, while three had gone on to gain their PPL. However, the scheme continued for a few more years, offering more scholarships to a wider public: in 1974 it attracted 91 applicants, of whom eight received awards, implying keen competition. It ended a few years later when the County withdrew its support and the Wing bequest was all spent.

Other events of the 1960s and 1970s included two which were organized externally but in which Sherwood took part. First, in 1967, was a national competition sponsored by the Wills tobacco firm, involving both flying instructors and students, working in pairs. Each instructor was assigned one student for training from scratch in limited time, after which heats were held to determine a short list of better students. The winners of these heats then met for a final, held at Kidlington, near Oxford. Three Sherwood instructors and their students took part: one pair reached the final, but they were not the national winners. The event does not appear to have been repeated.

A second was really two events, both held in 1972 and 1973: races for the John Howitt trophies awarded to winners of both the International Air Rally and the Formula 1 Air Race. These were sponsored to commemorate the 135th anniversary of the founding of Howitt Printers of Nottingham. The firm's director in the 1970s was Pat Howitt, whose father had been a member of the Nottingham Flying Club before the war. The winner of one of the trophies in 1973 was a Sherwood member. The events figured in the pageants of those years were staged by Truman Aviation and are outlined more fully in chapter 12.

Another more trivial event worth recording was the rescue of a politician. In 1969, Jeremy Thorpe, then leader of the Liberal party, found himself stranded at Tollerton when his aircraft broke down. It had to be taken to East Midlands Airport for repair, and he was flown by two Sherwood members to Castle Donington to be reunited with his plane. Sherwood's *Newsletter* commented, 'Presumably when Jeremy Thorpe becomes Prime Minister of England we shall receive our due reward!'

## Sherwood Flying Club - Comparisons between Past and Present

A senior instructor has made some observations on the way the Club has changed over the years:

Whilst early Club members were mainly self-employed businessmen and a large percentage wanted to emulate the fighter pilot, nowadays the typical student is a professional who is more interested in thinking of himself as a 747 pilot. This results in us no longer having an aerobatic aircraft but giving quite a lot of instruction in instrument flight and radio navigation.

Several students have gone on to become airline pilots.

A number of members have commented on the escalating cost of flying and the increasing web of regulations to be observed. It is a common misconception that all aviation fuel is tax-free. In fact this only applies to jet fuel, used by virtually all commercial airliners today. The fuel consumed by most propeller-driven aircraft of the type flown from Tollerton is closely akin to ordinary petrol, and bears both VAT and other fuel tax. Furthermore, it contains some lead, which requires special treatment by oil companies now serving a largely lead-free car market. This has resulted in a steep rise in the price of such fuel (called Avgas) in the past few years. Present flying charges of about £110 an hour (varying with the type of aircraft flown) just about cover costs (fuel, maintenance, periodic inspections and hangarage). As one is required to fly a minimum of 40 hours to gain a Private Pilot's Licence, this will cost a pupil starting from scratch at least £4,400. In 1960 flying charges were about £3 an hour, so there has been a 37-fold increase since then, while general inflation has been about half that. If not exclusively for the rich, the club tends to attract either young people with well-off parents, or those with a comfortable

**Plate 96:    A Robin DR40 with diesel (jet fuel) engine in the Truman Hangar.** *Rod Gill*

disposable income of their own. Unlike the 1960s, it now has few former servicemen who had learnt to fly at the RAF's expense.

To address the problem of costs, the Club has considered exchanging one of its Avgas-driven aircraft for a model which uses jet fuel. A Robin DR40 was given a three-month trial in the spring of 2007. According to the June 2006 issue of the *Newsletter*, the current fuel prices were 140p per litre for Avgas as against 55p per litre for tax-free jet fuel - amounting to a difference of some £30 per hour's flying. On the other hand the Robin is more expensive than equivalent Avgas-driven planes, both to buy and to maintain. At the end of the three-month trial, therefore, the Club decided against an exchange.

With regard to regulation, as airspace becomes busier, the scope for accidents to occur increases, and regulation has to be more stringent. To quote the Chief Flying Instructor:

> Recently, the standards of flying expected of 'weekend' pilots have been jacked up and we suspect pressure is being applied to make most general aviation the preserve of professionals. More and more airspace is being designated as 'controlled' and international airports are squeezing light aircraft out.

And, unlike fuel price increases, there seems to be no way of countering regulation inflation.

A minor example of the more stringent environment in which Sherwood operates today is Customs and Special Branch requirements – the latter introduced to combat terrorism, first from the IRA and now from potential suicide bombers. There are no Customs or Special Branch officers based at Tollerton, so those wishing to fly abroad have to obtain clearance elsewhere, which normally involves paying landing fees at a bigger airport. In the 1960s (when there were no Special Branch requirements) the newly emerging East Midlands Airport offered to waive landing fees to Sherwood members flying in to obtain customs clearance before setting off overseas. That no longer applies; indeed, Tollerton aircraft now tend to keep clear of East Midlands' airspace, which has become too busy to accommodate many light aircraft from elsewhere. Sherwood's days are by no means numbered, but it has to navigate in more difficult times.

## The Player Flying Club

The Player Flying Club, part of the Player Athletic Club, was based at Tollerton for only three years, from 1967 to 1970. It owed much to the enthusiasm of one of the company's directors, Geoffrey Kent, who became one of the first who learned to fly with the Club. It owned just one plane, a Piper Cherokee 140, which was used for recreational flying by members and for flying lessons by instructors and their students. It had a caravan on site accommodating a members' lounge and flight office. All members were employees of John Player. They included full members (instructors, qualified and student pilots) and associate members who could take part in non-flying activities and also travel as passengers with qualified pilots while waiting their turn to become student-members. Numbers were limited by the availability of 'instruction time' provided by the Club's one plane and the spare time of three instructors, who were all serving RAF officers. The Chief Flying Instructor was Squadron Leader Len Stapleton, then based at Syerston.

Flying instruction was provided free by these pilots, who also gave ground tuition on subjects like navigation and meteorology. In the three years of its existence, Player Flying Club gave training to some 50 students, mostly from the shop floor. Nineteen, including three women, gained their Private Pilot's Licence.

The non-flying activities, including ground instruction and socials, normally took place in the evening on company premises in Nottingham rather than at Tollerton. There was also a newsletter, *Lima Echo* (the call signal of the Club's plane), from which much of the information in this section has been gathered.

The Club was heavily subsidized by the company, so that flying lessons for Player students cost only about a third of the fee paid by Sherwood students. No doubt this caused some envy among Sherwood members but did not sour relations between the two Clubs, which were always cordial. They did not, however, share aircraft, facilities, or instructors.

The Player Flying Club closed in 1970, after objections from other members of the Company's Athletic Club that too much subsidy was being devoted to flying at their expense. The subsidy was reduced, student fees rose and many club members left until numbers were no longer viable (though fees were still well below those of Sherwood). The few remaining students as well as the Chief Flying Instructor were invited to join Sherwood. One Player member, Graham Whitehead, who had already gained his PPL with the Club, went on to become a Sherwood Flying Instructor. He stayed with Sherwood for over ten years before emigrating to the USA, where he gained a commercial airline pilot's licence and flew for American Airways until his recent retirement.

As a *quid pro quo* for taking on the remaining Player members, Sherwood was sold *Lima Echo* at a reduced price. It did not need the extra plane at the time but could not refuse the generous offer of what was a very fine plane. It is now in private hands and still flying, from a grass field near Widmerpool.

## The Air Training Corps

One of the founders of No. 2425 Squadron of the Air Training Corps (ATC) based at Tollerton is John Davis. A retired policeman, he has given us a succinct summary of its history. Dates have been confirmed from the Squadron's website. It was formed in Cotgrave Junior School in 1965, but soon outgrew these premises and in 1966 moved to unoccupied rooms on the ground floor of the Main Hangar at Tollerton Airfield. Immediately above were the office and stores of a firm selling Tupperware products, where in 1970 an electrical fault caused a serious fire which spread to the ground floor. 'The Squadron lost everything,' Davis says. It recovered with considerable help from Eric Johnson, then the airport manager, and moved successively to a scout hut in Tollerton village, Keyworth Junior School (where the Headmaster, John Hartley, a wartime RAF pilot, became Commanding Officer), and then, in 1984, to a new purpose-built headquarters on the north side of the Main Hangar, where it has remained ever since. John Davis succeeded John Hartley as Commanding Officer – he was also a pilot, having learnt to fly with Sherwood Flying Club in the 1960s. The present (2007) Commanding Officer is Rob Frost.

The ATC can be regarded as the youth branch of the RAF, for boys and girls aged 13 to 17 with an interest in aviation. As a national body it was founded in 1941, and the local Squadron commemorated the 50th anniversary in 1991 by dedicating a plaque on one of the wartime bunkers 'to all who served at Tollerton Airfield during World War II'. (The same bunker, near the control tower, has another plaque in memory of those who died when their Wellington bomber crashed near Tollerton in February 1941.)

Plate 97:  The Tribute to ATC Members who served at Tollerton during
World War II. *Nigel Morley*

Now known as the Tollerton Airport Squadron, it draws most of its members from nearby villages, West Bridgford and Nottingham. A recent issue of *Keyworth News* (May 2007) devotes a page to the Squadron, under the title 'What did your daughter or son do last weekend?' It begins by listing the kind of activities cadets (boys and girls) are offered – flying, target shooting, camping, adventure training and sports – and goes on to outline the diary of 'a typical day's flying', based on a recent trip to RAF Cranwell. It included taking turns in handling the controls of an aircraft in flight, and performing manoeuvres under the eye of an accompanying pilot. The flights on this particular 'typical day' took place from Cranwell rather than Tollerton, presumably because of the ATC's association with the RAF. Tollerton has, since 1956, been entirely civilian.

## The Clubhouse

Since the early 1950s the clubhouse/restaurant has been run by and for people with no necessary connection with flying. Before 1950, when Nottingham Flying Club was active, things were different. The original clubhouse, built in the thirties and still in use until it burnt down in 1982, was erected by National Flying Services and run by the Nottingham Flying Club. During the war the Club's activities, both flying and social, were suspended and the clubhouse, like the rest of the airfield, was taken over by the Air Ministry for use by the RAF.

When it returned to Tollerton in 1946 the Nottingham Flying Club re-opened its clubhouse and ran it along pre-war lines until activity was again suspended when the airfield was once more taken over by the RAF in 1949. During those three years, the Club's executive committee elected two committees, a Flying and a House committee. The latter was responsible for all arrangements relating to the clubhouse but was answerable to the main executive committee.

It is perhaps significant that the first two executive committee meetings were held in Nottingham and not in the clubhouse. An August edition of *The Aeroplane* has a picture of Club members outside the clubhouse, with a caption that states that the building 'is just reaching completion after being considerably ravaged by the occupation forces during the war'. It also seems to have been bereft of basic services and of furniture, much of the latter having been moved to RAF Newton during the war. Minutes of the second meeting reported that 'the services for lighting, water and telephone were to be installed in the next few days' and that 'a tender had been submitted to the Air Ministry ... for the following: 10 tables, 100 chairs, 4 bar stools, 6 fire extinguishers and one refrigerator'. The third and subsequent meetings were held in the clubhouse – it was back in business. Within weeks a kitchen steward (initial salary £4 a week) and stewardess (salary not known) were appointed, meals were being served and a bar opened.

The last minuted meeting of the executive committee was held on 22

November 1949. It is assumed therefore that Nottingham Flying Club, including the clubhouse, effectively ceased to function thereafter.

Two years later the clubhouse was revived as the Eagle Flying Club, headed by Freddie Cronk, formerly chief pilot of Trent Valley Aviation, and then of Eagle Airways. But this time the management was not answerable to the committee of a flying club. It offered food, drink and a pleasant ambience for all who used it, but entry was restricted to Club members. No doubt many flyers were members, but membership was also open to non-flyers. It was in effect purely a social club. Furthermore, casual visitors could join on coming through the door and received the same services as more regular members. The reason why Eagle retained the word 'flying' in its name was largely sentimental, though it no doubt seemed appropriate because of its location and use of former flying club premises. 'Club' had more practical significance: it was easier to obtain a licence to sell alcoholic drinks to club members than to the general public.

One who remembers the clubhouse in the late fifties is Anne Sweet. She recalls a small and cosy bar which she and her boy-friend used to visit frequently for drinks and darts. Neither she nor he took flying lessons – they couldn't afford to – but were sometimes given rides by members of the Sherwood Flying Club who also frequented the clubhouse bar. This implies that informal links between the clubhouse and the true Flying Club still existed

Plate 98: Advertisement for Country Club shortly before the Clubhouse was burnt down.

the club in the country!

Wine, dine and dance in the
**VINTAGE RESTAURANT**
Licensed till 2 a.m.
Table d'hote and a la carte. Cabaret Saturday
Sunday Lunch £3.50 inclusive
Children Special Tariff
Weddings, Birthdays, Special Occasions our speciality
Panoramic view of Nottingham Airport and activities
For reservations phone 816790
Tuesday to Saturday 7 p.m. till 12 midnight

**Tollerton Country Club**
NOTTINGHAM AIRPORT, TOLLERTON, NOTTINGHAM

though the two were no longer formally associated. A large room adjoining the bar was used from time to time as a dance hall, usually hired for the purpose by outside bodies. For most of the time however it was empty and unheated – Anne remembers it being uncomfortably cold in winter. Neither Anne nor Mrs Gani, who also frequented the clubhouse at this time, remembers there being a proper restaurant to serve more than sandwiches, as it had before 1950 and would do again later.

The clubhouse continued to function as a social venue and bar until 1982, though the business running it changed, as did the name: soon after Derek Truman founded Truman Aviation in 1963, it became the Tollerton Flying Club; in the 1970s the Tollerton Country Club; and in the early 80s the Rob Roy Steak House - the last two names more accurately reflecting its role and the clientele it served.

An article in *Nottingham Topic* (January/February 1981) describes Tollerton Country Club as a club with bar and 'excellent restaurant facilities' and the venue for Nottingham Flying School's regular social events. It goes on:

> [It] is open every evening from Tuesday to Saturday, 8 pm to 2 am; this is just for the use of members, membership being £12 for a single and £15 for a joint subscription. However the club is also now open for Sunday lunch and is proving very popular ... Non-members may come here for Sunday lunch.

On April Fool's Day 1982, not long after it had been completely refurbished and some fifty years after it was built, a disastrous fire destroyed the clubhouse. Remarkably, the fire was confined to the clubhouse; the adjoining club room of Sherwood Flying Club, and beyond that the Club Hangar, escaped damage. A report in the *Nottingham Evening Post* the next day read:

**Plate 99:** Miah's Restaurant in the post-1982 Clubhouse – exterior, 2007. *Rod Gill*

Fire raged through one of Nottinghamshire's newest restaurant nightspots last night and 30 customers escaped as flames quickly spread through the roof. The blaze ... which almost gutted the former Country Club, caused an estimated £80,000 of damage. Customers were still sitting at their meal tables when the fire alarm went off. ... Police said today that an electrical fault is believed to have started the blaze in the roof. Five small planes in the hangar near to the restaurant were moved to escape the danger of the blaze. A fire brigade spokesman said there was little they could do other than prevent the blaze spreading to adjoining buildings.

A new two-storey building was erected soon afterwards on the same site, this time mostly made of brick. It re-opened as a restaurant called The Tiger Moth, which struggled for customers and became run down. In July 2004 it was taken over by Moshahid Miah who had the interior thoroughly refurbished and turned into a high-class restaurant called Miahs with seating capacity for 160. There are also five bedrooms in which some of the staff sleep. The elegant décor of the dining area and bar contrasts with a plain exterior, rough car park and the unkempt area between it and Tollerton Lane. The restaurant, which offers Bangladeshi, Indian and Western cuisine, is open every evening of the week and at lunchtime on Sundays, but normally only gets busy at weekends. It is no longer a club and is open to the general public like any other restaurant.

**Plate 100: Miah's Restaurant – interior, 2007.** *Rod Gill*

# CHAPTER 15

# Manufacturing and Storage after Fields

Until the departure of Field Aircraft Services in the late 1950s, Tollerton airfield was almost wholly used for aviation related activities – flying from hangars or working on aircraft in hangars. The only exception was the restaurant-cum-clubhouse described towards the end of the previous chapter.

Field's move to Wymeswold left many buildings at Tollerton unused. Some were demolished or dismantled and taken away, including the Bellman and Bridge Hangars. Others were left standing, including the Main Hangar and its adjoining storerooms and offices. It is these, together with the ground on which removed buildings once stood, that became sites of a miscellany of non-aviation related activities.

When Derek Truman took out the lease on the airfield in 1963, he tried to establish a leisure centre alongside the aviation activity. As this did not materialize he began to look for businesses to which to sub-let some of the unused property. We do not have a comprehensive list of the businesses he attracted (they ran into scores, many of which stayed only briefly), but in the 1960s they included British Road Services and Robin Hood Transport (vehicle storage), Batching Plant (manufacturing plant), John Jardine Ltd (storage), N.Ginsby (sign manufacture), Long Metalcraft (engineering), Becorit GB (engineering), Agrati Sales UK (storage), O'Grady Engineering (storage) and Solomon (dress manufacture).

A 1981 report prepared for Rushcliffe Borough Council to consider the future of Tollerton Airfield includes a list of buildings occupied in March 1981 and their uses, together with a map, which is the basis of figure 10 on page 220. The longest-standing non-aviation business then was O'Grady Engineering, present since 1966 when it was using Tollerton for storage only, but by 1981 was doing some of its light engineering work there too. The second and third longest-standing businesses were Bardot Fabrics (textiles) and Rubber Supply (storage), who came to Tollerton in 1969 and 1970 respectively. Next came Progressive Joinery (joinery and storage) in 1971, and BMS Plastics (resin and fibre glass products) in 1975, followed by Mailwright Ltd (mail distribution) and A.E.Smith in 1979, and Ian Stewart Casuals (knitwear) in 1980. It will be seen on the map that all this manufacturing and storage is located either in parts of the Main Hangar or in adjoining and other buildings near Tollerton Lane.

Meanwhile most of the Main Hangar was used to park aircraft until a new hangar became available on the site of the old Bellman in the 1990s. Hangar space for other activities was limited and they were mostly small ventures. Probably the largest was Bardot Fabrics, which employed up to 70 people, though some were at what was initially a secondary centre at Radcliffe-on-Trent. The firm supplied jersey fabrics mainly to clothing manufacturers who in turn supplied garments to High Street shops such as Marks and Spencer and British Home Stores. Beginning in a small building north of the Main Hangar, it then built a self-contained factory within the hangar itself where it installed knitting machines, offices and its own canteen. It also used outbuildings for storage.

In 1982 the firm moved all its work to Radcliffe, transferring the lease at Tollerton to another knitwear firm, Belvoir Knitting, which continued in the Main Hangar until 1999, when Bardot Fabrics also ceased trading.

Bardot stayed at Tollerton thirteen years – much longer than most. In general there was a fairly high turnover of firms who had taken out short sub-leases from Truman Aviation. In a renewed lease agreement between Truman Aviation and Nottingham City Council dated 23 January 1984, thirteen such sub-leases are listed, the longest being for five years and the shortest for one year only. Only three of the names are the same as those who were there in 1981: Rubber Supply, A.E.Smith and Bardot Fabrics, by then a holding company which, as we have seen, had sub-let to Belvoir Knitting.

It would be tedious to catalogue all the businesses at Tollerton that have come and gone. By January 2007 (see figure 11 on page 221) none of those named in the previous paragraphs were present. About half the floor space in the Main Hangar was leased by Jacksons Recovery Ltd as a police compound. Cars damaged in accidents in Nottingham and south Nottinghamshire were brought here for inspection by insurance assessors. After assessment, those worth repairing were taken away to be restored to roadworthiness; the rest were sent to scrap yards in Dunkirk (Simms Metals) and Cotgrave (Chris Allsop

Plate 101: Jackson's Recovery in the Main hangar, 2006. *Nigel Morley*

off the A46). Most of the rest of the hangar was occupied by Monarch Acoustics, Monarch Computer Furniture, and Metric Precision, making metal goods. A few of the outbuildings stood empty and unkempt. Yards to the south and east of the hangar were used for storage by Tollerton Skip Hire Ltd, Frank Haslam Milan and Rushcliffe Home Services.

The general appearance of this part of the airfield today is unsightly and in need of either a drastic tidying-up programme or complete demolition and replacement by something different. If Nottingham City Airport plc, new owners of the whole airfield, obtain planning permission, it will mean demolition of all the buildings housing firms like those outlined above, together with the removal of the firms themselves; and their replacement by a business park with offices but no factories, warehouses or storage yards.

## Ormonde Aircraft Ltd

This enterprise differs from the others dealt with in this chapter in two respects: it is aviation-related, and it takes place in a relatively new hangar, some distance from the Main Hangar and its semi-derelict surroundings.

With the departure of Fields, no modification of aircraft or manufacture of aircraft parts took place at Tollerton until 2002. There was only routine maintenance, mostly of planes based at Tollerton and belonging to Truman Aviation, the Sherwood and Player Flying Clubs, and private individuals. This is dealt with on pages 217 and 225.

**Plate 102: The Front of the Main Hangar in 2006.** *Nigel Morley*

In 1991, Philip Tillyard of Trent Aero Ltd based at East Midlands Airport, took out a lease on a piece of land on Tollerton airfield from the owners, Nottingham Corporation, where he erected a small hangar, referred to here as the Ormonde Hangar after its present occupants. Tillyard had been involved in vintage aircraft reconstruction, but was by this time engaged in sub-contract work for aviation firms like Rolls-Royce, and used the hangar to store equipment. By 2002 he no longer had use for it and offered the space to a former employee at East Midlands, Alan Purdy, who had been engaged for many years in the reconstruction of aircraft in general and of Spitfires in particular, first at East Midlands Airport and then at Staverton in Gloucestershire. Alan accepted the offer and set up his own company to occupy the hangar, which he named Ormonde Aircraft Ltd.

The company is in the business of overhauling historic aircraft and the manufacture of new parts to replace items that have deteriorated beyond repair. Overhaul includes the reconstruction of Spitfires and Hurricanes – old wartime machines, rejuvenated and restored to airworthiness after years of neglect or worse. This inevitably requires the manufacture of replacements for worn out components. An extreme example is that of a Spitfire which had crashed on the beach at Dunkirk during the war and was so badly corroded by exposure to seawater for some 65 years that, apart from its original shell, it needed almost total replacement.

Contracts have gradually built up, and the company now employs eight men in addition to Alan and his wife Grace, who are co-directors. It supplies air

**Plate 103: Inside Ormonde Aircraft Ltd.** The tail section of a Spitfire is being finished.
*Nigel Morley*

museums and private individuals with a spare million or two pounds to spend; the latter may lend their purchases to organizers of fly-pasts at air pageants. There is also some specialization in the manufacture of components, with sales to and purchases from similar businesses. For instance, while Ormonde makes and sells exhausts and fuel tanks for Spitfires, it does not make aircraft engines or their parts. Its 'markets' include The Imperial War Museum and Historic Flying Ltd, both at RAF Duxford near Cambridge, and the Battle of Britain Memorial Flight based at RAF Coningsby.

Nothing here is mass-produced; every item is a one-off. If it is to fly, be it a whole aircraft or a small component, it must be certified as safe. Ormonde is in the process of gaining approval from the Civil Aviation Authority to certify some aircraft components, and is also currently seeking its approval to test for Certificates of Airworthiness for whole aircraft.

Work like this is time-consuming and requires meticulous attention to detail, often using original design drawings. In the four years of Ormonde's existence at Tollerton, concentration has been on making parts rather than completing whole aircraft ready for test flight. However, Alan Purdy has six such completions to his credit from his time at East Midlands and Staverton, and is looking to add to that at Tollerton.

The company is working to a niche market, which is unlikely to expand significantly – there are four or five small businesses in Britain doing similar work involving highly skilled craftsmanship with fairly basic tools and working off complex design drawings. However, there seems to be no shortage of work to keep Ormonde busy at its present scale of operations for the foreseeable future, while hangar space is fully used. And the company will continue to occupy the same hangar, still owned by Tillyard, if the development plans of Nottingham City Airport plc are realized.

# Postscript

In the summer of 2006, Nottingham City Council announced that it proposed selling Tollerton airfield in the following November. Bids were invited, and 24 were received. Coincidentally, Rushcliffe was being required to build 20,000 new homes to accommodate an expected rise in housing demand, and it seemed that if the airfield were sold to a development company, it would be a likely site for some of those homes – perhaps 3,000. That prospect, and particularly the amount of additional traffic it would generate, caused a good deal of alarm locally. In the event, the winning bid was made by a recently formed company, Nottingham City Airport plc, for an amount thought to be in the region of £5 million according to a report in the *Evening Post* of 23 November 2006.

The company became owner of all the airfield's buildings, runways and other facilities, and of nearly all the land on which the airfield stands – nearly, because two runways extend beyond the boundary of the land bought from the corporation (see Figure 8, page 98). These date back to World War II, when the runways were constructed, after the Air Ministry had requisitioned a sizeable tract north of the airfield's pre-war boundary. The tract was returned to its owners on final derequisitioning in 1960. Today, only one of the runway-ends is in use; that small portion of the airfield continues to be leased, the owner of the land being Nottinghamshire County Council.

In one sense, the change of ownership does not alter the position of Truman Aviation – it now leases the airfield from Nottingham City Airport plc instead of from the City Corporation, but is still a leaseholder; and its managing director

Figure 104:     The Hay Crop on Tollerton Airfield, 2007. *Rod Gill*

is still Derek Leatherland, who remains owner of the company. However, he is also one of the three directors and shareholders of Nottingham City Airport plc; the other two are an engineer, Victor Truman (no relation of the Truman family from whom the company's name derives), and the Edwalton corn merchant and farmer, Brian Wells. Rent paid by Leatherland of Truman Aviation is therefore received by Leatherland and his co-directors of Nottingham City Airport. Truman Aviation will continue to direct all aviation activity on the airfield; Nottingham City Airport will develop and maintain aviation and other facilities.

Development of the airfield is therefore the province of Nottingham City Airport plc. It has drawn up ambitious plans, currently the subject of negotiation with Rushcliffe Borough Council, the process and outcome of which will be a matter of keen interest to all those who use or live near the airfield, as well as to the authors of this book and, we imagine, to many of its readers.

October 2007

# Bibliography

## Unpublished documents

Files at     Nottinghamshire Archives Office
             Nottingham County Libraries Local Studies Section
             The University of Nottingham Department of Manuscripts
             The National Archives

Articles of Association of The Sherwood Flying Club Ltd. 8 July 1957

Lease Agreement between Nottingham City Council and
Truman Aviation Ltd, 1984

Nottingham Flying Club Minute Book 1938 to 1963, with Correspondence
and Bank Statements

Scrapbooks of Freddie Cronk, Herbert Houldsworth. Derek Truman and
Mary-Rose Vandervord

## Books

| | | |
|---|---|---|
| Allez-Fernandez | *Great Aircraft of the World* | 1988 |
| Austen Michael (ed) | *British Civil Aircraft Register 1919 - 1999* | 1999 |
| Blake Ron et al | *The Airfields of Lincolnshire Since 1912* | 1984 |
| Bowyer Charles | *History of the RAF* | 1977 |
| Brooks Robin J. | *Nottinghamshire and Derbyshire Airfields In the Second Word War* | 2003 |
| Chamberlain E.R. | *Life in Wartime Britain* | 1972 |
| Chorley W.R. | *Bomber Command Losses of the Second World War* | 1992 |
| Cruddas Colin | *Those Fabulous Flying Years* | 2003 |
| Curtis Lettice | *The Forgotten Pilots - A Story of the Air Transport Auxiliary 1939 - 45* | 1985 |
| Franks Norman | *Ton-Up Lancs* | 2005 |
| Halley James J. | *The K File - The Royal Air Force of the 1930s* | 1995 |
| HMSO | *Royal Air Force Builds for War* | 1997 |
| Holmes | *Avro Lancaster: The Definitive Record* | 1997 |
| Hunting Group | *Field's First Fifty* | 1986 |

| Hunting Penelope (ed) | *The Hunting History* | 1991 |
| Logan Malcolm | *The Civil Air Guard Book* | 1939 |
| Mondey David | *British Aircraft of World War II* | 2004 |
| Moyle H.R. | *The Hampden File* | 1991 |
| Penrose Harald | *British Aviation: Widening Horizons 1930 - 34* | 1979 |
| Penrose Harald | *British Aviation: Ominous Skies 1935 - 39* | 1980 |

## Periodicals and Newspapers – dates where referred to given in text

Airfield Review

Flight

Newsletters of Hunting Group (*Tally-Ho*) and of the Player and Sherwood Flying Clubs

Nottinghamshire Newspapers and Periodicals

Pilot

The Aeroplane

# INDEX

This index covers the significant subjects covered in the book. No journals are mentioned because these are covered in the bibliography.
Page numbers are in standard font and references to plates and figures in bold italic.
Aircraft are listed under their familiar name with the manufacturer's name following.